180

Hong Kong

Hong Kong

Gene Gleason

The John Day Company, New York

© 1963 by Gene Gleason

Library of Congress Catalogue
Card Number: 63-7957

MANUFACTURED IN THE UNITED STATES OF AMERICA

To all who helped—
particularly, Pat

Contents

*Sixteen pages of illustrations will
be found following page 160.*

Hong Kong

BRITISH CROWN COLONY OF HONG KONG
and Adjacent Areas

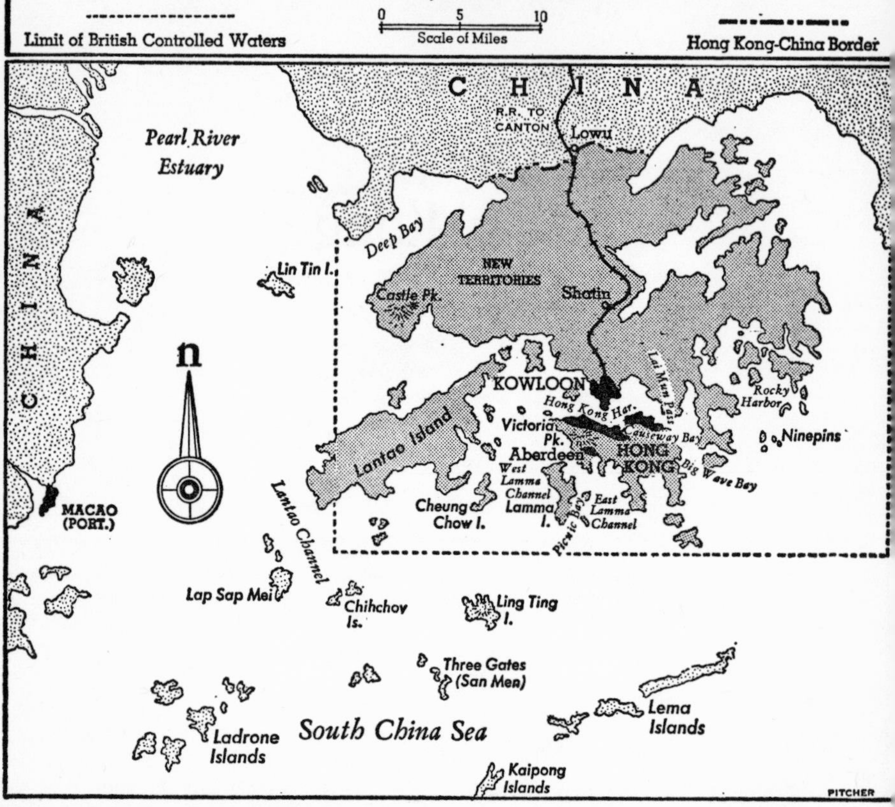

Limit of British Controlled Waters
0
5
10
Scale of Miles
Hong Kong-China Border
C H I N A
R.R. TO CANTON
Lowu
Pearl River Estuary
CHINA
Deep Bay
Lin Tin I.
NEW TERRITORIES
Castle Pk.
Shatin
n
KOWLOON
Lai Mun Pass
Rocky Harbor
Hong Kong Har.
Victoria Pk.
Causeway Bay
Ninepins
Lantao Island
Aberdeen
HONG KONG
West Lamma Channel
Big Wave Bay
MACAO (PORT.)
Cheung Chow I.
Lamma I.
Picnic Bay
East Lamma Channel
Lantao Channel
Lap Sap Mei
Chihchov Is.
Ling Ting I.
Three Gates (San Men)
Lema Islands
South China Sea
Ladrone Islands
Kaipong Islands
PITCHER

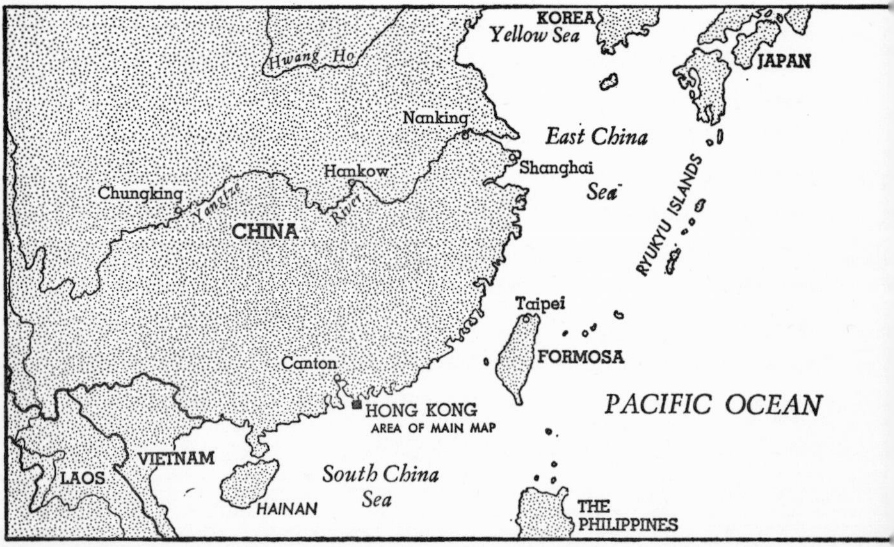

KOREA
Yellow Sea
JAPAN
Hwang Ho
Nanking
East China Sea
Shanghai
Hankow
Chungking
Yangtze River
CHINA
RYUKYU ISLANDS
Taipei
FORMOSA
Canton
HONG KONG
AREA OF MAIN MAP
PACIFIC OCEAN
VIETNAM
LAOS
South China Sea
HAINAN
THE PHILIPPINES

Introduction

Hong Kong is a high point on the skyline of the Free World. As a free port operating on a free-world basis, it is too valuable to lose.

—SIR ROBERT BROWN BLACK, Governor of the British Crown Colony of Hong Kong, 1962

Except for Portugal's tiny overseas province of Macao, Hong Kong is the last Western outpost on the mainland of China. It is the Berlin of East Asia, poised in perilous balance between two ideologies and two civilizations.

The government and people of Hong Kong have performed a matter-of-fact miracle by saving the lives of more than a million refugees from Red China. Without appealing for foreign aid or emergency subsidies from the home country, the colony's rulers have provided jobs, homes and freedom for the destitute. Private charitable organizations overseas and outright gifts from the governments of Great Britain and the United States have achieved miracles on their own in feeding, clothing and educating the poor of Hong Kong, but the main burden is too great to be borne by any agency except the full public power of the royal crown colony.

Most of Hong Kong's people are too poor to afford what an American would consider minimum comforts. They came to Hong Kong with nothing, yet every day they send thousands of food packages back to Red China, hoping to save their relatives from starvation.

These are only the workaday miracles of Hong Kong; the greatest miracle is that it exists at all. It has never had enough of the good things—land, water, health, security or money—but always a surplus of the bad ones—wars, typhoons, epidemics, opium, heroin, crime and corruption.

It is one of the most contradictory and baffling places in the contemporary world—a magnificent port and a teeming slum; a bargain-hunter's paradise and a nest of swindlers; a place of marginal farmland and superlative farmers, efficient and orderly, sly and corrupt. It has outlived a thousand prophecies of its imminent doom. Its people dwell between the claws of a tiger, fully aware of the spot they're on, but not at all dismayed.

Tourists and sailors come to Hong Kong by the hundreds of thousands every year, half-expecting to discover inscrutable Orientals, or to be followed down a dark alley by a soft-shod killer with a hatchet in his hand. The Orientals turn out to be the noisiest, most gregarious people the Westerner has ever seen. No one follows him down a pitch-black alley at midnight, unless it's a stray cat looking for a handout, or a shoe-shine boy working late.

The real magic of Hong Kong is that none of it is exactly what you expected. You prowl around for handicraft shops and find them next to an automated textile mill. You've been told to keep your eye open for the sprawling settlements of squatter shacks, and you find them slowly being swallowed up by multi-story concrete resettlement estates. You turn on the faucet in your hotel at noon and it issues a dry, asthmatic sigh; you try it again at six and it spits at you like an angry camel, splashing all over your suit.

You look for a historic hill in Kowloon, and there is what's left of it—a stumpy mound, shaved down by a bulldozer, with the rest of it already dumped into the sea to form the foundation of a new industrial city. You look for the romantic hallmark of Hong Kong, a Chinese junk with bat-wing sails, and it putt-putts past on a Diesel engine without a scrap of canvas on the masts.

You fear for your life as you stand on the crowded sidewalk, plucking up the courage to bull your way through a fantastic tangle of autos, motor-scooters, double-deck trams, rickshaws, massed pedestrians and laborers carting bulky loads on bamboo shoulder-slings, but the white-sleeved patrolman in the traffic pagoda parts the torrent with a gesture like Moses dividing the Red Sea and you cross without a scratch.

A small, slender Chinese beauty in a closely fitted Cheongsam strolls by with a skirt slit to the mid-thighs, and you begin to perceive the reason for the thousands of Caucasian-Chinese intermarriages in the colony. Such unions go so well they hardly merit comment in today's Hong Kong gossip; a generation ago, they would have overturned a hornet's nest of angry relatives in both racial groups.

Hong Kong is like the Chinese beauties in their Cheongsams; no matter how often you turn away, your next view will be completely different and equally rewarding.

CHAPTER ONE

Up from British Barbarism

The common disposition of the English barbarians is ferocious, and what they trust in are the strength of their ships and the effectiveness of their guns.

—GOVERNOR LU K'U OF CANTON, 1834

In 1841, the British crown colony of Hong Kong attached itself like a small barnacle to the southeast coast of the Celestial Empire. The single offshore island that constituted the whole of the original colony was a spiny ridge of half-drowned mountains forming the seaward rampart of a deep-water harbor. Before the British came, it had no geographic identity. They gave it the Chinese name "Hong Kong," usually translated as "fragrant harbor," which distinguished the one appealing feature of its forbidding terrain.

Sparsely inhabited from primitive times, Hong Kong, the more than two hundred rocky islands scattered outside its harbor, and the barren seacoast opposite them lay far out in the

15

boondocks of China. Its innumerable, deeply indented coves and mountain-ringed harbors made it a favorite lurking place for coastal pirates.

For centuries, fleets of pirate junks had apportioned their rapacity between pouncing on coastwise ships and pillaging isolated farms and fishing settlements. The Manchu emperors, lacking the unified navy necessary to sink these cut-throats, attempted to bolster the thin defenses along the pirate-infested coast of Kwangtung Province by offering tax-free land to any of their subjects who would settle there. Even so, there was no wild scramble to accept the gift.

Less troublesome than pirates but hardly more welcome to the rulers of China were the European traders who had been plying the Chinese coast since the beginning of the sixteenth century. In the middle of that century, Portuguese merchant-sailors overcame part of this hostility by employing their well-armed ships to help the Chinese emperor crush a pirate fleet. They were rewarded with imperial permission to establish a small trading outpost at Macao, forty miles west of Hong Kong Island.

Traders from Spain, Holland, England, France and America soon began to operate out of Macao, and the British East India Co. opened a trade base at Canton in 1681 to supply a lively English market with Chinese tea and silk. Canton, the only Chinese port open to world trade, stood due north of Macao and ninety-one miles northwest of the future colony at Hong Kong.

Throughout a century and a half of dealings at Canton, European traders enjoyed the same degree of liberty: they were all free to pay whatever prices or imposts the Chinese Hong merchants and customs officials chose to demand. The Chinese wanted neither foreign goods nor foreign traders, but if the latter persisted in buying and selling at Canton, they were expected to submit to strict Chinese regulations or get out.

There were rules forbidding any foreigner to live in Canton except during the six-month trading season, rules denying foreign women the right to enter the city, rules against possessing firearms and an absolute ban against bringing foreign warships past the Boca Tigris (Tiger's Mouth), the fortified strait on the Canton River estuary leading to the city.

In practice, the rules were a kind of game; few were consistently enforced unless the Western traders raised a howl over Chinese customs duties or bumptiously insisted on dealing directly with the officials of the Celestial Empire instead of its merchants. Then the reins were yanked up tight, and the commercial interlopers had to obey every restriction to the letter.

Foreigners at Canton remained in a weak bargaining position until a few European traders, particularly the English, discovered one product that the Chinese passionately desired. It was compact, easy to ship, extremely valuable, and it brought full payment in hard cash upon delivery. It could be brought from British India in prodigious quantities, and because it contained great value in a small package, it could slip through Chinese customs without the disagreeable formality of paying import duties. This was opium—the most convincing Western proof of the validity of the profit motive since the opening of the China trade.

The Chinese appetite for opium became almost insatiable, spreading upward to the Emperor's official family and draining away most of the foreign exchange gained by exporting tea and silk. The alarmed Emperor issued a denunciation of this "vile dirt of foreign countries" in 1796, and followed it with a long series of edicts and laws intended to stop the opium traffic.

The East India Co., worried by repeated threats of imperial punishment, relinquished its control of the opium trade and dropped the drug from its official list of imports. Private traders with less to lose immediately took up the slack, and after opium was barred from Canton, simply discharged their cargoes of dope into a fleet of hulks anchored off the entrance of the Canton River estuary. From the hulks it was trans-shipped to the mainland by hundreds of Chinese junks and sampans. Chinese port officials, well-greased with graft, never raised a squeak of protest.

The Emperor himself seethed with rage, vainly condemning the sale of opium as morally indefensible and ruinous to the health and property of his people. Meanwhile, the trade rose from $6,122,100 in 1821 to $15,338,160 in 1832. The British government took a strong official line against the traffic and denied its protection to British traders caught smuggling, but left the enforcement of anti-opium laws in Chinese hands. A joint Sino-British enforcement campaign was out of the question, since the Chinese had not granted diplomatic recognition to the British Empire.

This insuperable obstacle to combined action was the natural child of Chinese xenophobia. When Lord Napier broached the subject of establishing diplomatic relations between Britain and China in 1834, the Emperor's representatives stilled his overtures with the contemptuous question, "How can the officers of the Celestial Empire hold official correspondence with barbarians?"

The glories of a mercantile civilization made no impression on a people who regarded themselves as the sole heirs of the oldest surviving culture on earth. To the lords of the Manchu empire, English traders were crude, money-grubbing upstarts who had neither the knowledge nor the capacity to appreciate the traditions and philosophy of China. What could these cubs of the Renaissance and the Industrial Revolution contribute to a civilization of such time-tested wisdom? They could contribute to its collapse, as the Chinese were to learn when their medieval war-machine collided with the striking power and nineteenth-century technology of the British Navy.

After the East India Co. lost its monopoly on the China trade in 1833, the British government sent its own representatives to settle a fast-growing dispute between English and Chinese merchants. Once again the Chinese snubbed these envoys and emphasized their unwillingness to compromise by appointing a new Imperial Commissioner to suppress the opium trade.

For a time, the British merchants comforted themselves with the delusion that Lin Tse-hsu, the Imperial Commissioner, could be bought off or mollified. He dashed these hopes by blockading the Boca Tigris, surrounding the foreign warehouses at Canton with guards and demanding that all foreign merchants surrender their stock of opium. He further insisted that they sign a pledge to import no more opium or face the death penalty.

Threats and vehement protests by the traders only drove Lin to stiffer counter-measures, and the British were at last forced to surrender more than 20,000 chests of opium worth $6,000,000. Commissioner Lin destroyed the opium immediately. British merchants and their government envoys withdrew from Canton by ship, ultimately anchoring off Hong Kong Island. None of them lived ashore; the island looked too bleak for English habitation, though it had already been considered as a possible offshore port of foreign trade.

With the British out of the opium trade, a legion of freelance desperadoes flocked in to take it over, leaving both the British and Chinese governments shorn of their revenue. Further negotiation between Lin and Captain Charles Elliot, the British Superintendent of Trade in China, reached an impasse when Lin declined to treat Elliot as a diplomat of equal rank and advised him to carry on his negotiations with the Chinese merchants.

Having wasted their time in a profitless exchange of unpleasantries, both sides huffily retired; the Chinese to reinforce their shore batteries and assemble a fleet of twenty-nine war junks and fire rafts, and Captain Elliot to organize a striking force of warships, iron-hulled steamers and troop transports.

The junk fleet and two British men-of-war clashed at Chuenpee, on the Canton River estuary, in the first battle between British and Chinese armed forces. It was a pushover for the British; Chinese naval guns were centuries behind theirs in firepower, and the gun crews on the junks were pitifully inaccurate in comparison with the scientific precision of the British. Within a few minutes the junks had been sunk, dismasted or driven back in panicky disorder. The British on the *Hyacinth* and *Volage* suffered almost no damage or casualties.

No formal state of war existed, however, so Captain Elliot broke off the one-sided engagement before the enemy had been annihilated. He pulled back to wait until orders came from Lord Palmerston, British Foreign Secretary, directing him to demand repayment for the $6,000,000 worth of opium handed over to Lin. At the same time, Elliot was told to obtain firm Chinese assurance of future security for traders in China, or the cession of an island off the China coast as a base for foreign trade unhampered by the merchants and officials of the Celestial Empire. Palmerston, maintaining the calm detachment of a statesman 10,000 miles distant from the scene of battle, thought it would be best for Elliot to win these concessions without war.

Elliot, mustering the full strength of his land and sea forces, blockaded the Canton and Yangtze Rivers, occupied several strategic islands and put Palmerston's demands into the hands of Emperor Tao-kuang. Humiliated by the irresistible advance of the despised foreigners, the Emperor angrily dismissed Commissioner Lin. His replacement, Commissioner Keeshen, began by agreeing to pay the indemnity demanded by Lord Palmerston and to hand over Hong Kong Island, then deliberately dragged his feet to postpone the fulfillment of his promises. Elliot, fed to the teeth with temporizing, ended it by throwing his whole fleet at the Chinese. His naval guns pounded their shore batteries into silence, and he landed marines and sailors to capture the forts guarding Canton.

The Chinese land defenders were as poorly equipped as the sailors of their war junks; when they lighted their ancient matchlocks to fire them, scores of soldiers were burned to death by accidentally igniting the gunpowder spilled on their clothing.

In a naval action at Anson's Bay, the flat-bottomed iron steamer *Nemesis*, drawing only six feet of water, surprised a squadron of junks by pushing its way into their shallow-water refuge. A single Congreve rocket from the *Nemesis* struck the magazine of a large war junk, blowing it up in a shower of flying spars and seamen. Eleven junks were destroyed, two were driven aground and hundreds of Chinese sailors were killed within a few hours. Admiral Kwan, commander of the shattered fleet, had the red cap-button emblematic of his rank shot off by the British and was later relieved of the rank by his unsympathetic Emperor.

Keeshen hastened to notify Elliot that he stood ready to

hand over Hong Kong and the $6,000,000 indemnity. But even the shock of defeat had not flushed the Emperor from his dream world of superiority; he repudiated Keeshen's agreement and ordered him to rally the troops for "an awful display of Celestial vengeance." Well aware of the hopelessness of his situation, Keeshen tried to hold out by postponing his meetings with Elliot. Elliot, not to be put off this time, countered by opening a general assault along the Canton River. Within a month, his combined land and sea offensive had reduced every fort on the water route to Canton and his ships rode at anchor in front of the city.

British preparations to storm the city were well advanced when a fresh truce was arranged. The entire British force sailed back to Hong Kong, having retreated from almost certain victory. Elliot, however, felt no disappointment; he had never wanted to use more force than necessary to restore stable trade conditions. He feared that full-scale war would bring down the Chinese government, plunging the country into revolution and chaos.

Hong Kong had become *de facto* British territory on January 26, 1841, when the Union Jack was raised at Possession Point and the island claimed for Queen Victoria. Its 4,500 inhabitants, who had never heard of the Queen, became her unprotesting subjects.

The acquisition of the island produced ignominy enough for both sides; Keeshen was exiled to Tartary for giving it up and Elliot was dismissed by Palmerston for accepting "a barren island with hardly a house upon it," instead of obeying the Foreign Secretary's orders and driving a much harder bargain.

A succession of disasters swept over the colony in its first year of existence. "Hong Kong Fever," a form of malaria thought to have been caused by digging up the earth for new roads and buildings, killed hundreds of settlers. Two violent typhoons unroofed practically every temporary building on the rocky slopes and drowned a tenth of the boat population. The wreckage of the ships and buildings had scarcely been cleared away when a fire broke out among the flimsy, closely packed mat sheds. In a few hours, it burned down most of the Chinese huts on the island.

The flavor of disaster became a regular part of Hong Kong history. Its own four horsemen—piracy, typhoons, epidemics and fires—raced through the colony at frequent but unpredictable intervals, filling its hills and harbor with debris and death. There is still no reason to assume that they will not return, either singly or as a team, whenever the whim moves them.

Even imagining Hong Kong as an island bearing no more than a minimum burden of natural hazards, it is difficult to understand how it became settled at all. The London *Times* scorned it editorially in 1844 with the comment that "The place has nothing to recommend it, if we except the excellent harbor."

The original colony and the much larger territory added to it in the next 120 years have no natural resources of value, except fish, building stone and a limited supply of minerals. Only one-seventh of its total area is arable land; at best, it can grow enough rice, vegetables and livestock to feed the present population for about three months of a year. There is no local source of coal, oil or water power. Fresh water was scarce in 1841, and in 1960, after the colony had constructed an elaborate system of fourteen reservoirs, the carefully rationed supply had to be supplemented with additional water bought and pumped in from Red China.

Hong Kong has an annual rainfall of 85 inches—twice that

of New York City—but three-fourths of it falls between May and September. At the end of the rainy season, ten billion gallons may be stored in the reservoirs but by the following May, every reservoir may be empty. Water use, especially during the dry winter, has been restricted to certain hours throughout the colony's history. Running water, to the majority of Hong Kong's poor, means that one grabs a kerosene tin and runs for the nearest public standpipe. Those lucky enough to reach the head of the line before the water is cut off may carry home enough to supply a household for one full day.

The industries of the colony, which expanded at a spectacular rate after World War II, could never have survived on sales to the local market. Most of its residents have always been too poor to buy anything more than the simplest necessities of food, clothing and shelter. No tariff wall protects its products from the competition of imported goods, but resentment against the low-wage industries of the colony continually puts up new barriers against Hong Kong products in foreign countries, including the United States.

From its thinly populated beginnings, Hong Kong has been transformed into one of the most dangerously overcrowded places on earth, with 1,800 to 2,800 persons jamming every acre of its urban sections. Eighty percent of its population is wedged into an area the size of Rochester, N.Y.—thirty-six square miles. About 325,000 people have no regular housing. They sleep on the sidewalks, or live in firetrap shacks perched on the hillsides or rooftop huts. A soaring birth rate and illegal infiltration of refugees from Red China add nearly 150,-000 people a year.

Fire is the best-fed menace of contemporary Hong Kong. In the 1950-55 period, flash fires drove 150,000 shack and tenement dwellers out of their homes, racing through congested settlements with the swiftness and savagery of a forest in flames. Tuberculosis attacked the slum-dwellers at the same ruinous pace. No one dares to predict what would happen if one of the colony's older, dormant scourges—plague or typhus—were to break out again. But the colony found cause for relief and pride when a 1961 cholera scare was halted by free, universal inoculations.

More than a century of turmoil and privation has taught the colonists to accept their liabilities and deal with their problems, yet they prefer to dwell on the assets and virtues which have enabled them to endure, and in many cases, to prosper tremendously.

Hong Kong harbor has always been the colony's greatest asset. Of all the world's harbors, only Rio de Janeiro equals its spacious, magnificent beauty, with its tall green mountains sloping down to deep blue water. Perhaps Rio has a richer contrast of tropical green and blue, but the surface of Hong Kong harbor is so irrepressibly alive with criss-crossing ferry lines, ocean freighters riding in the stream, and tattered junk sails passing freely through the orderly swarm that it never looks the same from one minute to the next and is incapable of monotony.

An oceanic lagoon of seventeen square miles, the harbor lies sheltered between mountain ranges to the north and south and is shielded from the open sea by narrow entrances at its east and west ends. Vessels drawing up to thirty-six feet of water can enter through Lei Yue Mun pass at the eastern end of the harbor. Through the same pass, jet airliners approach Kai Tak Airport, roaring between the mountains like rim-rock flyers as they glide down to the long airstrip built on re-claimed land in Kowloon Bay, on the northern side of the harbor.

The intangible ramparts of the colony are as solid as its peaks: the sea power of the British and American navies, and the stability of British rule. At their worst, the colony's overlords have been autocratic, stiff-necked and chilly toward their Chinese subjects.

The same British administrators who nobly refused to hand over native criminals for the interrogation-by-torture of the Chinese courts could flog and brand Chinese prisoners with a fierce conviction of their own rectitude. Nevertheless, they brought to China something never seen there before; respect for the law as an abstraction, an objective code of justice that had to be followed even when it embarrassed and discommoded the rulers.

Almost from its inception, the colony attracted refugees from China. Many brought capital and technical skills with them, others were brigands and murderers fleeing Chinese executioners.

Banking, shipping and insurance services of the colony quickly became the most reliable in Southeast Asia. Macao, in spite of its three-century lead on Hong Kong, was so badly handicapped by its shallow harbor, critical land shortage, and unenterprising government that it sank into a state of suspended antiquity. Hong Kong merchants, eager for new business, kept in close touch with world markets. Labor was cheap and abundant, still it was more liberally paid than in most of the Asiatic countries. Labor unions numbered in the hundreds, but they were split into so many quarreling political factions that they could rarely hope to win a showdown fight against the colony's business-dominated government, although the Seamen's Union did obtain many concessions after a long strike in 1922.

Notwithstanding the social gulfs between the British,

Portuguese, Indian and other national elements in the colony, all of them march arm-in-arm through one great field of endeavor; the desire and the capacity to make money. Hong Kong lives to turn a profit, and its deepest fraternal bond is the Fellowship of Greater Solvency.

Motivated by this common purpose, the British and Chinese dwelt together in peaceful contempt during the first fifteen years of the colony's history, sharing the returns of a fast-growing world trade. The opium traffic resumed as though there had never been a war over it. The only enemy that worried the merchants became the Chinese pirates who preyed on their ships.

From Fukien to Canton, pirate fleets prowled the China coast. Two of their favorite hangouts were Bias Bay and Mirs Bay, within easy striking range of Hong Kong. With the arrival of the British, they began looting foreign merchant-ships with the same unsparing greed they had previously inflicted on Chinese ships and villages.

British warships, superior to the pirate craft in all but numbers and elusiveness, hunted them down with task forces. In four expeditions between 1849 and 1858, the Queen's Navy sank or captured nearly 200 pirate junks. Thousands of prisoners were taken, and a fair share of them were hanged. British landing forces, storming up the beaches from the warships, leveled every pirate settlement they could find.

The land-and-sea offensive had a temporarily restraining effect, but new-born pirate fleets sprang up like dragon's teeth to turn to the practice of seaborne larceny. A fifth column of suppliers, informers, and receivers of stolen goods within the colony obligingly assisted the pirates in plucking their neighbors clean. Hong Kong's oldest industry has retained its franchise down to present times; in 1948, airborne pirates attempted to high-jack a Macao-Hong Kong plane in flight. The plane crashed, killing all but one person who was detained and questioned, then released for lack of jurisdiction and sent back to China.

Piracy was the fuse that touched off a second Sino-British war in 1856, when the Chinese government charged that a Chinese ship manned by a British skipper was, in fact, a pirate vessel. While the skipper was absent from the Chinese lorcha, the *Arrow*, his entire crew was taken prisoner and accused of piracy by China.

The incident landed in the lap of Sir John Bowring, a former Member of Parliament and one of the most curiously contradictory of all colony governors. Philosophically a liberal and a pacifist, he was markedly sympathetic toward the Chinese. A prolific author, economist and hymn-writer, he had a brilliant gift for linguistics and was credited with a working knowledge of 100 languages, among them Chinese. He initiated wise and far-reaching improvements, including the first forestry program, which were enacted into law by later governors. With all these gifts, his five-year term (1854-1859) was marred by a series of hot and futile wrangles with his subordinates.

This mercurial man reacted to the capture of the *Arrow*'s crew by demanding an apology and their release. When the apology was not immediately dispatched, he assembled a military force and set out to capture Canton. War in India delayed the arrival of British reinforcements, and Canton withstood the assault. Meanwhile, Chinese collaborators in Hong Kong poisoned the bread supplied to Europeans; Bowring's wife was one of scores of persons who suffered serious illness by eating the bread.

Shortly afterward the French joined forces with the English. Canton and Tientsin were captured, and the Chinese government was forced to agree to add more trading ports to the five provided by the 1842 Nanking Treaty.

The ensuing short-term armistice was broken by sporadic Chinese attacks on British supply lines and a general resumption of hostilities, ending in the occupation of the Chinese capital at Peking.

The Kowloon Peninsula, jutting from the Chinese mainland to a point one mile north of Hong Kong Island, became involved in the war when its residents rioted against British troops encamped there. The British had considered the annexation of Kowloon for several years, realizing that if the Chinese decided to fortify it their guns would command Hong Kong harbor. Treating the riot as a compelling reason for taking possession, the British obtained an outright cession of the peninsula and Stonecutters Island, a little body of land about one mile west of Kowloon, under the terms of the 1860 Convention of Peking.

Bowring, meanwhile, had created a public Botanic Garden —still a beautiful hillside haven at the heart of the colony— laid down new roads and erected a number of public buildings. But his daily relations with other colony officials had degenerated into a battle-royal of insults and counter-accusations. The home government, appalled at Bowring's un-British disregard for good form, rushed in a new minister to direct negotiations with China and replaced Bowring as governor with Sir Hercules Robinson, an unusually able colonial administrator. Bowring left the colony with his reputation at low ebb, snubbed by its English residents. The Chinese of Hong Kong, inured to snobbery but grateful for Bowring's attempts to help them, saw him off with parting gifts.

Sir Hercules began his administration with a piece of good

fortune; practically all the contentious subordinates who had made Bowring's tenure a long nightmare resigned or retired. The colony's military leaders kept the pot simmering by demanding most of Kowloon for their own use, although Robinson wanted to preserve it for public buildings and recreational grounds.

In England, where the brimstone smell of the Bowring affair lingered for many months, the London *Times* was moved to describe the China outpost as a "noisy, bustling, quarrelsome, discontented and insalubrious little island" whose name was "always connected with some fatal pestilence, some doubtful war, or some discreditable internal squabble." Robinson's skirmish with the military attracted no more attention than a stray pistol-shot after a thundering cannonade.

Between wars and internal bickering, the colony was growing up. The California gold rush of 1849, followed by a major gold strike in Australia two years later, created a surge of prosperity as goods and Chinese laborers funneled through the port on their way to the goldfields. Japan was opened to world trade in 1853, and American whalers and seal hunters had begun to call at Hong Kong. Total shipping tonnage cleared through the port rose 1,000 percent in the fifteen years after 1848. With skilled labor and well-equipped dockyards at hand, the building, refitting and supplying of ships became the colony's most important industry.

Overseas shipment of Chinese laborers from mainland China to perform work contracts in Central America, Australia, and the islands of the Indian Ocean created grave human problems.

Chinese were being kidnaped, abused like slaves and packed into the airless, filthy holds of sailing ships where they died at an alarming rate. From 1855 on, the colony imposed tighter and tighter restrictions on the trade, prescribing better living conditions aboard ship and prosecuting kidnapers of labor. But the labor suppliers evaded the laws of the colony by taking on provisions at Hong Kong and calling at other ports along the China coast to shanghai contract workers.

The first of many waves of refugees to seek asylum in Britain's "barbarian" enclave arrived with the outbreak of the Tai Ping Rebellion in 1850. Led by Hung Siu Tsuen, a Christian student, the rebels attacked the ruling Manchu Dynasty and fomented wild disorder in Canton. Thousands of apprehensive Chinese fled to Hong Kong, throwing themselves on the mercy of the foreign devils.

Governor Robinson and the land-hungry generals eventually compromised their conflicting claims to Kowloon real estate, but the colony government spent years of patient effort in straightening out the fuzzy, inexact and spurious titles to individual land-holdings on the peninsula. On the whole, British courts achieved a fair adjudication of claims.

Sir Hercules did not permit his administrative successes to alter the colony's reputation for day-to-day blundering. He housed prisoners in a hulk off Stonecutters Island where it was accidentally swamped by an adjoining boat with a loss of thirty-eight lives. On a kindly impulse, he belatedly moved the hulk closer to shore, and a group of convicts ran down the gangplank to dry land and freedom.

Such oversights were exceptional; when Sir Hercules ended his term in 1865, he could look back on an administration which had put the unpopular colony on its feet by reforming its courts and modernizing and expanding its public works. This was no fluke, for he went on to similar successes in Ceylon, Australia, New Zealand and South Africa before being elevated to the peerage.

During its formative period, the colony was predominantly

a society of adult males. Its merchants and workers came from China to earn a living and to send their savings back to their wives and children; when they grew too old to work, they returned to their native cities and villages. But there was always a number of families among the population, and after the refugees began pouring in, the percentage of children rose. In 1865, children numbered 22,301 in a total population of 125,504. Only 14,000 of these were of school age, and less than 2,000 of them attended school.

Missionaries began to run schools for Chinese and European children almost from the time the colony was established, but the scale of their undertakings was modest. The Chinese organized native schools, and like the missionary ventures, floundered along with ill-trained teachers, inadequate buildings and loose supervision. Government schools, low in quality and enrollment, freed themselves of religious control in 1866. A private school with advanced ideas instructed Chinese girls in English, only to discover that its pupils were accepting postgraduate work as the mistresses of European colonists.

Five Irish governors, starting with Sir Hercules Robinson in 1859, ruled Hong Kong in succession, and three of them ranked among the ablest executives in its history. Each one was in his separate way a strong-minded, individualistic, and occasionally rambunctious chief. After the Hibernian Era came to an end in 1885, no later governors emulated their mildly defiant gestures toward the home government.

Sir Richard Graves Macdonnell, second of the Irish governors, was a tough and seasoned colonial administrator who tackled the unsolved problems of crime and piracy with perception and vigor. He saw that naval action against the pirate fleets would bring no lasting results while the sea-raiders had the assistance of suppliers, informers and receivers of stolen goods within the colony. He put all ship movements in Hong Kong waters under close supervision, and assigned police to ferret out every colonist working with the pirates. To a greater degree than any of his predecessors, he succeeded in checking piracy, but no governor has ever stamped it out.

Macdonnell also intensified the campaign against robbery, burglary and assault. Commercial interests applauded his increased severity in the treatment of prisoners and his frequent reliance on flogging, branding and deportation of offenders. Macdonnell himself saw no contradiction between such rough-shod methods and, on the other hand, his generosity in donating crown land for a Chinese hospital where the destitute and dying could be cared for in a decent manner. Previously, relatives of ailing, elderly paupers had deposited them in empty buildings with a coffin and drinking water, leaving them to suffer and die alone.

Sir Arthur Kennedy, who followed Macdonnell, was one of the colony's most popular governors. He knew his job thoroughly and he combined this knowledge with sound judgment, a lively sense of humor, and a rare talent for pleasing the traders and the Colonial Office. He initiated the Tai Tam water-supply system and continued Macdonnell's relentless fight against crime.

Kennedy threw his more orthodox colleagues into a dither by entertaining Chinese merchants at official receptions in Government House, his executive residence. He went so far as to invite these Chinese to suggest improvements in the laws of the colony, and they promptly asked for a law to punish adulterous Chinese women. Knowing that each of the petitioners had several wives and concubines, Sir Arthur realized that his volunteer legal advisers were actually looking for government sanction to hobble their restless bedmates. He tabled the petition with tact.

External changes produced surprising mutations in the progress of the colony. Its isolation diminished with the opening of the Suez Canal in 1869 and the completion in the next year of direct overland telegraph connection with England. No longer was a governor left to his own devices for days and weeks, improvising policy at the peril of his job until orders arrived from home.

The hazards of life on the South China coast remained. In 1874, the colony was devastated by the worst typhoon since 1841. Flying rooftops filled the skies above the island, and 2,000 Chinese fishermen and their families drowned in the ruins of their floating villages.

Sir Arthur's departure to become the Governor of Queensland was a melancholy time for the colony's Chinese. They were openly devoted to him—the first governor who had treated them more or less as equals. Even the English liked him, and he became the first and only governor to have a statue erected to his memory in the colony's Botanic Garden. The statue disappeared during the Japanese Occupation of World War II.

Kennedy's successor, Sir John Pope Hennessy, not only preserved this solicitude for the Chinese but provoked a storm of protest from European residents by practicing leniency toward Chinese prisoners. When murders and burglaries increased, his humanitarian policies were blamed. Hennessy, a resourceful debater who was at his best in defending his own policies, was not intimidated. The weak side of his administration showed in a quite different area—his habitual neglect of essential paper work.

Hennessy's friendliness toward the Chinese unexpectedly involved him in controversy with the Chinese themselves. For centuries, wealthy Chinese families had "adopted" little female domestic slaves by purchasing them from their parents or relatives. In the households of the rich, these Mui Tsai could be identified at once by their shabby clothing and their general appearance of neglect.

Even families of limited means purchased Mui Tsai, so that the mother of the family could take a job outside her home while the juvenile slavey cared for the children and contended with the simpler household drudgery. For the poorest families, sale of a daughter as a Mui Tsai was the natural solution to an economic crisis. But the institution, unacceptable to Western eyes from any aspect, had become the vehicle for gross abuses—the kidnaping and sale of women as prostitutes in Hong Kong or for transportation overseas. Kidnapings had become so numerous and flagrant by 1880 that Governor Hennessy and Sir John Smale, the colony's Chief Justice, condemned the Mui Tsai system as contrary to British law.

The Chinese protested that Mui Tsai was not slavery; it was an ancient, respectable adjunct of family life. Indeed, it was quite humane, for it saved the daughters of many impoverished families from being drowned. The English didn't want that, did they? The Chinese offered no defense of kidnaping and forced prostitution arising from the institution of Mui Tsai.

Under pressure of the colony government, influential Chinese set up the Po Leung Kuk, or Society for the Protection of Virtue, to rescue women and girls from flesh peddlers, provide a home for them in a section of the Chinese-operated Tung Wah Hospital, and train them for respectable occupations.

Hennessy, like Governor Bowring, entangled himself in a

series of acrimonious disputes with other colony officials, antagonizing them in groups by lashing out at the school system, prison maladministration and the harsh treatment of convicts. His most combative foe was another Irishman, General Donovan, head of the colony's armed forces. Their verbal Donnybrook erupted over the perennially thorny question of how much Kowloon land the military was entitled to.

General Donovan hit back at Hennessy with a sneak attack; he complained to the home government about the outrageous sanitary conditions in the colony—the lack of proper drainage, the polluted seafront, and the verminous tenements where entire Chinese families shared one room with their pigs and other domestic animals. All these conditions had existed in Hong Kong since 1841, but no one had called them to the home government's attention with the holy indignation of Donovan.

Osbert Chadwick was sent from England to investigate and he found sanitary conditions every bit as bad as Donovan had described them. Chadwick's report became the basis, after long postponement and inaction, for the creation of a Sanitary Board and fundamental sanitary reforms.

Hennessy left the colony in 1882 to become Governor of Mauritius and to lock horns with a new team of associates. Four administrators and two governors passed through the colony's top executive position in the next decade, but none effected any substantial improvements in sanitation. Every attempt to clean up pesthole tenements was balked by cries of persecution and government interference from the landlords; they would consent to no improvements unless the government paid their full cost.

In other directions the colony advanced steadily. It completed a new reservoir system and central market and rebuilt the sewage and drainage system. Ambitious land-reclamation projects were pushed ahead at Causeway Bay and Yau Ma Tei to meet the unabating demand for level sites in the crowded, mountainous colony. Kowloon, a wasteland of undulating red rock, in the 1880s began cutting down its ridges and using the spoil to extend its shoreline—a process that continues at an amazingly accelerated rate today.

Hong Kong has never known an age of serenity; its brief interludes of comparative calm have always been followed by cataclysmic upheavals. In the spring of 1894, the colony was invaded by plague, long endemic on the South China coast. Within a few months, 2,485 persons had died of pneumonic, septicemic and bubonic plague, and Western medicine had no more power to check it than had Chinese herb treatments.

The onset of plague was so terrifying that long-deferred sanitary reforms were rushed through and rigidly enforced. Deaf to the protests of all residents, British military units began regular inspections of Chinese homes. Sanitary teams condemned 350 houses as plague spots and evicted 7,000 persons from infected dwellings. Resenting foreign invasion of their privacy and mistrustful of Western medicine, the Chinese retaliated by posting placards openly in Canton and furtively inside the colony accusing British doctors of stealing the eyes of newborn babies to treat plague victims.

Business came to a stop and ships avoided the plague-stricken port. The plague abated for a year, then returned in 1896 to take another 1,204 lives. The Chinese kept up a rearguard action against sanitary measures with strikes and evasions, hiding their dead and dying or dumping their bodies in the streets and harbor. Sometimes they exposed their dying relatives on bamboo frames stretched across the narrow streets, hoping that the departing soul would haunt the street instead of its former house.

The benighted traditionalism of the colony's Chinese awoke the British administration to one of its most serious weaknesses; a half-century of British rule had failed to give to 99 percent of the colony's residents any clear idea of the civilization they were expected to work and live under. The tardy lesson eventually took effect, and the British embarked on a long and intensive program of improving and enlarging their school system. In the Tung Wah Hospital, English and Chinese doctors learned to their surprise that therapies unlike their own were not necessarily sheer quackery, and that they could work together for the benefit of their patients.

With the population of the colony exceeding 160,000 in the early 1880s, military and commercial leaders turned to the possibility of acquiring more land on the Chinese mainland. They pressed the British Foreign Office to seek the territory running north from the Kowloon Peninsula to the Sham Chun River, about 15 miles away. The suggestions were rejected as prejudicial to Sino-British relations until other foreign powers started to thrust into Chinese territory for commercial concessions and spheres of political influence.

France, Russia and Japan were the spearheads of this infiltration of the Celestial Empire, which had been weakened by internal rebellion. Japan defeated China in the 1894-95 war and exerted ever-stronger commercial control over the mainland. Russia made its bid by advancing through Manchuria and occupying Port Arthur. Germany hastened to join the commercial invaders. Hacked at from four directions, the Chinese people attempted to close ranks in defense of their homeland.

The United States, with no apparent desire to annex Chinese territory, nevertheless heightened both British and Chinese apprehension by launching its naval attack on Manila from Mirs Bay in May, 1898. The Chinese feared another land grab, and the British felt they could best protect Hong Kong if they were able to deal with a strong, unified China.

Despite its earlier reluctance to disturb the status quo, Great Britain was now convinced that it had to acquire the territory between Kowloon and the Sham Chun River as a protective buffer for Hong Kong. On July 1, 1898, Britain obtained a 99-year lease to this mainland territory and 235 adjacent islands with a total land area of 365 ½ square miles.

Chinese guerrilla forces in the New Territories—as this leased area is still called—opposed the British occupation but were defeated and driven out by British troops in a ten-day campaign. That was the easiest part of it. It took four years of wrangling with the uncooperative Chinese residents to establish valid titles to private plots of land in the New Territories. Kowloon City, an eight-acre patch on the border of Kowloon and the New Territories, became a kind of orphan in the transaction, with the British firmly insisting it was part of the lease and the Chinese arguing somewhat inconclusively that it was not. Nationalist China claimed it as recently as 1948, but Red China has not so far pushed a similar claim. Britain regarded it as hers in 1960, and sent in her police to clean out the robbers and murderers who had long used it as a hiding place.

A general deterioration of Sino-British relations followed the leasing of the New Territories. The two empires were at odds over the maintenance of Chinese customs stations in the New Territories, the presence of Chinese warships in Kowloon Bay and the treatment of Chinese prisoners in Hong Kong jails. Moreover, each disagreement was intensified by the patriotic fervor which led to the Boxer Rebellion.

At the opening of the twentieth century, the Chinese Empire had been driven into a hopeless position. Bound and crippled like the feet of her women, she had neither the weapons nor the industrial capacity to repel the encroaching armies of Europe and Japan. By any reasonable standard, she was beaten before she started to fight back.

Out of China's desperation grew a super-patriotic secret society, The Fist of Righteous Harmony, or Boxers, who claimed that magical powers sustained their cause, making them invulnerable to the superior weapons of foreigners. Occult arts and a rigorous program of physical training, the Boxers professed, would carry them to victory. It was a crusade of absurdity; foolish and foredoomed, but plainly preferable to unresisting surrender.

The Boxers opened their offensive by murdering missionaries and Chinese Christians, causing a new rush of refugees to Hong Kong. They burned foreign legations in Peking and sent the surviving Chinese Christians and foreigners fleeing to the British legation for safety. An international army, composed of French, German, Russian, American and Japanese units, lifted the siege of the legation on August 14, 1900, and remained in Peking until peace was signed eleven months later.

Recurrences of plague killed 7,962 persons in the colony at the turn of the century, but the discovery that plague was borne by rats prompted a war to exterminate them. Rewards of a few cents were paid for their carcasses, and profit-hungry Chinese were suspected of importing rats from Canton to claim the bounty. The threat of plague gradually decreased, but malaria tuberculosis, pneumonia, and cholera remained to ravage the refugee-jammed colony.

On September 18, 1906, a two-hour-long typhoon hit the colony without warning, drowning fifteen Europeans and from 5,000 to 10,000 Chinese. No one could accurately estimate the deaths, which were concentrated among the fishermen and boat people, but nearly 2,500 Chinese boats of all types were hammered into kindling wood or sunk without trace. Fifty-nine European ships were badly damaged and a French destroyer broke in two. Piers and sea walls were breached and undermined, and 190 houses were blown down or rendered uninhabitable. Roads and telephone lines were washed out, farm crops and tree plantations were laid low by the power of the worst storm in local history. Damage estimates ranged far into the millions.

In the aftermath of the typhoon, all elements of the population cooperated to raise a relief fund. The money collected was used to repair wrecked boats, recover and bury the dead, feed and house the homeless and provide for the widows and orphans of storm victims. (The horror of this catastrophe was reenacted on September 2, 1937, when a typhoon and tidal wave engulfed a New Territories fishing village, drowning thousands.)

The dawn of the twentieth century marked the final collapse of the Celestial Empire. Dr. Sun Yat Sen, who had been banished from Hong Kong in 1896 for plotting against the Chinese government, steadily intensified his revolutionary activities until, in 1911, he led the revolution which overthrew the tottering monarchy and replaced it with the Republic of China. The unrest that accompanied this violent change-over caused more than 50,000 refugees to cross the Chinese border into British territory.

The transition from empire to republic did not end China's internal turmoil, and for many years afterward its political disturbances were felt in Hong Kong. Piracy flourished in the waters around the colony; one band of corsairs set fire to a steamship, causing the deaths of 300 passengers. Brigands and warlords preyed on southern China, sometimes making forays across the colony's border to pounce on villages in the New Territories. China was torn by political struggles during the 1920s, and these provoked strikes within the colony and Chinese boycotts of Hong Kong goods. All through this period, refugees poured across the border in unending lines.

The world-wide depression of the 1930s brought a sharp drop in colony trade, but the government created jobs for thousands with road-building and other public works.

Japan opened its war against China in 1937, and within a year Hong Kong was bursting with the addition of 600,000 refugees. Poverty and overcrowded housing offered ideal conditions for epidemics of smallpox and beriberi which killed 4,500 persons in 1938. Still, the total population climbed to 1,600,000. Government refugee camps housed about 5,000 people; another 27,000 regularly slept in the streets.

Emboldened by victories in China and an alliance with Nazi Germany, the Japanese militarists launched their "Greater Far Eastern Co-Prosperity Sphere" by attacking Hong Kong, Pearl Harbor and the Philippines on December 7-8, 1941. Crossing the Chinese border at Lo Wu in the New Territories, two Japanese divisions supported by overwhelming air power invaded and conquered the colony within three weeks. They proceeded without pause to loot its warehouses and strip its factories of machinery for shipment to Japan.

The Japanese imprisoned the remaining British residents and raped and pillaged at will. By torture, starvation, and main force they drove a million Chinese residents from the colony and maintained a merciless control over the survivors by propaganda, intimidation, imprisonment and the use of Chinese fifth-columnists.

With their smashing victories in the Philippines, East Indies and at Singapore, the Japanese should have found it comparatively easy to unite Asiatics against the whites who had once lorded it over them. But they suffered from the same compulsion as the Germans; at a time when they had a chance to win allies among the people they had conquered, they botched it by senseless cruelties. When their firecracker-like string of victories had burned out, they had gained no friends, but instead had earned millions of new enemies.

Nearly four years passed before the Japanese were beaten into unconditional surrender and the British rulers returned to Hong Kong. Their return had a kind of spectral quality as the British Pacific Fleet, commanded by Rear Admiral C. H. J. Harcourt, steamed through Lei Yue Mun pass, gliding under the silent muzzles of Japanese guns emplaced along the mountainsides with their crews standing at attention beside them.

This was on August 30, 1945. The British went ashore to find thousands of their countrymen and other Allied prisoners gaunt and starving in prison camps. Many had been crippled and deformed by torture. Others had been killed in Allied bombing raids on Hong Kong. Seven large and seventy-two small ships had been sunk in the harbor, 27,000 homes had been destroyed. The fishing fleet was in ruins and the fishermen were in rags. Nine-tenths of the surviving residents were dead broke, while a few collaborators and black-marketers had accumulated fortunes. Livestock had virtually disappeared. Millions of carefully cultivated trees, planted to check erosion and retain the run-off of tropical rainfall for drainage into the reservoirs, had been chopped down to provide firewood. Schools were almost entirely suspended. Railroads and ferry lines were in an advanced stage of disrepair. Disease and crime had reached their highest rates in many years.

The British, who are inclined to procrastinate in the solution of small crises, can be indomitable in the face of major emergencies. Within six months after reoccupying the colony they had restored its government and society to working order. Six years after the British return, the colony was more prosperous, more congested, and more progressive than it had ever been before.

Nationalist China was driven from the mainland in 1949, and a new Communist state took its place. Britain promptly recognized Red China as the ruling power on the mainland, but relations between the Chinese Reds and Hong Kong were strained by Communist-caused disturbances in the colony and shooting "incidents" at sea and in the air. There was no apparent danger of war, however. In 1951, the colony's trade amounted to $1,550,000,000, the highest point it had ever reached.

If there were signs of complacency in Hong Kong, they were erased by the outbreak of the Korean war. The United Nations clamped immediate restrictions on the colony's trade with Red China, and Red China slashed its imports from Hong Kong. Trade volume declined still further when Hong Kong voluntarily halted its exports to Korea and the sending of strategic materials to Red China. The United States at first included Hong Kong in its embargo of all trade with Red China, but the colony prevailed upon America to ease the ban. America agreed to accept goods from Hong Kong, provided that they were accompanied by a Certificate of Origin attesting that they were made in Hong Kong and had not simply been transshipped from Communist China through the colony.

With the China market gone, as well as Hong Kong's traditional role as a transshipper to and from China, the colony executed its most spectacular economic somersault since 1841; it switched from trading to manufacturing. In six years, the great entrepôt became an important industrial producer. By 1962, over 70 percent of the goods it exported were made in the colony, and about half its workers were employed in industry.

Having performed this overnight flip-flop without suffering an economic set-back, Hong Kong has become more prosperous than ever. Except that it has too many people, hasn't enough land to stand on, can't raise enough food or store enough water, is incessantly harried by rising tariffs and shipping costs, and has no idea what its testy, gigantic neighbor to the north will do next, Hong Kong would appear not to have a worry in the world.

CHAPTER TWO

An Avalanche from the North

"When one reads of 1,000,000 homeless exiles all human compassion baulks and the great sum of human tragedy becomes a matter of statistical examination."

—"A PROBLEM OF PEOPLE," Hong Kong
Annual Report, 1956

From the end of World War II until the fall of 1949 the mainland of China rumbled with the clash of contending armies. Thousands of Chinese, uprooted and dispossessed by the Nationalist-Communist struggle, streamed southward across the Hong Kong border in a steady procession.

The orderly nature of the exodus ended when Mao Tse-tung, having beaten and dispersed the Nationalist forces of Chiang Kai-shek, turned his guns on all people suspected of thinking or acting against the People's Republic of China. What had been a slow withdrawal became a headlong flight for life.

For six months after the Reds took over the mainland,

Hong Kong clung to its free-immigration policy. Then it reluctantly adopted a formula of "one in, one out"—accepting one immigrant if another person returned to China. But the refugee flow continued at a reduced rate in spite of land and sea patrols on both sides of the international boundary.

In 1956, the British relaxed immigration rules for seven months, hoping the refugees would go home. Instead, 56,000 new refugees arrived from China, and the colony reimposed its restrictions.

The Chinese side of the frontier unexpectedly opened in May, 1962, and 70,000 refugees dashed for Hong Kong. The colony, alarmed and already desperately overcrowded, strengthened and extended its boundary fence and returned all but 10,000 of the new arrivals to China.

This race for freedom aroused the Free World's tardy compassion. The United States moved to admit 6,000 Hong Kong refugees, including some who had applied for admission as long ago as 1954. Taiwan, Brazil, and Canada also expressed willingness to accept a limited number. Until this change of heart, Taiwan had taken only 15,000 colony refugees, and the United States only 105 a year. None of these offers will materially reduce the number of Hong Kong refugees, whose total is officially estimated at 1,000,000. Unofficial estimates set the total around 1,500,000.

Whatever the total within this range, it stuns the imagination. The well-intentioned observer who has come to sympathize finds himself backing away from this amorphous mass, unable to isolate or grasp its human content of individual misery, privation and heartache. He wants to help, as he would do if he saw a child struck down in the road, but when the whole landscape is a panorama of tragedy, he hardly knows where to begin.

There are a dozen landscapes like that in Hong Kong; the hills of Upper Kowloon with thousands of flimsy shacks perched uncertainly on their steep granite faces; the heights above Causeway Bay where squatter settlements flow down the mountainside like a glacier of rubbish; the rooftops of Wanchai, maggoty with close-packed sheds; the rotting tenements of the Central District strewn in terraces of misery across the lower slopes of Victoria Peak; the sink-hole of the old Walled City in Kowloon with its open sewers and such dark, narrow alleys that its inhabitants seem to be groping around in a cave with a few holes punched through the roof.

Yet there are people in the colony who have chosen to cut their way through this thick tangle of indiscriminate suffering. Going beyond that first fragile desire to help and the secondary conclusion that no one person can do anything effective against a problem of such vast dimensions, they have learned to stand in the path of an avalanche and direct traffic. They have opened a way to solve the refugee problem by the simple process of starting somewhere. Ultimate solutions, in the sense of housing and feeding all the refugees by giving them productive jobs in a free economy, lie many years and millions of dollars away. Meanwhile, people of courage and resolution, dealing with individual human needs instead of wallowing in statistics, have achieved wonders in improving the lot of Hong Kong's refugees. Who they are and what they have done offer the real key to Hong Kong's problem of people.

Sister Annie Margareth Skau, a Norwegian missionary nurse of towering physical and spiritual stature, began her work among Hong Kong's refugees with invaluable postgraduate training. She herself was a refugee from China, driven out by the Reds.

Born in Oslo, she studied nursing at its City Hospital and decided to become a "personal Christian," dedicating her life to labor as a missionary nurse of the Covenanters, or Mission Covenant Church of Norway. The work was certain to be arduous, for the Covenanters sent their workers to such remote corners of the world as Lapland, the Congo or the interior of China. Annie, who has an almost mystical intensity of religious faith, had no qualms about her probable assignments. Besides, she looked about as large and indestructible as Michelangelo's Moses, and possessed a temperament of ebullient good nature.

After serving successfully in several other missions, she was sent to China in the late 1930s. Establishing herself at a mission in Shensi, northeastern China, she was the only Western-trained medical worker among the 2,000,000 residents of this agricultural region. In all likelihood, she was the largest woman ever seen by the Chinese children under her care—over six feet, four inches tall, with a Valkyrie's frame—but so gentle that none of the children were awed by her presence. Her appearance anywhere was a signal for laughter and games; she never seemed too tired to play with children and teach them little songs.

Invading Japanese armies passed within two miles of her mission and clinic in 1938, but none of the villagers ever betrayed the foreigner's presence. She had a quick, retentive mind, and learned to speak Mandarin Chinese almost as well as she knew her own language. On the rare occasions when an English-speaking visitor reached the out-of-the-way settlement, he was surprised to find Sister Annie speaking his language quite capably. Throughout the war and into the postwar era, she continued to bring Christianity and expert medical care to her adopted people.

When the Communists seized control of China, however, the Christian missionaries were doomed. The Christian God became a hateful image in a shrine reserved for Lenin, Stalin and Mao Tse-tung, and a beloved missionary nurse in a farming village was transformed into an enemy of the people. The commissars and their lackeys began by hedging Annie about with arbitrary regulations, then they confiscated medical supplies intended for her patients.

None of these measures succeeded in halting her work. Exasperated at their failure, the local party leaders finally dragged her before a kangaroo-style People's Court. The word had been passed that any villager who arose to denounce her for crimes against the state would be handsomely rewarded. Not a single accuser appeared. Having lost face before the entire village, the Reds were more determined than ever to punish her.

If no one who knew Sister Annie could be lured into a denunciation of her, the obvious solution was to haul her off to a distant village where no one knew her. Having done this, the Reds threw her into jail as an object-lesson to anyone who befriended Christians. An old woman, knowing nothing of Annie but remembering the humane work of other missionary nurses in the village, begged the Communists to put her in jail with the foreign prisoner so that she could comfort her.

"Even the guards were kind to me," Annie recalls. "The village people didn't jeer at me or try to hurt me; they kept trying to pass food to me. They were loyal to the last minute!"

Under the relentless persecution and mistreatment, Annie's strong body broke down, and in the summer of 1951, she was close to death from pneumonia and malaria. The Reds, who refused to let her leave the country when she was well, hurried to get rid of the ailing woman. Exhausted and gravely ill, she left China and returned to Norway for a long rest and the slow regaining of her normal health.

Eighteen months later she came back to Asia knowing that she would never be readmitted to a Communist China. But there was still work to be done, and she turned her efforts to a squalid shacktown in Hong Kong called Rennie's Mill Camp.

Three years earlier the routed remnants of Chiang's army, left behind on the mainland, had thrown together a cluster of shacks beside Junk Bay, a backwater of the British colony without roads, water, light or sanitation. Nearly 8,000 persons, wounded soldiers and their wives and children, camped haphazardly on the steep shores of the bay, ran up the Nationalist flag and claimed the forlorn site as their own.

When Annie reached the camp in March, 1953, traveling by sampan and clambering over the high hills like a lost Viking, she found it haunted by despair; a dirty, disease-ridden place, dragged down by the decline of the Nationalist cause. Another nurse had started a small clinic in a wooden hut, eight by ten feet in floor area, which treated 600 patients a day. Annie and the other nurse shared sleeping quarters in a cubicle attached to the hut.

Sometimes the cases were so numerous and critical that the two nurses put the worst cases in their own cramped beds and spent the night on their feet treating other patients. Their medical equipment consisted of one thermometer, a few antiseptics and dressings, and a rickety table that wobbled groggily on the half-decayed floorboards.

With the approach of Christmas, 1953, the fortunes of the clinic sank to a new low. Both nurses were quite broke, unable to buy the food and medical supplies their patients needed so critically. Acting more from faith than reason, Annie set out to pick her way over the precipitous rocks to Lei Yue Mun pass and cross by sampan to Hong Kong Island, hoping to beg for help.

To her delighted surprise, the mission's post-office box on the island produced a windfall—$200 in contributions from ten persons overseas. Charging into the shopping crowds, Annie spent every cent on food and medicine. She scarcely noticed the weight of her purchases as she trekked the hard route back to Rennie's Mill. Until three o'clock Christmas morning, the two nurses were on their feet, handing out life-saving presents and exchanging holiday greetings in Mandarin and Cantonese.

"The money problems weren't so bad after that," Annie says. "Gifts came in from welfare organizations and individuals, and we were able to build a little stone clinic and a home for ourselves."

At the same time, health problems grew worse at Rennie's Mill. Drug addiction and tuberculosis spread through the camp as its inhabitants abandoned hope of an early return to China.

"Bad housing and poor food started the TB," she explains. "But it got much worse when people gave up hope, or heard about their relatives being killed by the Communists. Chinese people are devoted to their parents, and to be separated from them, or learn they've been killed—it's heartbreaking.

"That was when we realized we'd have to build a rest home for those patients," Annie says. "We didn't have any money; all we had was a mission to do the best we could. One day I boarded a sampan with a group of children and we rowed out into Junk Bay until we came to a little inlet. I saw a hill just above us, jutting right out to the shore. I knew right then we would build our chapel on that hill."

Annie discusses the incident with the fervor and conviction of one who has received a private revelation.

"I saw the whole rest-center arranged around that chapel
almost as if it were already completed, built around love. I
had no idea where the money was coming from, not any kind
of an architect's plan, but it didn't matter. I knew that Christ
would find a way."

A way began to appear when a nurse who had worked with
Sister Annie visited the United States in 1954, telling children
in Wisconsin schools about their work. The response was elec-
trifying. One small boy stood up beside his desk to announce
with utter seriousness, "I want to give my heart to Jesus." The
appeal spread like a prairie fire; by February, 1955, Wisconsin
school children had sent more than $2,500 for the new rest
home, which was called Haven of Hope Sanatorium. An
anonymous contributor donated another $5,000 through the
Church World Service, Hong Kong welfare agency of the
National Council of Churches of Christ in America.

"Now our sanatorium had walls and a roof," Annie says.
"So we prayed for furniture and food for our patients—and
for bedpans, too.

"It was a hand-to-mouth existence," she remembers without a trace of self-pity. "Our staff had no resources—we were
so short of staff that some of us worked for two years without a day off. We didn't mind it at all; we worked with one
mind and one spirit, as if that sanatorium and what it stood for
was our one reason for living."

In its early stages, the sanatorium was nothing more than a
rest home. One day, almost as an afterthought on a busy
round of duties, Annie asked a few of her patients to help her
with some routine tasks. They pitched in at once and returned
the following day to volunteer for more duties. They kept at

the work for several days, then called on Annie in a kind of delegation.

"Give us instructions, show us what to do," they respectfully demanded. "We want to learn how to be real nurses."

Annie agreed, taking care to see that none of the volunteers exerted themselves beyond the limits of their precarious health. After three months, they insisted on examinations to show what they had learned.

From modest and tentative beginnings, the courses multiplied and expanded into a full-scale nursing school, offering a two-and-a-half-year progression of classes in eleven different subjects, with stiff exams. Most of the pupils are girls between eighteen and twenty who specialize in TB nursing. The eleventh class was graduated in February, 1962, and the demand for new enrollments was so brisk that Annie, as Director of Nursing Services, could accept only five out of sixty eager applicants.

The sanatorium grew into a 206-bed institution of modern and spotless appearance, and a 40-bed rehabilitation center for chronic and infectious TB patients has been built nearby. Church World Service cut a road through to the isolated site and it was later paved by the colony government. Tuberculosis has been brought under control at Rennie's Mill Camp, and the Haven of Hope is drawing many of its patients from outside. There is no danger of a shortage; TB strikes everywhere among Hong Kong's poor.

Haven of Hope is administered by the Junk Bay Medical Council, which also operates a clinic at Rennie's Mill. Four doctors comprise the sanatorium staff. Except for Annie and Miss Martha Boss, the assistant matron, from Cleveland, Ohio, all the nurses are Chinese. Miss Boss, trained in the same diligent tradition as Annie, spends three days a week at the sanatorium, three days on church work and school duties in Rennie's Mill, and the seventh day on an industrial medical project.

Rennie's Mill Camp no longer looks like a shacktown. Catholic and Protestant mission schools have been established, and many residents are employed in handicraft shops. A new police post has been erected beside the camp, and a bus line carries camp residents to the business and shopping districts of Kowloon. Soon a reservoir is to be constructed with government aid on a hill above the camp, and a modern housing development will replace inadequate dwellings.

Taiwanese flags still fly in the breeze at many places in the camp, and Nationalist Chinese contribute to its support. But its main lease on life comes from the churches and the colony of Hong Kong.

Although the scope of Annie's activities has become much wider, she has lost none of her personal and religious attitude. When she walks through the wards she is followed by the smiles of hundreds of children. At any moment, she will stop to lead a grinning group of little girls, perched on their beds like sparrows, in a song. With Annie joining in the gestures, the kids sing out in Cantonese "Jesus loves little children . . . like me . . . (pointing to themselves) . . . like you . . . (pointing at Annie or the girl in the nearest bed) . . . like all the others" (with a big, wide-open sweep of the arms).

Annie hugs a lively, black-haired youngster and says quietly, "Her mother was seven months pregnant when she swam from China to Macao with this little one on her back. The girl's been here two years, and she's gradually getting better. Her mother went back to China, and has probably been liquidated by the Communists."

Another girl reacts to Annie's pat on the head with the wiggly cordiality of a puppy.

"This little one was scared to death of 'imperialists' when she came here," Annie explains. "It took us a long time to persuade her that the Red propaganda wasn't true."

Her first two patients at Haven of Hope, a brother and sister, have now completely recovered. Both had seen their parents tortured and killed by the Reds.

"When the girl came to us, her face was like stone," Annie says. "For two years I played with her, trying all kinds of funny things to bring her out of that frozen stupor, but she never smiled once.

"I wasn't getting anywhere," she continues. "Then I tried something different. On July 6, 1955, I put her in a sampan with eleven other kids, and took them all to see the wonderful new building we'd just finished. You know, the first time she got a look at it she broke into a big smile! It was the first time she looked happy. Now she's fourteen, and her greatest ambition is to be a nurse."

A magnificent chapel, built exactly where Annie had visualized it, was completed in time for Christmas services in 1961. A group of Norwegian seamen donated an illuminated cross to surmount its roof. At night, when their ships sail out from Hong Kong, they can see it glowing above a line of hills that cut back from the sea like the fiords of Norway.

To Annie, the chapel embodies the same spirit she expressed in naming the eleven wards at Haven of Hope Sanatorium: Love, Peace, Joy, Patience, Kindness, Goodness, Faithfulness, Neatness, Temperance, Hope and Courage.

For qualities like these, exemplified in her work at Rennie's Mill Camp and the sanatorium, Sister Annie Margareth Skau was given the Florence Nightingale Award of the International Red Cross on May 18, 1961. Annie regarded the award not as a personal tribute, but as an honor earned and shared by everyone who worked or contributed to make the Haven of Hope a reality.

"There is so much that needs to be done for these poor, homeless people," she says. "Why, we've hardly begun the job."

In 1951, the same year that Annie Skau was exiled from Red China, the Communists drove out a remarkable European-Chinese couple who had been helping moneyless families to support themselves by setting up home industries. Their house, with all their savings invested in it, was seized by the state and they reached Hong Kong with a total capital of thirty-four cents.

The husband, Gus Borgeest, had been a production expediter in a Shanghai textile mill for twenty years. His background was almost as international as the U.N.; a British subject, he was born in Shanghai of mixed British, Danish, Portuguese, Italian and German ancestry. Mona, his Christian-Chinese wife, was born of Cantonese parents in the Hong Kong fishing town of Aberdeen.

During the Japanese invasion, Gus was interned for two years. He spent his time in prison reading about the Quakers and became converted to their ideal of helping others. When the war ended, he returned to his Shanghai job until Mona contracted tuberculosis. To aid her recovery, the couple moved to the more favorable climate of Hangchow. It was only a stopover, for the political climate that developed after the Reds took control made the survival of Christian welfare workers an impossibility.

Arriving in Hong Kong, Gus found a job in the Fish and

Vegetable Marketing Organization of the colony government. Mona had regained her health, and the two of them spent their spare hours doing refugee welfare work in the squatter settlements. It was thoroughly discouraging; living conditions were deplorable and the refugees, subsisting on handouts, were losing their pride and initiative.

"We aren't accomplishing anything," Gus told Mona. "It's a waste of time—unless we can do something, find some way to help people earn their way out of these miserable firetraps."

After a long series of discussions in which they considered and discarded a variety of self-help schemes, Gus and Mona agreed to stake all their resources on one hopeful but wholly untried plan. They put aside every spare penny until they had saved $700. Now Gus was ready to present their plan to the appropriate officials of the colony government.

He went to K. M. A. Barnett, District Commissioner and the colony's top authority on the Chinese people and their customs. Mr. Barnett listened in some wonderment while Gus outlined a proposal to build a refugee rehabilitation center on a desolate island seven miles west of Hong Kong Island. He would teach people how to make a living by farming marginal land—and there was plenty of such land lying idle in the colony.

The Commissioner was friendly, but he needed the answers to certain questions. What was Gus's farming experience? Twenty years in a textile plant. Why did Gus think he could grow anything on that island? Hadn't the Chinese farmers abandoned it?—and they could grow almost anything, anywhere! Gus was positive he could make it go. Did he have any money? Gus mentioned the $700 and said he was sure it would be enough for a starter. On the face of it, the plan looked highly unfeasible to Mr. Barnett, but he sensed something out of the ordinary in Gus's determination. Besides, the Commissioner reflected, his office was never crowded with people who intended to do something simply for the benefit of their fellow men.

Having weighed the matter thoroughly, District Commissioner Barnett recommended that the strange couple from Shanghai be given a chance. The colony government leased the barren, 200-acre island to Gus for thirty-four dollars a year, and he and Mona spent most of their savings to buy two tents, bedding, a sack of rice, cooking utensils and farming tools.

On June 5, 1953, Gus, Mona, their five-year-old daughter, Naomi, and two refugee farmers set sail for their new home, which Gus had rechristened Sunshine Island, in a hired junk. On their first night ashore it rained four inches in two hours, but they stuck it out with Mona doing the cooking and Naomi scampering around for field grass to ignite the fire. Twelve days after they landed, a refugee fisherman, his wife and daughter nosed their leaky boat against a sandy beach and became the next settlers.

Within a month, Gus and his helpers had tilled a small patch of land and were raising some chickens, geese and nanny goats. Three-fourths of his capital had been consumed by these improvements and the farming books he pored over every night. An interest-free loan from a Quaker friend kept the venture afloat, and they sweated through the humid summer building grass huts, planting crops, and slashing paths through the shoulder-high sword grass.

Any heavenly blessings they received did not cover weather conditions, for Typhoon Tess flattened their huts and tore up their garden. Yet the improbable colony earned its first income at the end of five months—$2.60 from the sale of rab-

bits they had raised. Loans and small gifts from friends overseas furnished additional support. Virtually nothing went
swimmingly; the first few families who joined them on Sunshine couldn't stomach the solitary island and had no interest
in working to pay their way.

One of the worst catastrophes in Hong Kong history—
the Shek Kip Mei fire that destroyed the shacks of more than
60,000 squatters—created an unsought opportunity for Gus.
Strapped for cash, he landed a temporary job helping to re-
locate the fire victims and sent his earnings back to Mona, who
kept the Sunshine Island project breathing. He returned in a
few months to find the island earning about one-third of what
the Borgeests had spent on it.

Both of them decided on some major changes. He talked to
welfare agencies and secured their help in selecting people
who had the desire and the qualifications to benefit from the
scheme; farmers and those who wanted to learn simple trades,
or people like Professor Ting, a former lecturer at Hangchow Christian College, who was willing to mind the geese
while building up his shattered health. Every worker on the
island earned $.35 a day, plus food and lodging for his family;
a puny income, even by Hong Kong standards, but in their
view, infinitely preferable to handouts.

Welfare organizations in Hong Kong had been watching
the progress of the fledgling colony and were quick to appreciate its value. The United Church of Canada donated $960,
the Hong Kong Welfare Society put up $30 a month to pay
families working on the island, and other agencies joined in—
Church World Service, Catholic Relief Services and the Lutheran World Federation—sending cash, supplies and carefully
chosen settlers.

When the first stone houses on the island were completed in

1955, Gus struck a note of triumph by giving them the high-sounding name of Villa Borghese—a salute to his Italian ancestors. Twenty families, comprising 100 persons, had entered wholeheartedly into the spirit of the plan, digging terraced gardens from the rocky hillsides and planting pineapples. Bamboo, banana, and pine trees were set firmly on the hillsides or in the sheltered hollow between Sunshine's two highest hills. Refugee students, earning their tuition from welfare agencies, excavated a fish-breeding pond.

For the first time Gus was able to pay himself a salary of $36 a month, but as often as not in succeeding months he turned it right back into the kitty to balance his accounts. Periodic crises like typhoons, crop failures, and the death of valuable livestock regularly badgered the colony, but Gus contrived to ride them out.

In 1957, Gus was laid low by a serious case of tuberculosis. For six months he reluctantly remained in a chair placed on a sunny terrace in front of his house. From there he directed Mona in the management of the colony. Gradually regaining his strength, he recovered fully in two years and resumed active charge of the enterprise.

Increased aid from the outside enabled Gus to raise every worker's daily pay to 70 cents. Sunshine Island lost its bleak look; besides its new stone buildings, it had over 800 fruit trees and 300 pigs, including 30 breeding sows. Roads had been chopped through its spiny ridges, knitting the whole project together.

Hong Kong's government staff, satisfied that Gus was doing something solidly beneficial for refugees, furnished district officers, agriculturists, forestry and fisheries experts as consultants on various Sunshine Island jobs.

But the human dividends of Sunshine Island were far more

impressive than its physical achievements. More than 700 men and women, including a number of drug addicts, had found new hope on the island. After working there for six months or a year and creating a small nest-egg from their savings, they applied their newly acquired skills to start their own farms on marginal land or get jobs in the city. A large majority of them are now earning their own living in the British colony.

Gus, having conceived Sunshine Island as a pilot project for farming marginal land, schooled a group of his "graduates" in a marginal-farm resettlement at Cheung Sheung, in the New Territories. Each new farmer received two acres from the Hong Kong government, plus a cow, farm tools and a small cash allowance. Practically all of them made the grade as independent farmers.

Activities expanded once more on Sunshine Island when the Hong Kong Junior Chamber of Commerce donated $2,500 to build a piggery for 30 animals, and 20 more sties were added to it in 1961. Papaya and pomegranate trees were added to the orchard. The island became a local attraction for visitors, with Boy Scouts and other youth organizations camping and swimming at a beach on the side of the island most distant from the farm area.

With the knowledge he paid a steep price for on Sunshine Island, Gus has set up marginal-farm projects at three more locations besides Cheung Sheung.

"I think that Mona and I have reached our first major objective," he said, early in 1962. "That is to show refugee families a better way of living than handouts and squatter settlements, and to help strengthen the over-strained economy of Hong Kong."

Several other organizations have adopted the self-help

system pioneered by the Borgeests, and Gus is ready to move on to fresh challenges once the Sunshine Island settlement becomes self-supporting. He believes this can be done within three years; from there on, he would like to turn Sunshine over to an administrative committee capable of running it without him.

The island has become a bustling work center. A one-handed stonemason who has built hundreds of feet of stone-and-cement walls for pig pastures is erecting the walls of another piggery. Dozens of Hakka women in their black-fringed straw hats are transporting dirt in straw baskets to clear the site of a new road. One man tirelessly splits boulders with a heavy hammer and a chisel; while he works, he listens to Cantonese music issuing from his transistor radio, perched on an adjoining rock. A sampan taxi, operating between Sunshine and the nearby island of Peng Chau, supports a family with several children and a seaworthy chow dog.

Gus is absorbed in new plans to help others. Two years ago he undertook a complete survey of the island of Shek Kwu Chau, two miles west of Sunshine, to determine whether it could be made into a rehabilitation center for some of Hong Kong's 250,000 narcotics addicts. With only slight modifications, the survey has become the blueprint for the center, opening in 1962 under the administration of the Society for the Aid and Rehabilitation of Drug Addicts. He was one of the early developers of Hei Ling Chau, the island leprosarium run by the Mission to Lepers, and remains a member of its administrative council.

On the last day of August, 1961, Gus and Mona became winners of a Ramon Magsaysay Award, the "Nobel Prize of the East," for their Sunshine Island accomplishments. The award also carried a $10,000 prize, and the Borgeests decided to save it for the education of their three daughters.

"We have no other funds," Gus explained. "But a lot of people who heard about the prize must have decided that old Gus is on easy street. Our contributions fell off, and our debts started shooting up again."

At fifty-two, Gus is a ruggedly built man whose face and bald head have been burned dark brown by the sun. His one gospel is the doctrine of helping others to help themselves.

"The Chinese people don't want to live on anybody's charity," Gus said. "And that's doubly true of the refugees; they wouldn't have come here, most of them, if they'd been willing to become stooges for a government that did all the thinking for them."

Gus has a well-defined conception of the way he prefers to spend his own future:

"I'd like to devote the rest of my life to work among the lepers and drug addicts. We couldn't do much for the addicts on Sunshine; we'd get them accustomed to living without drugs, but they'd slip back into addiction when they met their old companions back in the city.

"And if there's time enough, I'd like to go to one of the rural areas in the Philippines with Mona and set up another place like Sunshine Island. With what we've learned here, I know we could do a lot better."

The heroic works of the Borgeests and Sister Annie Skau, outstanding though they are, have directly affected the lives of less than one percent of Hong Kong's refugees. But the dimensions of the crisis are so great that they have engaged the attention of scores of humane and intelligent people. They have gone far beyond routine assistance to devise creative and practical solutions to the colony's refugee problems.

Monsignor John Romaniello, a Maryknoll missionary from New Rochelle, N.Y., used his noodle to produce millions of meals for hungry refugees. A roundish man with nothing on his mind but the Lord's work and noodles, he revels in his title as "noodle king of Hong Kong." He sings about noodles, writes about noodles, puns about noodles and buttonholes every American tourist he meets for contributions to buy more noodles.

It is showmanship with a purpose. Behind the kidding lies an idea so obvious that no one ever thought of it until Monsignor Romaniello came to Hong Kong in 1957 as director of Catholic Relief Services. He noticed that millions of dollars' worth of American surplus foods like milk powder, corn meal, and wheat flour being sent to the colony to feed refugees were winding up on the black market. Having lived among the Chinese for thirty years, he decided to keep a close eye on the surplus-food traffic.

One day he observed a young girl taking a sack of surplus flour into a bakery, then paying the baker to convert it into noodles. The simple incident stayed in his mind, nagging at him. Later, while riding across the harbor on the Star Ferry, the answer to a gigantic riddle came to him in one reflective flash; the little girl was paying to have the flour made into noodles because her mother, like most refugee mothers, had no way of turning the flour into an edible meal. The same was true of corn meal; there was neither space nor cooking facilities for it in the average refugee cubicle. In their raw state, the surplus foods were alien to a Chinese palate.

Why not convert these foods into noodles? No colony baker was equipped to handle the job on the scale Monsignor Romaniello envisioned. On any scale, the cost was too high for the refugee feeding program. Monsignor Romaniello, helped by other Maryknoll fathers, constructed a noodle-making machine out of scrap parts and an old engine. It looked like nothing ever designed by engineers, but it rolled out the noodles.

The Maryknoll noodles caught on at once with the Chinese, who found them easy to prepare and agreeable to eat. With funds provided by Catholic Relief Services and the Hong Kong Junior Chamber of Commerce, the first noodle-making contraption was replaced by a production-line model. Within four years, Hong Kong noodles were pouring out of the machines at the rate of 5,000,000 pounds a year, and welfare organizations like the Church World Service had adopted them. Noodle machines were exported to the Philippines, Macao, Taiwan, Korea and Vietnam as the noodle mania grew.

Another Catholic priest, working in a phase of welfare work wholly unlike that of the "noodle king," has achieved a degree of success comparable to that of Monsignor Romaniello. He is Father P. J. Howatson, an Irish Jesuit who has become a key figure in the colony's youth leadership program.

Welfare workers will tell you, holding their breath as they do so, that gangs of young hoodlums have not yet infested Hong Kong. Widespread poverty, overcrowded housing, and a predominantly young population seem to offer fertile soil for their growth, but welfare people believe juvenile gangs have not appeared primarily because of the integral unity of the Chinese family, with its respect for parents and elders.

There is a second line of defense, the Boys' and Girls' Clubs Association, which embraces 13,000 of the poorest youngsters in its recreational and leadership programs. Father Howatson is the prime mover in the Association, doing some of its finest work among rooftop squatters in Wanchai, a waterfront jungle of bars and cabarets where shiploads of pent-up sailors are regularly turned loose.

Because of the magnitude of Hong Kong's welfare needs and the bewildering assortment of private organizations attempting to deal with them, there is an absolute necessity for a central clearinghouse to eliminate overlapping in some areas and neglect in others. This is the function of the Hong Kong Council of Social Service, a coordinating agency of ninety welfare organizations which regularly checks the balance sheets of its affiliates. If they pass muster, the colony government grants them substantial aid to supplement their own resources.

The Council, under its executive secretary Madge Newcombe, is also charged with discovering where and what the needs of poor people are, and then of assigning the religious or welfare societies best equipped to satisfy them. There is no shortage of needs; the Council's concern is to avoid imbalance and wasted effort in meeting them.

Five years ago the Council created the Central Relief Records Office. With its file of approximately 200,000 cards, listing the name of every relief client and the aid he is receiving from each agency, the office has drastically reduced the duplication of welfare-agency work and chiseling by potential recipients. There is no need for begging; relief is so well organized that any hungry person can get a meal at a welfare agency.

Apart from feeding and housing the colony's displaced persons, there is a human problem of especial poignance. A resettlement estate, at its outset, is an assembly of strangers from all over China, some from big cities, some from back-country hamlets, tossed together like beans in a bowl.

At Wong Tai Sin, one of the largest resettlement estates,

60,000 people are packed into long rows of multi-story concrete blocks. Physically, they are far better off than they were in the shacktowns they came from, but when they first moved in they were strangers lost in a crowd, rootless and with no sense of community interests.

During World Refugee Year (1959-60), the United States government met the problem of building community consciousness at Wong Tai Sin with one of its most effective gifts—$210,000 to build a community center there. Now completed and in full operation, it is a large, modern, five-story building teeming with community enterprises.

The variety of its activities is bewildering: classes for the deaf, courses in Diesel mechanics and refrigeration engineering, Chinese opera, day nurseries, social events, libraries, movies and a hundred other interests—all of them designed to form a congenial community out of thousands of isolated families.

The idea worked so well that the United Kingdom put up an equal amount of money to build a second center in the new-born industrial city of Tsuen Wan. The Toronto and Canadian World Refugee Year committees donated $75,000 for a third community center at Chai Wan, on Hong Kong Island. Others are planned, and the public response to the centers has been so enthusiastic that the colony hopes to establish one in every resettlement estate.

The Hong Kong branch of Church World Service, a department of the National Council of the Churches of Christ in America, picked up fresh vigor a few years ago. Dr. Elbert E. Gates, Jr., pastor of the First Baptist Church of Westfield, N.J., made an incidental stop at Hong Kong during a trip to Australia. He and his wife, June, had a closeup look at the colony's refugees, and what they saw made an unforgettable impression on them. In 1959, he gave up his pastorate and took a one-third cut in salary to become director of the Church World Service branch in Hong Kong.

Working together, the couple have become leaders in colony refugee activities. The statistical side alone is enormous—distributing 53,000 quarts of powdered milk a day and 2,500,000 balanced-ration biscuits a month, and operating a noodle factory and a central kitchen with a daily capacity of 40,000 meals. There are scholarships for young people, dental clinics, foundling homes, homes for orphaned girls and a dozen other undertakings.

Dr. Gates, a cheerful, tireless advocate of the colony's poor people, interrupts his work many times to show overseas visitors what is being done, and still needs to be done, to help the refugees. He takes most pleasure, perhaps, in displaying the "self-help" projects of Church World Service.

At one school in the hills of Kowloon, he directs a home where girls are taught to make dresses, sweaters and ties for the American market. All were formerly homeless, most are under twenty years old, some are blind, others have only one hand or one arm. They have all learned to knit, including the girl with one arm, and are earning their living by making high-quality products for sale in the best stores.

"We don't want to produce curios, or something that tries to play on people's sympathy by calling itself a refugee product," Dr. Gates says. "These girls have proved they can turn out goods that will hold their own in a competitive market."

It is obvious that Doctor and Mrs. Gates are enjoying themselves as much as those they help when they drop into the Faith Hope Nursery, a joint enterprise of Church World Service and the YWCA. The nursery children, two to five years old, are shack-dwellers whose mothers work during the day. At the nursery, the kids receive daytime care, meals, clothes and a daily bath, with plenty of time left over for group singing and dancing. When the pastor and his wife appear, moppet grins spread the width of the classroom and there is a spirited exchange of Cantonese greetings.

Church World Service, together with CARE, Catholic Relief Services and the Lutheran World Service, form the recognized "big four" of Hong Kong's private welfare organizations. Each one does its own work and cooperates willingly with the other three, as well as scores of other Catholic, Protestant and non-denominational groups. One hears a certain amount of subdued muttering about this or that religious group pushing hard for new members, but there is no sign that it has seriously impaired their aim, which is to help all poor people without regard to finicky distinctions of race or religion.

CARE, the non-denominational American member of the big four, made a brilliant and original addition to its long-established welfare program in 1961. This was the Ap Chau Island settlement, built for the families of fishermen.

The people who fish the waters around Ap Chau, a three-acre island in the northeastern corner of the New Territories, had for generations spent their entire lives on fishing junks, never establishing homes on shore or attending schools. But the technical demands of the modern fishing industry put them at a competitive disadvantage, and they petitioned the colony government for permission to build homes on Ap Chau and send their children to school.

Graham French, a Philadelphia philanthropist who was in Hong Kong to observe CARE operations, heard about the petition and became curious enough to investigate it thoroughly. He discovered that the petitioners were so deeply indebted to loan-sharks that they had no real chance to finance housing ashore unless they got outside funds. He offered to give $17,500 to get the settlement started, CARE added another $20,000 and the colony government spent $14,000 to clear a site for the houses.

With these combined funds, a settlement consisting of houses for forty-eight families, or 360 people, was completed in December, 1961. The Royal Engineers laid an undersea 1,000-yard pipeline from a mainland reservoir to supply the island with fresh water. The fishing families, for their part, formed a community cooperative to administer the scheme. Rents go into a revolving fund, and members of the co-op can borrow from it at one percent interest to repair and mechanize their boats.

The fishermen's wives were at first so naïve about living on shore that they tried to furnish their houses with a piled-up heap of boards and braces resembling the poop deck of a fishing junk.

After a time, the seagoing ladies learned to adjust themselves to conventional tables and chairs. Using sewing machines supplied by CARE, they took instructions from the government teacher on the island and learned to sew their own curtains. Their husbands took carpentry instruction at the same school and produced some acceptable furniture. Ultimately, the entire project will become self-supporting.

A similar cooperative settlement has been launched at Sai Kung, a market town in the New Territories. Lawrence and Horace Kadoorie, Hong Kong industrialists and philanthropists, donated pigs to bolster the domestic economy of Sai Kung. Three other allied ventures have been okayed by the government for construction at Tai Tam, on Hong Kong Island, and on the outlying islands of Tsing Yi and Po Toi.

Numerically, the most extensive of all private welfare groups in Hong Kong are the Kaifongs, or Chinese neighborhood welfare associations, with 665,000 members. Operating on slim budgets, they have nevertheless managed to provide medical care, distribute emergency relief supplies, conduct hundreds of free classes, set up noodle factories and give anticholera shots.

The Kaifongs are a departure from the older Chinese practice of limiting charity to your own family or clan; they branch into such community-wide interests as traffic safety and antinoise campaigns. Once they even put on a drive to persuade Kowloon kids not to fly their kites in the path of airliners approaching Kai Tak Airport! (This last one sounds a bit overzealous, but not to anyone who has stood in the streets of Kowloon Tong while the jets roared overhead, all but untying his shoelaces with their vibrations.)

Although the United States government has conducted no regular foreign-aid program in Hong Kong, it has given the colony almost $30,000,000 worth of aid, either as surplus foods or as part of its Far East Refugee Program.

The main burden of relief falls, as it should, on the colony government. The Hong Kong administration spends $10,000,000 annually on social welfare work and more than $55,000,000 a year on every form of direct and indirect aid to its millions of poor residents.

The problem of what to do about its refugees had been with the colony throughout its history. Whenever China was afflicted by famine, unrest or revolution, thousands of its people sought temporary haven in Hong Kong.

Perhaps the most noted refugee of the pre-British era was Ti Ping, the last boy Emperor of the Sung Dynasty, who was driven out of China by the Mongols in 1279 A.D. He encamped on the Kowloon Peninsula for almost a year, then resumed his flight to the west, where he was defeated and drowned in a sea battle with the Mongols. An inscribed rectangular rock called the Sung Wong T'oi, or Terrace of the Sung Emperor, stands near Kai Tak Airport to commemorate his stopover.

The British had barely settled in their new colony when a group of refugees who had been plotting to overthrow the Manchu emperors fled there in the 1840s. Unwilling to endanger their relations with the Manchus, the British branded the plotters under the arm and shipped them back to China. The Tai Ping Rebellion of 1850, fomented by a Christian Chinese, Hung Siu Tsuen, to depose the Manchus, provoked serious disorder in Canton and brought another wave of frightened Chinese to Hong Kong.

Thousands of Chinese streamed into the colony during the next decade, but most of them moved on to the goldfields of California and Australia, or to contract labor in the Americas and the islands of the Indian Ocean. Their passage was expedited by labor-traders who often recruited manpower by kidnaping Orientals and shipping them out in barbarously overcrowded vessels.

The Boxer Rebellion of 1900, bringing a rash of murders of missionaries and Chinese Christians, forced thousands to seek safety in Hong Kong. A far greater number arrived in 1911 when Dr. Sun Yat Sen overthrew the Manchu Empire. In the early chaotic days of the Chinese Republic about 100,000 refugees came to the crown colony, jamming its housing and creating prime conditions for a plague outbreak which presently killed nearly 2,000 persons.

There was a brief reversal in the direction of the refugee procession when Britain entered World War I and 60,000 Chinese turned back home. But continuing disorders in China brought many right back to Hong Kong, and the southward drift persisted through the 1920s.

When the Japanese invaded China in 1937, the drift became a tidal wave; in two years 600,000 refugees crossed the border. The population had reached 1,600,000 when the Japanese attacked Hong Kong in December, 1941.

Having no desire to support such a large population, the Japanese conquerors set to work to reduce the head-count. Their methods were a model of brutality; starvation, execution and driving the Chinese back to their homeland with bayonets. All who attempted to detach themselves from the northbound herd were instantly killed. By the end of the war, the Japanese had cut the colony population to less than 600,000.

During the war, the colony came perilously close to losing its chances of ever being returned to its place in the British Empire. At the Yalta Conference, President Franklin D. Roosevelt told Stalin privately that he thought Hong Kong should be returned to China or made into an internationalized free port after the Japanese were defeated.

Nothing was said to Prime Minister Winston Churchill, who had flatly opposed every attempt to whittle down Britain's colonial possessions. Ten years after, when asked about the Roosevelt proposal, Churchill replied, "According to the American record [of the Yalta Conference], President Roosevelt said he knew I would have strong objections to this suggestion. That was certainly correct—and even an understatement."

Chiang Kai-shek also campaigned for the return of Hong Kong to China and almost as soon as the war ended, James F. Byrnes, American Secretary of State, announced that the future status of Hong Kong would be determined at a meeting of the Council of Foreign Ministers. As soon as they learned about this, the British, led by Prime Minister Clement Attlee, registered their emphatic disapproval and the idea died without further discussion.

Although Hong Kong did not go back to China, the Chinese went back to Hong Kong. During the postwar struggles of Nationalist and Communist forces, thousands of their Chinese countrymen removed to Hong Kong, including virtually all who had been driven from the colony by the Japanese. But the great human avalanche came in 1949, when the Reds gained absolute control of the country. Fugitives from Communist "liberation" swarmed into Hong Kong at the rate of 10,000 a week.

One year after the Communists took over, the colony's population reached 2,360,000. More than 330,000 people were living in hillside squatter settlements, sleeping on the sidewalks, on tenement rooftops, even in the center strip of the widest Kowloon streets. A shacktown fire in 1950 drove 20,000 persons from their homes. The next year a single fire dishoused 10,000 people, and a series of fires in 1952 burned out 15,000 others.

Sooner or later, colony officials told themselves, the refugees would return to China as the immigrant waves of other years had done. The government took a firm stand on the doctrine that it was not supposed to become the landlord for millions of its residents, but it yielded sufficiently to erect temporary wooden huts and bungalows for 40,000 squatters.

All the high-principled resolutions to stay out of the public housing business were swept away on Christmas Night, 1953. A roaring conflagration broke out at Shek Kip Mei, in Upper Kowloon, racing up the tiers of hillside shacks as if it were mounting a flight of steps. Somewhere between 60,000 and 70,000 people were left homeless. About half of them found shelter with friends or relatives, and the government was plunged into the enormous task of feeding, clothing and re-housing the fire victims.

Pausing just long enough to permit the displaced people to sift their few remaining possessions from the ashes, the government bulldozed the 45-acre site, leveled the ground, and had erected emergency accommodations on it in fifty-three days. The streets had hardly been cleared of homeless people when a new shack fire at Tai Hang Tung dishoused 24,000 others.

Simultaneously, the colony recognized the inadequacy of its cottage-and-bungalow housing, which required too much land and provided for too few people. It began the construction of multi-story resettlement estates—six- and seven-story blocks of reinforced concrete clustered together in populous communities. Eleven such estates, lodging 360,000 people in fireproof and typhoon-proof structures, have been completed since 1954 at a cost of $32,000,000. One toilet is shared by hundreds of people and there is no electric light in the rooms unless the tenant pays extra for it. But when they are seen beside the remaining shacks, the multi-story blocks seem immeasurably superior. In addition to the multi-story estates, 80,000 persons have been housed in fourteen cottage resettlement areas.

An apartment in a resettlement block is a concrete-walled room, renting for $1.60 to $4.60 a month. The Hong Kong Housing Authority has built a higher-quality low-cost apartment in skyscraper developments, renting from $8 to $23 a month, and 106,000 persons are to be accommodated in them by 1964.

Around 30,000 people live in flats built by the Hong Kong Housing Society, a voluntary group aided by government loan funds, and this number will be doubled in a few years. If the colony maintains its present rate of building, it can provide new apartments for 100,000 persons annually for the next five years.

This small mountain of statistics looms large on the land-scape until you consider that there are now about 500,000 to 600,000 people living in squatter shacks, on sidewalks and roof-tops and in tumbledown firetrap tenements. Theoretically, they could all be rehoused in five or six years, but the colony's population is rising meanwhile at the rate of 150,000 a year.

The dreams of Hong Kong housing officials are haunted by figures; a baby born every five minutes and illegal immi-grants sneaking across the border at an incalculable rate. Illegal immigration is never estimated at less than 10,000 a year and often set as high as 40,000. Popular guesswork may jack it up to 20,000 a month.

In its own protection, the colony has been forced to for-bid further immigration, except at an approximate rate of fifty a day. Its only shield against a smothering horde of advancing people is the effectiveness of its land and marine police. To the extent that the border police can restrain illegal immigration, the colony may be able to catch up with its housing needs, provided, of course, that the birth rate tapers off.

The colony's marine police are a small, well-trained force contending with overwhelming odds. Their fleet of 27 boats and 610 men is charged with patrolling 400 miles of coastline and 728 square miles of territorial waters. They have one 58-foot boat with a top speed of 22 knots and three jet boats of 20-foot length, useful in hot pursuit, with a maximum speed of 42 knots. Their 70-foot launches mount a 50-caliber

Browning machine-gun on the foredeck and carry a cache of smaller arms, but they deliver no more than 11 knots.

As many as five of the patrol boats may be out on duty at one time, but the sea lanes from Macao and China are crowded with ships at all hours. A police launch cruising along the western edge of Hong Kong waters on a clear day will often have forty vessels within its sight.

There are red sails in every sunset off Lantau, largest and westernmost of Hong Kong's 237 islands. The skipper of a police launch may spend every spare moment scanning the horizon for suspicious-looking craft, but even in full daylight he cannot hope to detect and halt all the smugglers. At night, when the smugglers slip through fog or run without lights, the skipper's chances are considerably slimmer. The Red Chinese gunboats are also on the prowl just beyond territorial limits, hoping to catch their runaway countrymen, but they are often unsuccessful.

The Hong Kong courts charged 1,551 illegal immigrants in 1961; another 1,763 were intercepted by the marine police and sent back to China. Thousands of others slipped through the net either at Macao or Hong Kong. Here are a few typical incidents that occurred during two months in the winter of 1961-62.

Eighty-three men, women, and children stole a Chinese military launch and escaped to Macao. Marine police caught seventy-three illegal immigrants in a motor junk off Lamma Island. Police discovered thirty-two men and women attempting to slip past Castle Peak in a sailing junk. A woman and two children were arrested in Tai Tam Bay, Hong Kong Island. A Communist gunboat intercepted a sampan near Lappa Island, opposite Macao, firing shots into the hull and driving the dozen women and children aboard back to Red territory.

A Red gunboat fired on a junk at the mouth of the Canton River estuary, sinking it with all twenty-nine immigrants aboard.

During the same period, an unknown number of illegal immigrants swam across Starling Inlet from the Chinese mainland to Hong Kong, using rafts and basketballs to keep themselves afloat. A middle-aged man swam from Lappa Island to Macao under the muzzles of Communist guns to visit his son. On every dark night or at any time there is a chance of screening their passage in foggy or overcast weather, the immigrants keep coming in.

Marine police inspectors say there is a well-organized traffic in smuggling illegal immigrants. Smugglers can buy a second-hand junk in Macao and stuff its hold with twenty to forty immigrants. They have a regular scale of prices based on the financial blood-count of each customer; $40 for well-heeled Shanghai Chinese, $30 for a moderately solvent Fukienese, and $13 to $20 for a Cantonese farmer or laborer. If the smugglers fall into the hands of the marine police, they may spend a year in prison, and their passengers will be sent back to an ice-cold reception in Red China. Jail sentences seldom keep smugglers from returning to the trade; the profits justify the risk.

"If we catch a boat with people that look like genuine fishermen, we may warn them to get a Hong Kong operating license and let them go," a marine police inspector said. "If we spot one that looks like a regular smuggler, we arrest the whole bunch."

The marine police crews are predominantly Cantonese; first-class seamen and courageous policemen, but at best they can scarcely hope to snare more than a minority of those who are determined to break through the blockade. When the successful ones reach Hong Kong Island or one of the sheltered coves of the New Territories, they are met by friends, relatives or confederates of the smugglers. They vanish into the almost impenetrable masses of Chinese and emerge a few months later to register as residents. In most cases the British have no alternative but to accept them.

Many of the police are themselves refugees from Red China. They perform their antismuggling duties conscientiously, but if refugees get through despite their best efforts and vigilance, they may be something less than heartbroken.

Protection of the land border with Red China is the responsibility of the 200 uniformed men of the Frontier Division, with headquarters at Fanling, four miles south of the border. Measured in a straight line, the border is only thirteen miles long, but 22 miles as it follows a snaky line from Deep Bay in the west to Mirs Bay in the east. On the colony side, it is backed up by a closed zone which varies in depth from a few hundred yards to a mile. No one except police, farmers living in the area, or persons carrying special passes from the Commissioner of Police is allowed to enter or move about in the closed area.

Before the dramatic refugee surge of May, 1962, only nine-tenths of the border was fenced on the British side, and the stoutness of the fence was variable—high and topped with barbed wire at some places, but no more than a plain, low fence at others. The storming of the barrier in 1962 caused the British to build an entirely new one which stretched the full length of the border. Crowned with many strands of barbed wire, it stood 10 feet high and was laid out like a long cage, with 20 feet of enclosed ground between the outer, parallel fences.

Between the marshlands on the west and the hilly country in the east, the Frontier Division police have three main stations and nine police posts. From each of these, police observers scan the border with binoculars. Foot patrols also keep a continuous watch along the boundary. At night, when the closed area is under curfew, searchlights and dogs are added to the regular patrols. When the integrity of the border is as seriously threatened as it was by the spring invasion of 1962, the closed area may be increased to a depth of three miles, as Governor Black ordered on May 19, 1962.

Under normal conditions, farmers who live along the border enjoy a kind of twilight-zone immunity. Known to the patrols, they may cross the border during the day to work either in Hong Kong or China without molestation, but they must be home before nightfall, because the border, with all its rail and road connections, shuts down at dark. Night crossings, even before the 10-foot barrier went up, were discouraged by peremptory challenges and bullets.

The Reds have no fence on their side of the border. They do not need it; nobody wants to get in.

Why did the Red Chinese permit the transborder flight of May, 1962? At first it was interpreted as a deliberate attempt to embarrass the British, and certainly the colony's police and military units had a thankless assignment. When they transported the captured refugees back to the border, they were jeered at and reviled by colony residents. Protests were issued by international relief officials.

The onus soon shifted to Red China, which was revealed by the exodus as a land of hunger. All news from Communist China is censored or second-hand, so no accurate explanation of the flight could be made at the time. It appeared, however, that industrial retrenchment in the cities of China had caused many city-dwellers to move to rural areas, perhaps to seek food, perhaps to bolster the country's sagging farm production.

Most of those who crossed the border in the big May surge were from the adjoining province of Kwangtung, indicating that free movement of people within China was confined to this one southern area. Most of those interviewed in Hong Kong complained that they were hungry, and that they had lived on a substandard diet for months with no real hope of improvement.

There was a momentary temptation to regard the flight as a sign that civil government had collapsed in Communist China, but this hope faded on May 25, when the Reds again sealed off the border. No official explanation for the turn-about was made, but newspapermen in the colony suspected that a sharp British protest to Peking may have prompted the clamp-down.

To the refugees in Hong Kong, the world spotlight meant very little, except that it may have made other countries aware that no place in the world has shielded so many fugitives from Communist tyranny as the crown colony.

CHAPTER THREE

Conflict and Coexistence with Two Chinas

"There is a saying in China; 'If the east wind does not prevail over the west wind, then the west wind will prevail over the east wind.' I think the characteristic of the current situation is that the east wind prevails over the west wind; that is, the strength of socialism exceeds the strength of imperialism."

—MAO TSE-TUNG, MOSCOW, 1957

So spoke the chairman of the Chinese Communist Party at a time when all the winds seemed to be blowing his way. For eight years the People's Republic of China had performed with the disciplined enthusiasm of a collegiate cheering section, expanding its industrial capacity at a prodigious rate and disseminating its political influence throughout Asia. Soviet Russia had given complete ideological support and technical assistance to its junior partner in world Communism.

Since then, the winds have shifted to a new quarter. The Great Leap Forward that began in 1958 has struck a dead calm. Backyard factories and foundries have failed to attain either the standards or quantity of production anticipated, but they succeeded for a time in clogging the country's transportation system and in interfering with the distribution of food and other consumer goods. The same confused planning that turned the emphasis from large-scale industrial production to backyard factories also transformed the traditional small Chinese farm and the medium-sized collective farm into titanic agricultural communes. By a combination of mismanagement and adverse growing conditions, the communes have brought about the worst food shortage in China's recent history.

In the summer of 1961, the prevailing winds from Moscow turned unseasonably icy as an ideological split developed between Russia and China. No one outside the Communist partnership could assess the full significance of the break, but it offered very little prospect of increased Soviet assistance to Communist China.

Every change in the political winds of mainland China creates an eddy in Hong Kong. In the eight years when Red China was swept along by the momentum of its revolutionary spirit, the colony was beset by a succession of incidents. British ships and planes became the target for Chinese Communist guns. Long after the mainland fell under the unchallenged domination of the Reds, the grim warfare between Communists and Nationalists continued in the streets of Hong Kong.

Whether by coincidence or direct cause, the second year of the Great Leap Forward brought an unexpected lull in the Communist harassment of the colony. Left-wing agitation in the schools and trade unions persisted, but colony officials noticed that Communist sympathizers, once so avid for violent strikes and street demonstrations, seemed to have lost their appetite for both. The assumption was that Peking had told them they could expect no further support from that source. At the same time, shooting incidents and border clashes virtually ceased.

There was no disposition in the colony to regard this undeclared armistice as a bid for reconciliation. The news that the Great Leap had made its first big stumble was already in circulation, and the colony administration, quite unofficially, reached its own conclusion; Communist China was temporarily too busy mopping up its own mess to indulge its normal passion for badgering Hong Kong. When China's house had restored order, its Communist leadership would be right back at the colony's throat.

Hong Kong's colonial administration has never deluded itself with the belief that it could survive a massive assault by Red China. In population and the size of its armed forces, Hong Kong is outnumbered by approximately 200 to 1. Against Japan in 1941, Hong Kong's resistance lasted less than three weeks; against Red China, it might last about half as long.

But there are certain restraining factors unreflected in the comparative strength of the opposing land forces. The most tangible of these are the ships of the British and United States navies, continually riding at anchor in Hong Kong harbor or cruising in the surrounding seas. Aircraft carriers, submarines, cruisers and destroyers equipped with planes and missiles tend to put the brakes on impulsive acts of aggression by an inferior naval power.

A Communist grab for Hong Kong would almost inevitably involve Red China in a major war. Great Britain has shown no disposition to surrender this profitable possession without a fight, and although the United States has made no specific pledge to defend the colony, it is not likely to let the Chinese Communists snatch it from her principal ally.

Red China's instinctive belligerence may be tempered by the fate of its first outright aggression, which did not keep the United Nations out of Korea, but did a great deal to keep Red China out of the United Nations for years thereafter.

Aided in part by these considerations, Hong Kong has sat since 1949 on the doorstep of a country dedicated to its destruction. In the late 1940s, it was felt that a substantial cut in the colony's trade with China would ruin the British enclave by purely peaceful methods. Most of the trade has been lost since then, but Hong Kong has perversely grown more prosperous than ever before.

The overriding reason why Hong Kong continues to thrive in the shadow of its hostile neighbor is economic. Ideologies apart, they need each other.

Despite the drop in their total trade, Hong Kong remains Red China's chief non-Communist trading partner. In recent years it has become a lop-sided arrangement, with the Chinese Communists shipping ten times more goods to the colony than they purchase from her. Yet the imbalance appears to suit the purposes of both sides.

Hong Kong, which cannot produce enough food to sustain its population for more than a few months of the year, has imported an average of $200,000,000 worth of goods from Red China in each of the last three years, and food represents more than a third of the total. In the same years, Red China imported about $20,000,000 annually from the colony. Thus the Reds earned a favorable trade balance of $180,000,000 a year, giving them the foreign exchange they need as critically as Hong Kong needs food.

It may be wondered why the Chinese Communists, with three successive crop failures, are willing to export any of their food. But they must earn foreign exchange to pay for grain, flour, powdered milk and sugar to save themselves from starvation, and their food purchases in the world market during 1960 and 1961 ran up a bill of $360,000,000.

The whole pattern of mainland-colony trade has been reversed since 1950. In that year, their trade came to $406,000,-000, or about a third of Hong Kong's total world trade of $1,314,000,000. By 1960, the total colony-mainland trade had skidded to $228,000,000 and represented only one-seventh of the colony's world trade volume of $1,716,000,000.

In 1950, Hong Kong exported $255,000,000 to Red China, but imported only $151,000,000 from her. The crown colony still serves as a major transshipment port for China's trade with other countries, but her importance as an exporter and re-exporter from other countries to China was painfully diminished by United Nations and United States embargoes during the Korean war.

The pinch of those embargoes was so tight that it looked for a while as if Hong Kong, which had prospered on its Chinese export trade for 110 years, would wither from the loss of it. To the amazement of its economic obituary writers, the colony side-stepped its assigned grave by developing its own industries. Within a few years, Hong Kong became bigger as a manufacturer than it had ever been as a trader.

Red China's benefits from the existing trade with Hong Kong go further than the earning of foreign exchange from a favorable trading balance. She also trades profitably in human misery. The Chinese refugees who fled to Hong Kong are the prime victims of this merciless squeeze.

No matter how intensely the refugees dislike the Communist regime on the mainland, they have not severed their ties with friends and relatives in China. They are the first to know of economic reverses and crop failure inside China because the news is brought to them by travelers crossing the colony border. It is a story repeated by almost every new refugee who escapes from the homeland to Macao or Hong Kong.

The effect on the Chinese in Hong Kong is irresistible; by every tradition of family loyalty they are compelled to help their starving kinsmen in China. In obedience to this obligation, the Hong Kong Chinese sent 13,000,000 two-pound packets of food and other household needs through the colony's post office in 1961 to friends and relatives across the border.

The squeeze takes the form of customs duties which often exceed the value of the goods shipped. If the sender mails his parcel from a Hong Kong post office, the receiver in China pays the duty when it arrives. But the duty can be any amount the Red Chinese officials choose to assign, and many recipients refuse the parcels because they cannot pay for them. If a parcel agent handles the shipment, sending it through the Chinese post offices across the frontier or through his own agents inside China, the Hong Kong sender has to pay all the duties in colony currency before it starts on its way.

One Chinese resident who came to the colony in 1962 told *The South China Morning Post*, a Hong Kong English-language daily, that the Red Chinese government was taking in about $53,000 a day on these parcel duties, with the peak of the loot coming at Chinese New Year, when presents are shipped home in the greatest numbers. A vast percentage of the parcel-senders were poor people, and each parcel cost them anywhere from a day's to a week's wages, or more.

The external harmony which has prevailed between the

colony and the mainland since 1959 offers a glaring contrast to the discord that preceded it. Ever since 1949, the Reds have been taking angry swipes at the colony, a game in which their worst enemies, the Chinese Nationalists, frequently joined.

In the year that the Reds gained control of the mainland, trade relations and communications between China and Hong Kong were broken off. The Kowloon-Canton Railway suspended transborder operations and Communist guerrilla forces lined up threateningly along the frontier.

While the Communists pressed the colony from the north, the Nationalists launched a blockade of all ports along the Chinese coast. Caught between the opposing forces, the colony banned political societies with outside allegiance and bolstered its own defenses. Additional lands and buildings were requisitioned for military use and 900 volunteer soldiers were added to its garrison.

Great Britain sought to relieve the existing tension by recognizing Red China on February 6, 1950, but there was no exchange of diplomatic representatives. Swelling tides of Chinese refugees continued to pour across the frontier and the colony instituted its first immigration controls in May, 1950.

The initial breach in Hong Kong's policy of cautious neutrality came on June 5, 1950, when two Nationalist warships, enforcing their own blockade against the Reds, attacked the 800-ton British merchant vessel *Cheung Hing*. This dreadnought, steaming along with a cargo of fertilizer from Amoy, was raked with Nationalist shells which killed six of her passengers and wounded six others.

Early in August, 1950, the Reds produced their own series of incidents. Communist gunboats fired on three British ships just outside Hong Kong territorial waters and an armed Red junk bombarded the American freighter *Steel Rover*. The day after the *Rover* incident, a Communist shore battery on Ling Ting Island, a few miles outside the southern limit of Hong Kong waters, directed its cannon and machine guns against the British freighter *Hangsang*, wounding two British officers. Communist forts in the same area fired on the Norwegian freighter *Pleasantville* on August 6, but no hits were scored.

The shootings were collectively interpreted as a Red warning to keep all Allied shipping away from her installations on Ling Ting and the nearby Lema and Ladrone islands. On August 17, the British destroyer *Concord* replied to the warning by exchanging a half-hour of shellfire with the Communist forts.

None of these incidents was as disruptive as the Communist agitation inside the colony. Here the core of the trouble arose from the Hong Kong Federation of Trade Unions, or FTU, an openly pro-Red group with more than sixty member unions whose power was concentrated in shipyards, textile mills and public utilities. The FTU succeeded in fomenting a streetcar strike in 1949. With zealous devotion to the party line, the FTU unions shoved themselves into every labor dispute they could penetrate. They also displayed a touching concern for the unhappy living conditions of the refugees, undeterred by the fact that most of the refugees obviously preferred them to conditions in Communist China.

A flash fire in a refugee settlement on November 21, 1951, drove 10,000 persons from their shacks and enabled Red China to rush in with the offer to send a relief mission. The Communist angels of mercy were to be met at the Hong Kong terminus of the Kowloon-Canton Railway by a banner-waving group of left-wing welcomers. They failed to show up, and a riot broke out in which there was one fatality and thirty injuries before police brought it under control.

The left-wing unions trumpeted their public concern for the refugees by a number of street demonstrations which police barely managed to keep from exploding into new riots. Wearying of the skirmishes, Police Commissioner Duncan MacIntosh tried a new tack. With the consent of Governor Alexander Grantham, he offered to satisfy the strident Communist demands to improve the refugees' lot by paying full transportation costs and expenses of ten Hong Kong dollars to every person who wanted to return to any part of Red China. The only acceptance came from an old man who wanted to be buried with his ancestors in Northern China.

The sea-lane incidents resumed on September 25, 1952, when a Communist gunboat halted the Macao ferry with a burst of warning shots, searched the ship and removed a Chinese passenger. In the same year, there were two other Communist and three Nationalist attacks on British ships.

A Communist warship came upon a Royal Naval launch in the Pearl River estuary on September 10, 1953, riddled it with shells and killed six men, wounding five others. A stiff British protest was delivered to Peking without bringing either an apology or compensation. The Nationalists kept up their end of the harassment in that month with one of their warships firing on the British destroyer *St. Bride's Bay* off the China coast.

Each of these incidents stirred the British government to send protests to Peking or Taipeh, but they usually elicited only transient interest outside the countries directly involved.

The Chinese Communists' capture of two American newsmen and an American merchant-marine captain on March 21, 1953, brought the United States government into the long succession of Hong Kong incidents. The reaction was quick and angry, for the Reds had subjected the United States to an unceasing campaign of vilification and had already imprisoned more than thirty American civilians in China. The Dixon-Applegate case came as a kind of climactic tail-twister.

Richard Applegate, National Broadcasting Company correspondent in Hong Kong, and Donald Dixon, International News Service correspondent in Korea, were sailing five miles west of Lantau Island on Applegate's 42-foot sailboat, the *Kert*, when they were stopped by a Chinese gunboat manned by Chinese soldiers. The newsmen, accompanied by merchant marine Captain Benjamin Krasner, his Chinese fiancée and two Chinese sailors, were in international waters, bound for Macao on a pleasure cruise. Protests that they were violating no law had no effect on the Reds, who accused them of straying into Chinese waters.

The *Kert* and its six passengers were towed to the Communist base at Lap Sap Mei, transferred to Canton and held prisoners until September 15, 1954. The United States protested vehemently to Peking, and Great Britain joined in demands that the group be set free. Harry J. Anslinger, United States Commissioner of Narcotics, had a private revelation which he duly reported to the United Nations: The *Kert* had been captured by Chinese narcotics smugglers, led by Lu Wang-tse, a notorious woman pirate! Nothing more was heard of the lady known as Lu—Applegate said after his release that he could not imagine how the preposterous tale had originated, but the Red Chinese let many months pass before they admitted the capture.

When the three Americans were finally released, they had suffered physically from a skimpy diet of practically inedible food. Captain Krasner's fiancée, and one of the crewmen, a British subject living in Hong Kong, were subsequently allowed to leave China, but the other Chinese crewman remained a prisoner.

The international repercussions of the Dixon-Applegate affair were intensified by a fresh provocation which called ships and planes of the United States, Britain and France into emergency action. This was the callous and apparently senseless shooting down of a British-owned Cathay Pacific Airways C-54 Skymaster on July 23, 1954, with the loss of ten lives, by three Red Chinese LA-9 Lavochkin piston-engined fighter planes.

The Skymaster, carrying twelve passengers and a crew of six, took off from the Bangkok airport at 8:28 P.M., heading northeast in bright moonlight over Thailand and Indochina for the 1,071-mile flight to Hong Kong. The passenger load was light, so most people occupied window seats. The sun rose soon after the plane flew out over the South China Sea. Cape Bastion, the southeastern tip of Hainan Island, a Communist possession about the size of Denmark, became visible 50 miles away. Below, a brisk southwest wind whipped the sea into whitecaps.

Co-Pilot Cedric Carlton suggested a time-saving route nearer to Hainan, but Captain Phillip Blown decided to hold his present course, keeping far away from Hainan to avoid another of the Red charges that their twelve-mile limit was being violated by non-Communist flyers. At 8:45 A.M., Carlton looked out a starboard window and shouted to Captain Blown that two cream-colored fighter planes with Red Chinese markings were coming up fast from the rear on his side. Captain Blown put the plane on automatic pilot, took a quick look back through the port window and saw a third fighter zeroing in on his side of the tail.

"Without any warning, they opened up with machine-gun

and cannon fire," Captain Blown later wrote in his report. "The noise and the shambles from their guns was terrific. It was obviously a premeditated attack."

The hail of bullets from short range immediately set fire to the Skymaster's left outboard engine, and the No. 4 engine on the far right. Flames burst from the auxiliary and main fuel tanks beside the No. 4 engine at almost the same moment.

Captain Blown, flying at 9,000 feet, instantly went into a dive. He turned sharply left and right as he descended, trying to shake the pursuing fighters, and headed for the sea at 300 miles an hour. He was fighting to get out of the line of fire long enough to dump his gas and check the flames that were eating away a broad section of the skin on his right wing.

The guns of the LA-9s kept up their clatter on his tail and bullets tore through the plane cabin, splintering the interior and killing several passengers. Bullets whizzed past the two pilots and smashed the boost pressure and fuel-flow gauges. At 5,000 feet, the rudder controls snapped; at 3,000, the right aileron control was shot off. The No. 4 engine was feathered, but its extinguisher failed to stifle the raging flames.

The Skymaster began to stall groggily toward the right, but Captain Blown checked it by throttling back his two left-wing engines and pouring full power on No. 3, the only operative engine on the right side. The ship's speed dropped to 160 miles an hour, and the right wing began to dip.

With the small degree of control remaining, Captain Blown plunged the Skymaster through the shoulder of a 15-foot wave as the right wing and No. 4 engine snapped off, then slammed into the middle of the next wave. The solid impact of the water caved in the cockpit windows. The tail broke off, up-ended in unison with the fuselage and headed for the sea bottom. Less than two minutes elapsed between the attack and the ditching.

Thirty seconds after hitting the water, the fuselage sank out of sight. Two of the Red fighters executed a U-turn around the wreckage before heading back to their base at Sanya, on the southern end of Hainan Island. Few of the victims had time to put on life jackets. When the cabin went down, only those washed clear of it had a chance to survive.

The eight survivors clambered or were dragged aboard the twenty-man inflated rubber raft. Captain Blown spread a weather awning over the raft and warned all passengers to keep out of sight under it in case of another attack.

Steve Wong, the Chinese radio operator, had died in the wreck. Captain Blown remembered seeing him talk into the mike all during the dive toward the sea and sending a final message, "Losing altitude, engine on fire." The message was heard at Kai Tak Airport in Hong Kong and rescue operations started immediately.

Two hours later, rescue planes began to circle over the raft —Hornets, a Sunderland, Valetta, York and a French B-24, but none could land on the water. A pair of U.S. Air Force SA-16 Grumman Albatrosses were dispatched from Sangley Point in the Philippines. One of the big amphibians landed in sheltered water on the lee side of Tinhosa Island and taxied out to the raft in a perilously rough sea.

The rescuers were guided to the spot by smoke flares dropped by the French B-24. Dozens of Chinese junks wallowed and rocked on the waves at some distance from the raft, making no attempt to interfere as American fighter planes flew cover over the raft. The survivors had been on the raft for seven hours before being rescued.

Besides the three fatalities among the crew—Stewardess Rose Chen, Steve Wong and Flight Engineer G. W. Cattanach—there were seven passenger deaths, including a tea merchant, a Hong Kong University student, an American exporter and his two sons, and the owner of a Hong Kong curio shop. Captain Blown, who continued as a Cathay Pacific Airways pilot for many years, received a Queen's Commendation for his cool-headed efforts to save the Skymaster and the lives of those aboard.

Humphrey Trevelyan, British Chargé d'Affaires at Peking, delivered his government's strongly worded protest, and the Red Chinese ultimately paid $1,027,600 indemnity for the loss of the plane. No explanation of the shooting was given, except for undocumented guesses that the Communists may have been trying to kill or kidnap some person on the plane or to scare off all ships approaching her territorial limits.

The shooting prompted John Foster Dulles, American Secretary of State, to issue a hot denunciation of the "further barbarity" of the Chinese Reds. The U.S. Navy Department dispatched two aircraft carriers, the *Hornet* and the *Philippine Sea*, to join in the rescue. Their planes raced to the rescue scene, ready to start shooting if there were any Red Chinese interference. It was one of the angriest moments between the U.S. and Red China since the Korean war. It passed without further raising of American tempers, but reinforced the already intense American antipathy for Mao's Communist state.

Less than one year later, the destruction of a second airliner in the South China Sea thrust Hong Kong into the Communist-Nationalist crossfire. A Lockheed Constellation of Air-India International took off from Kai Tak Airport, bound for the first Afro-Asian Conference at Bandoeng carrying eight

Red Chinese delegates. The conference was intended to assure the uncommitted nations that Communist China had put aside its warlike ways to become an exemplar of peaceful coexistence.

There was an appalling roar as the Constellation approached Sarawak; a bomb burst in the baggage compartment, setting the aircraft afire. Pilot Captain D. K. Jatar, showing incredible skill and nerve, managed to guide the shattered plane to a jolting belly-landing at 150 miles an hour. But the impact with the sea tore the Constellation apart and it sank in moments, leaving a circle of flames on the surface. Before the radio went dead, the ship had issued an international distress call.

Eleven passengers and five crewmen, including Captain Jatar, died in the crash and explosion. Three surviving crew members drifted in a life raft for nine hours until they were picked up by the British frigate *Dampier*. All the Chinese delegates were among those killed, and Peking charged sabotage. The accusation proved to be well-based; the bomb had been planted by a Nationalist saboteur, employed as a cleaner by the British maintenance company at Kai Tak Airport. Hong Kong police offered a $17,500 reward for his arrest, but he escaped to Taiwan on another airplane.

The Hong Kong government issued a warrant for the bomber's arrest, but the Nationalist authorities replied that they had no legal basis for his extradition to the colony. There the matter rested, with the abiding hatred between Peking and Taipeh continuing as before.

Each of the sea and air incidents threatened the security of the colony to some degree, but none rocked its internal structure with the earthquake power of the Double Ten riots of October, 1956. No other crisis since World War II has presented such a frontal challenge to its ability to preserve law and order. Three days of savage guerrilla warfare raged through thickly congested streets, and when the fight was over, the British administration had had the fright of its life.

Statistics convey none of the heat of these bloody battles, but they measure a few of their dimensions: 59 people killed, 500 injured, nearly $1,000,000 in property damage, 6,000 arrests, 1,241 prison sentences and four executions for murder. Nearly 3,000 police and several army battalions were engaged in subduing the rioters. From east to west, the riots extended across eleven miles of Upper Kowloon and the New Territories, and were marked by fifty-four skirmishes between mobs and the uniformed forces.

If the genesis of the riots were to be narrowed down to a single proximate cause, it would have to be something as trivial as an argument over a few paper flags pasted on a concrete wall. Physically, that was where they started, but their true origin goes back at least three centuries.

The riots took their name from the common designation of a patriotic holiday on October 10, the tenth day of the tenth month, marking the anniversary of the establishment of the Chinese Republic in 1911. In Hong Kong, it is preceded by the October 1 celebration of the birthday of Red China. Each holiday gave Nationalist or Communist sympathizers an opportunity to explode strings of firecrackers, hold rallies and fly their national flags. On both days, police were out in full force to prevent riots between the opposing Chinese groups, and they managed to keep the lid down fairly well until 1956.

The October 1 holiday in 1956 passed without undue commotion and October 10 began with no indication of Communist violence. Nationalist flags were displayed by refugees all over the colony, particularly in the heavily populated resettlement estates of Upper Kowloon. The refugees were predominantly pro-Nationalist, having been driven from their homeland by the Reds. After years of exile and grinding poverty, many of them were steeped in bitterness and yearning for revenge against the Communists.

The Triad gangs, whose members played a key part in the Double Ten riots, had been established in China three centuries ago as a patriotic society dedicated to the overthrow of the foreign Manchus who dethroned the native Ming Dynasty. Their professed ideals slowly rotted away and they devolved into a band of thugs, living on protection rackets, shakedowns of street peddlers and petty criminals, enforced by fear and strong-arm brutality. Since World War I, crime has become their primary business and their patriotism survives only as a front.

On October 10, 1956, pro-Nationalist residents of the Shek Kip Mei Resettlement Estate began to take down the paper flags they had pasted on the concrete walls of the housing blocks. Housing officials had objected that the pasted flags were difficult to remove after the Double Ten holiday was over, and the tenants, who could still fly flags from poles or ropes, accepted the cleanup job unprotestingly.

At Li Cheng Uk, a resettlement estate about a quarter of a mile to the northwest of Shek Kip Mei, housing officials themselves removed Nationalist flags and symbols stuck on the walls. It was early in the morning of the Double Tenth, when an unfriendly crowd of about 400 gathered quickly and demanded that the flags be restored. Police were called, but the crowd swelled to more than 2,000 by early afternoon and its demands became more extravagant. Impatient for action, some of the crowd attacked two resettlement officials, beating them severely. Police units, hurrying to help the injured men, were met with a barrage of flying bottles. They replied with tear gas and the mob, turning its anger on the police, showered them with rocks. A resettlement office was set afire but police reinforcements succeeded in dispersing the mob. By midafternoon, with two persons arrested and four injured, peace appeared to have been restored.

Right after the dinner hour, a newly formed mob at Li Cheng Uk renewed the rock-throwing attacks on police. Nationalist flags were unfurled and a shouting mass of rioters charged into police lines. Four riot units of 240 men were called out and the strengthened force threw a cordon around six blocks while a sporadic exchange of rocks and tear gas continued. The area enclosed by the cordon became relatively quiet, but new disorders broke out along its southern edge. Police vehicles were attacked, and members of Triads were sighted in the center of the commotion.

Rioting became general and violent by 10:30 P.M. and police set up roadblocks on main routes into the area. The mobs altered their tactics, splitting into small fighting squads that pounded a segment of the police lines with a swift, sharp attack, then scattered and ran before police could bring up reserves. Within a few minutes, the attack squads would re-form on another block and hit police lines again. As the evening advanced, the riot zone kept expanding into other parts of Kowloon. Police units were alerted on Hong Kong Island to forestall possible riots there.

Police were only one of the mob targets. A fire engine returning from a minor blaze near the Kowloon resettlement estates was bombarded with bricks, bottles and chunks of concrete. The engine driver, struck on the head by a flying object, lost control of the truck and it plunged erratically into a crowd, killing three and injuring five. Ambulances were stoned as they arrived to pick up the casualties. An Auxuliary Fire

Service vehicle was dumped over and set on fire. Hordes of rioters swarmed into the area, more police were summoned and a four-hour battle ensued.

The looting phase of the riots began with an attack on a bakery in the heart of the disturbed area. After smashing the bakery windows and setting it afire, rioters turned their rock-and-stone batteries on firemen called to put out the flames. Two floors of the building were destroyed before the firemen could extinguish the blaze. Meanwhile, rioters went berserk on the streets, looting and burning shops until the massed strength of police laboriously regained control of the neighborhood.

Another battle was fought in the crowded streets of Mongkok. Rocks were dropped on the police from balconies while Triad gangs embarked on the looting of shops. Marauding gangs roamed the Kowloon streets down to Austin Road, the northern edge of the tourist and luxury shopping section, before police hammered them into submission.

General restoration of order in Kowloon was still far off. October 11 was only a half-hour old when police learned that a mob infiltrated by Triad gangsters was preparing to set fire to a pro-Communist private school. Police sent to investigate were pelted with rocks and forced to withdraw with five men injured. A riot unit used tear gas to pen the rioters inside the resettlement buildings while other police went to the school. They found looters and arsonists busily at work and arrested eleven men.

About 3:45 A.M., hoodlums became active near Kai Tak Airport, a mile and a half east of Tai Hang Tung, wrecking a traffic pagoda.

Sunrise on October 11 brought a lull, but at 10 A.M., there was renewed rioting at Li Cheng Uk. Triad thugs peddled

Nationalist flags by threatening to beat up anyone who refused to buy. Looting and mob barricades again confronted police who had been hard-hit by injuries.

One mob launched a full-scale attack on the Sham Shui Po police station, but were repelled by gunfire and scattered into the side streets when an armored car pursued them. Mobs of ever-increasing size were fast-moving and elusive, and tear gas did little more than drive them to another location where they attacked again. They lighted bonfires in the streets and then heaved rocks at the firemen called to extinguish them.

The Kowloon rioters displayed no signs of a unified battle plan, nor any concerted push toward a strategic objective. But their actions revealed a consistent pattern of criminality after the looting and extortion began, confirming the police belief that Triads were in control. Police decided to shoot to kill, but realized that even this last-ditch measure would be useless unless they deployed their units to surround the rioters and take them prisoner. Shortly after noon of October 11— and very late by many people's judgment—three battalions of the Hong Kong army garrison were thrown into the fight.

With army battalions in action, the mob spirit began to die down throughout Kowloon by evening. A curfew was imposed, cross-harbor ferry service suspended, and the main impetus of the Kowloon riots came to an end.

Rigid enforcement of the curfew slowly cleared the streets of bystanders, but failed to drive the active rioters to cover. Looting and stoning of police persisted in Mongkok until after midnight, when riot guns and tear gas finally halted it. Strong-arm gangs armed with rocks, hammers, and iron bars prowled through eastern Kowloon, extorting money from shop-keepers, looting factories and battling police. Three rioters were killed and more than 400 arrested before the plundering was checked.

Looting and arson continued for the third day, October 12, at many places in Kowloon. The mass riots of the first two days were replaced by a merciless street war between bands of gangsters and the uniformed services of the colony. Three looters were shot to death in a raid on a provision shop in Mongkok. Firemen, ambulance crews and practically every man in a uniform was stoned or beaten if he ventured into a riot area.

On the afternoon of the 12th, police began dragnet raids on the hideouts of rioters and looters, taking 1,170 prisoners. The next day, raids at Li Cheng Uk by police and military units took 1,000 prisoners, and 700 others were rounded up at Tai Hang Tung.

On the morning of October 14, the curfew was lifted in Kowloon and most of the army units were relieved. But a night curfew continued for three more nights in northwestern Kowloon.

The day after the Kowloon riots erupted, a related but different kind of rioting broke out in Tsuen Wan, a New Territories factory town five and one-half miles west of Li Cheng Uk. In this area of textile and enamelware factories, most of the workers lived in company dormitories; physically close, but divided into intensely hostile pro- and anti-Communist unions.

Tsuen Wan had experienced some friction over the refusal of factory owners to display Nationalist flags on plant buildings during the Double Ten holiday, although pro-Nationalist workers could display the flags in their dormitories. No open protest was made until the afternoon of the next day, when a mob gathered outside a cotton mill and insisted that Nationalist flags be shown. The company acceded, and even granted the crowd leaders a small amount of money.

But the right-wing unions were in no mood for peaceful solutions that same evening when they launched a series of raids on Communist union offices; they looted and burned the offices and beat some leftist workers so savagely that five of them died. Sixty other leftist union members were collared by a mob and dragged off to a Nationalist rally where they were kicked and punched until many were unconscious. Meanwhile, another group of right-wing unionists continued to raid Communist union offices, assaulting any members they could find. Army troops were called to restore order, and their heavy vehicles crashed through mob barricades to remove the injured and clamp a strict curfew on Tsuen Wan.

One mile south of the town, mobs were still on a rampage, attacking a canning factory and setting it on fire. Four other factories on the outskirts of Tsuen Wan were besieged by mobs carrying Nationalist flags. Their demands were identical; either the plant would put out Nationalist flags and pay protection to the mob, or the place would be burned down. Management officials hastened to comply.

Several large textile mills were also favored with mob visits and a peremptory demand that they fire all pro-Red workers. Four miles west of Tsuen Wan, a Nationalist union group combined forces with a Triad gang, looted a textile factory, set fire to an automobile, stole a factory truck and withdrew after having their demands satisfied by management. Five houses and shops identified with Communist interests were invaded and wrecked.

The Tsuen Wan curfew was extended to surrounding areas and remained in force until October 16 while police and the army locked horns with the Nationalist rioters. Left-wingers were not an immediate problem, most of them having fled to the hills for their lives. But the rightist demonstrators were tough; they were disciplined fighters, ably led and guided by whistle-blast commands. Eight persons were killed, 109 seriously injured and 684 arrested before the rioters capitulated.

Long after the restoration of law and order, fear continued to keep workers away from their jobs. Full production did not resume at factories and mills in the Tsuen Wan area until early in November.

When the last of the Double Ten disorders ended, the hard-pressed colony government had a chance to assess events. Most of the property damaged by mobs belonged to Communists or their sympathizers, but Nationalist vengeance was by no means the only reason for its destruction; the longer the riots continued, the more inescapable became the conclusion that they were directed by criminals bent on manipulating patriotic emotions to enrich themselves.

The Double Ten riots did more than weaken the prestige of the Triads, whose leaders were either arrested or deported; it helped to illustrate the futility of waging a street war in Hong Kong over the Nationalist-Communist issue. Partisanship toward either side still burns strongly among the older Chinese, but it is a dwindling flame. Younger people, and many Chinese intellectuals within the colony, seem indifferent or hostile to both camps. Practically no one wants to return to Red China, and Taiwan had shown little inclination to welcome Chinese immigrants from Hong Kong until the border rush of May, 1962.

The turmoil occasioned by the Double Ten riots was succeeded by a period of comparative calm between Red China and the colony. But it ended in 1958, when the Chinese Communists clamped tight restrictions on inshore fishing by boats from Hong Kong. The Reds, perennially belligerent over the suspected invasion of their territorial limits, demanded that any boats fishing in their waters must have a Communist registration in addition to their colony registry. The registration also involved a Communist share of the fisherman's catch, and Hong Kong boats resented the gouge. The apparent solution was to keep their craft out of Communist waters.

The Reds made the problem more complex by invading Hong Kong waters on numerous patrol swoops to seize Hong Kong junks. The first of these came in October, 1958, when Red patrol boats grabbed several junks near Po Toi Island, on the southern edge of colony waters. In December, a Communist gunboat fired on junks in colony waters, killing two fishermen and injuring several others. A month later, a Chinese gunboat crossed into colony waters and captured two fishing boats with six persons aboard. In May, 1959, an armed Communist tug pushed nine miles into Hong Kong waters to round up a pair of large fishing junks.

In self-defense, many Hong Kong fishermen abandoned inshore fishing, and ventured much farther out to sea. Without intending to, the Reds helped to stimulate the mechanization of the colony's fishing fleet and improve its efficiency.

The colonial administration at Hong Kong carefully avoids comment on the Nationalist-Communist issue. It can, of course, initiate no foreign policy of its own, but must keep precisely to the line set down by the British government. It is expected to get along as best it can with both Red China and Taiwan, and leave the high-level thundering to London.

While the colony's officials are well aware that the United States and other Western powers are using Hong Kong as an observation post on Red China, and that both Red China and Taiwan have their corps of spies in the colony, they take no official cognizance of such activities until they become too conspicuous. Unfortunately, they often do. Toward the end of 1961, the colony had 21 Nationalist spies in custody, including a former leader of guerrilla forces in Southeast Asia.

Even more embarrassing are the cases in which one of the colony's officials turns out to be a foreign spy. On October 2, 1961, the colony government arrested John Chao-ko Tsang, an Assistant Superintendent of Police and one of its most promising career men, and deported him to Red China on November 30. The case created a sensation, for Tsang had the highest post of any colony official ever involved in an espionage case.

With its customary delicacy in matters affecting Red China, the government announced only that Tsang was being deported as an alien. Fourteen other "aliens" were rounded up for questioning in the case, and four of them were sent across the border at Lo Wu with John Tsang. Tsang was later rumored to be in charge of public security for the Reds at Canton.

Tsang's arrest was pure luck. A Chinese detective returning from Macao on another case noticed a man dressed as a common laborer take a bundle of $100 banknotes from one pocket and put it into another. The detective questioned him about the large amount of money, but found his answers pretty thin. He was accordingly hauled to a police station, questioned further and searched. A letter found on him was eventually traced to John Tsang. Unofficially, the letter was said to contain instructions from a Communist espionage cell in Macao.

The former Assistant Superintendent was thirty-eight years old, and so intelligent and popular that he looked to be headed

for a top place in the department. Born in China, he had come
to Hong Kong before the Reds ruled the mainland, joined the
police in 1948 and rose rapidly from the ranks. He had gone
to Cambridge University in 1960 for advanced studies, married while there, and returned to the colony in mid-1961. He
was then one of the highest-ranking Chinese officers in the department.

The nature of Tsang's work gave him an expert's knowledge of the colony's defenses and internal security, information of obvious value to the Reds. His associates in the police
force still doubt that he came to Hong Kong as a spy, believ-
ing that he turned Communist after he became established in
the colony. His wife and mother remained in Hong Kong
after his deportation.

The Tsang case was also an embarrassment to Hong Kong
Chinese who aspired to high office in the colony. It bolstered
the anti-Chinese bias of old-school colonialists, giving them an
opportunity to say, "See! When you give those Chinese a good
job, they sell you out."

The stream of political abuse which Peking had directed at
Hong Kong for a decade was superseded in 1960 by a stream
of fresh water flowing at the rate of 5 billion gallons a year.
On November 15, 1960, the two governments signed an agreement under which Red China was to tap its newly built Sham
Chun reservoir, two miles north of the colony border, to provide an auxiliary supply for Hong Kong. The colony put up its
own pumping station and laid ten miles of steel pipeline, four
feet in diameter, to convey the water to its own large reservoir
at Tai Lam, near Castle Peak. The water began flowing in December, 1960, and the arrangements for receiving and paying
for it have proceeded smoothly since then.

No one has assessed the symbolic or political significance of the deal, which meets only a small fraction of the colony's water needs, but it disconcerts many American tourists.

"Do you mean to tell me I've been drinking Communist water?" they ask. Most of the food they ate in Hong Kong probably came from Red China, but water is different. Some of them eye it suspiciously, as if they expected it to have a reddish hue or to contain traces of poison. The water is purified and filtered in Hong Kong, however, and thus far it has maintained a crystal-clear neutrality.

The life-or-death issue between Red China and Hong Kong is one that may not be decided until June 30, 1997, the termination date of the New Territories lease. If it is not renewed, more than 90 percent of the colony's land will revert to China, leaving Great Britain with Hong Kong Island, most of the Kowloon Peninsula and Stonecutters Island.

If China refuses to renew, as she has a clear legal right to do under the terms of the 99-year lease, she will get much more than the land itself. With it will come the colony's only modern airport, practically all its productive farmland, its chief industrial centers at Tsuen Wan and Kwun Tong, by far the greater part of its reservoirs and water-supply system, from one-third to one-half its population and all its mineral resources except a few quarries and clay pits.

"It would be folly to try to foresee what will happen in thirty-five years," said one of the colony's principal officials in 1962. "In this age of fission and fusion, it's impossible to see even five years ahead."

On one point, there is little doubt among the colony's officials: without the New Territories, Hong Kong would be untenable.

Outside of the colony, the 1997 deadline looms like doom; inside, it is just another of those far-off worries, like an epidemic or a catastrophic typhoon. Everyone knows it is coming; meanwhile, they go on making money, putting up new factories and hotels and planning gigantic public works.

Some of the colony's leading businessmen expect the Chinese Communists, or any other power ruling the mainland in 1997, to drive a tough bargain for the New Territories and then renew the lease for another 99 years.

Red China, which holds all the cards, hasn't tipped its hand.

CHAPTER FOUR

Industrial Growth
and Growing Pains

"Some are born great, some achieve greatness, and some
have greatness thrust upon them."

—SHAKESPEARE, *Twelfth Night*

In 1951 the economy of Hong Kong set two memorable
precedents; it reached the highest level in the colony's 110-year
history and then fell flat on its face. When the year ended, it
looked as if Hong Kong was finished as a world trading port.

Twelve months earlier all indicators had pointed toward a
continuing boom. Red China, frantically buying goods to
equip itself for the Korean war, had pushed the colony's trade
volume to an all-time high of $1,314,000,000 in 1950. Buying
continued at the same furious rate until May 18, 1951, when
most of the trade was choked off by the United Nations embargo on shipments to Red China. Even so, Hong Kong's total
trade volume reached a new high of $1,628,000,000 in 1951.

The U. N. embargo administered the *coup de grâce* to the crown colony trade with Communist China, but it was only the last of a series of trade restrictions arising from the Korean war. The United States embargoed all its trade with Red China when the conflict broke out in June, 1950, and at first included Hong Kong in the ban. The colony voluntarily stopped its trade with North Korea in the same month and banned a list of strategic exports to Red China in August, 1950. In December, 1950, and March, 1951, the colony increased its list of strategic items banned for export to China.

The cumulative effect of these restrictions, which were critically important in checking Chinese Communist aggression, was to push Hong Kong to the edge of economic disaster. With the loss of the China trade, the colony lost half its export market and about one quarter of its imports. This was the trade which had always been the main reason for the colony's existence.

Prospects for reviving the China trade when the Korean war was over did not look encouraging. Long before the embargoes and restrictions had gone into effect, the Chinese had begun to shift their trade from Hong Kong to Soviet Russia and Europe.

Hong Kong had grown and prospered on its ability to receive, process and reship the products of others, but its own productive capacity was insignificant. With a few minor exceptions, its industries—chiefly the building, repairing and supplying of ships—existed to serve its trade. Its banks and insurance companies, too, lived almost entirely on the colony's trade. Accordingly, when trade collapsed toward the end of 1951, the whole economy of the colony came crashing down with it.

In the aftermath of the 1951 debacle, there was at first no

thought of substituting industry for trade. For a variety of reasons, industry in the colony had never been developed independently of trade. Certainly Great Britain had not established the colony to produce goods which would compete with English manufacturers. The Hong Kong market was too small and its people generally too poor to support its own industries. There was no tariff wall to protect the colony's goods from outside competition, and this factor alone had stifled several early attempts to launch local industries.

Many natural handicaps combined to make the colony a most unlikely place for industry. Its mineral resources were few and limited in quantity. It had no local source of power to run a plant. Its water supply was chronically short of ordinary needs and suitable land for factories was scarce and expensive. The colony could not raise enough food nor provide enough housing to take care of its potential factory workers. And if anyone were imprudent enough to invest his money in an expensive industrial establishment, how could he be sure that the Reds would not move in and take it over, just as they had grabbed the mills and plants of Shanghai?

The colony had a few assets worth noting, however. Its government was stable and orderly, and had attracted a heavy influx of capital from pre-Communist China and the shaky regimes of Southeast Asia. Its banking, shipping and insurance services were the most efficient on the mainland of Asia, and its merchant community had well-cultivated connections with the world market. Its sheltered deep-water harbor was one of the best in Asia.

The colony's possibilities as a future industrial power were further enhanced by an unlimited supply of cheap labor and the immigration of skilled workers and experienced industrialists from Red China. Its labor unions numbered in the hundreds, but were so weakened by factional fights and political objectives that they were unable to drive a hard bargain in wage negotiations. Under Imperial Preference and the Ottawa Agreements of 1932, colonial products paid a lower tariff rate within the British Commonwealth than their foreign competitors.

Finally, any industry in Hong Kong could rely on one intangible asset of unique value; the character of the average Chinese workman. In most cases he was a refugee, uneducated and penniless but determined to reestablish himself with any job he could find. Having landed a job, he worked at it with a diligence, energy and skill that astounded Western observers.

Although industry had accounted for a very minor part in the colony's economy before 1951, its beginnings go back to the earliest years. Its first recorded product was the eighty-ton vessel, *Celestial*, built and launched by Captain John Lamont at East Point, on Hong Kong Island, on February 7, 1843. The California gold rush of 1849 and the Australian gold strike two years later caused a shipping boom in Hong Kong as scores of sailing ships carried Chinese labor to work in the goldfields. Shipbuilding expanded rapidly, a dry dock was constructed on the island and a whole new industry of refitting and supplying ships came into being. A foundry for the casting of ship cannon was established in the same era when cannon were the only valid insurance against South China's coastal pirates.

A group of ship-repair yards was consolidated in 1863 as the Hong Kong & Whampoa Dock Co., which subsequently sold its Chinese facilities and established its headquarters at Hung Hom, on Kowloon Bay. The Taikoo Dockyard & Engineering Co. began operations at Quarry Bay, on the north shore of Hong Kong island, in 1908. Between them, the two yards have completed nearly 1,400 ships, ranging from large cargo and passenger vessels to light harbor craft. Each company employs about 4,000 men, which is still the largest number employed by any Hong Kong industrialist.

These two companies, equipped to build 10,000-ton ships and capable of repairing practically any ocean liner that enters the harbor, remain the giants of local industry. But where they and about two dozen smaller shipyards employed 28 percent of the colony's industrial workers in 1938, they now hire around 3 percent. Theirs is not a declining industry, but it has become a hopelessly outnumbered one.

The colony's oldest export industry has a rather spicy history, antedating the establishment of Hong Kong by at least twenty years. A Cantonese hawker with an eye for trade discovered that the roots of the ginger plant when boiled in syrup had a strong appeal for British traders. Following the line of the most susceptible palates, the merchant, Li Chy, moved his ginger-preserving plant to Hong Kong in 1846. Some helpful soul introduced the product to Queen Victoria, who was so taken with its flavor that she made it a regular dessert at royal banquets, and suggested that it be named the "Cock Brand." Whether or not the Queen's intervention actually occurred is open to question, but there is no doubt that preserved ginger became a favorite English and European delicacy. Li Chy's Chy Loong Co. and a dozen eager imitators kept Caucasian tongues tingling until 1937, when U Tat Chee, the Ginger King, formed a syndicate to standardize quality and prices. During the Korean war, the United States detected a perceptible Marxist taint in the ginger that grew in Red China and banned its importation. A more democratic strain was then planted in the New Territories, and with suitable documentary evidence, permitted to enter the United States. Preserved ginger exports currently bubble along at 225 tons a year, pleasing overseas tastes and being credited by the Chinese with curing the lesser debilities of old age.

Sailing ships were insatiable rope-consumers, and from this demand grew the Hong Kong Rope Manufacturing Co., formed in 1883, and still doing business in Kennedy Town at the west end of Hong Kong Island.

The Green Island Cement Co., founded in Macao and transferred to Hong Kong in 1899, drew most of its raw materials from outside the colony to supply the local building industry. After replacing a kiln and four grinding mills hauled away by the Japanese in World War II, it got back into production in time to ride upward with the postwar building boom.

The Taikoo Sugar Refinery Co., established in 1884, was one of the first local companies to provide houses for its workers. Extensively modernized in 1925, it prospered until the Japanese looted and wrecked its plant so thoroughly that it was unable to resume production until the fall of 1950.

A 55,000-spindle cotton mill made a pioneer beginning in 1898, but the unrelieved humidity of the climate damaged its machinery and impaired its efficiency. Stiff competition did the rest and it was out of business before World War II. Flour mills and shell-button factories prospered for a time, then wilted in the heat of competition.

As cattle country, Hong Kong is slightly superior to the Sahara Desert. Nevertheless, Sir Patrick Manson, a doctor who specialized in tropical medicine, decided to establish a dairy company in 1886. He leased 330 acres of semi-vertical pasture from the crown and his first herd of 80 cows clambered and skidded around its dizzying slopes for a decade until an epizootic of rinderpest exterminated them. A new herd which soon outgrew its pasturage was stall-fed thereafter, living on fodder grass hand-gathered by patient Chinese women. Today's herd includes about half the colony's 3,000 dairy cows and is the chief domestic source of milk and butter. The dairy company has proliferated into a nutritional combine called The Dairy Farm, Ice & Cold Storage Co., which runs a chain of food stores, restaurants, soda fountains and ice and cold storage plants.

The match-making industry, dating from 1938, offers a gloomy illustration of Gresham's Law. Factories were built on Peng Chau, To Kwa Wan in eastern Kowloon and at Yuen Long in the New Territories, turning out tiny, cheap wooden matches. Factory equipment was primitive, wages low and the matches, more often than not, splintery and unpredictable. At its peak in 1947, the industry employed almost 1,000 workers, chiefly women. Then Macao entered the market with still lower wages and skimpier matches. Every box of Macao matches ought to bear the warning: "Take Cover Before Striking Match," but they far outsell the colony product. They have also done a lot to stimulate the manufacture of low-cost cigarette lighters.

Because of the colony's habitual preoccupation with trade, many of its industries existed for decades without attracting much attention outside their own circle of customers. With the collapse of trade in 1951, they assumed such unexpected importance that they seemed to have been invented for the occasion. Some of them, like the printing and beverage industries, were a century old. Cosmetics, furniture manufacturing and the fabrication of nails and screws dated from the early 1900s. Three industries of considerable importance in the export market—electric batteries and flashlights, rubber footwear, and canned goods—had been around since the

1920s. Enamelware, electro-plating, machinery, tobacco, and motion picture industries appeared during the depression decade, and the leather industry emerged in 1947.

Cottage industries, or small enterprises operating out of the home or a back-room workshop, are as old as Chinese civilization, embracing everything from wood and ivory carvings to musical instruments, jade, coffins, toys, beadwork, lanterns and silk-covered New Year's dragons. They average perhaps a dozen employees each, and number in the thousands.

The colony government has kept a careful record of total employment in registered factories (with 20 or more employees and subject to government inspection) and recorded workshops (15-19 workers and subject to inspection), but it has never had a statistical record of the number of industrial workers outside these two categories.

There are government estimates, but no precise figures, for the number of persons working in cottage industries, or such major industrial groups as building construction, engineering construction, agriculture, fishing and public transport. Estimates of the number of people working in shops, offices, and other commercial establishments are even hazier.

A purely statistical assessment of changes in Hong Kong industry that followed the 1951 trade collapse must necessarily be limited to the registered and recorded industries. Luckily, it has been the registered and recorded factories which most clearly reflected the colony's recent economic revolution.

Between 1947, when the postwar boom began moving, and 1951, when the U. N. embargo was imposed, the number of registered and recorded industries rose from 1,050 to 1,961 and their employed force nearly doubled. The colony's trade had been shooting upward at almost the same rate, and the

Net Domestic Product (the total value of all its goods and services) had increased by 75 percent.

The embargo halted the trade boom and reduced its volume by almost one-third in 1952. Not until 1960 did the total climb back to the record level of 1951. Colony traders, abruptly cut off from the China mainland market, had to find new markets or liquidate their accumulated stocks. Some found new markets in Southeast Asia; others liquidated their stock for whatever it would bring. Colony imports rose uncomfortably above exports, investment capital began searching around for better opportunities outside Hong Kong and unemployment became an additional cause for anxiety.

One obvious need was to step up the colony's export volume at once. It was in this situation that the "poor relation" in Hong Kong's economy—its industry—came into its own.

Despite its rapid postwar growth, the colony's industry had supplied only about ten percent of the products it exported. In simple desperation, the traders invested their Korean war profits in local industry. So also did the transplanted Shanghai industrialists who had lost their factories to the Chinese Communists but had retained their capital and managerial skills. The effect on Hong Kong was basic and far-reaching.

After a two-year period of readjustment, the number of industrial undertakings, or individual registered and recorded manufacturers, increased at the rate of 500 a year. Employment in the industries more than doubled; by the end of 1961, the colony had 6,359 companies with 271,729 workers. The climb continued into 1962.

Local industry, which had once contributed only ten per-

cent of the value of colony exports, contributed more than
seventy percent by 1962. Trade had made its comeback by
then, but it showed no sign of regaining the dominant position
it had occupied until 1952.

Entirely without warning and almost against its will, Hong
Kong had become a manufacturing center instead of an entrepôt. New industries had cropped up from nowhere, taken a
firm hold and climbed to the most important positions in the
colony's productive economy. A few of the old industries
had slumped, but most were expanding with the general prosperity.

During the uneasy two-year period of transition from trade
to manufacturing, the colony had to lay down two sets of
regulations to stabilize its trade relations with Japan and the
United States.

Japanese industry, swiftly reviving during the American
Occupation, began pouring cotton yarn and piecegoods,
household utensils and metalware into the Hong Kong
market. In 1952, Hong Kong imported four times more from
Japan than it exported to her. But the colony was less concerned about export-import balances than it was over reducing the Sterling Area's adverse balance of payments with
Japan. Japanese imports were tightly restricted or suspended
from early in 1952 until the second half of 1953. Meanwhile,
local industries enjoyed a welcome breather from Japanese
competition, especially in their home market.

Restoration of trade with the United States was essential.
The volume of this trade had taken a steep dive after the U. S.
and U. N. embargoes on trade with China, and the United
States wanted no Communist products funneled through
Hong Kong, nor any Red Chinese raw materials fabricated in
the colony. The Hong Kong Commerce and Industry De-

partment and the U.S. Treasury Department finally worked out a solution: the Comprehensive Certificate of Origin, covering every kind of goods that might be suspected of Red Chinese origin. Among these were silk, linen, cotton, jade, furniture, Chinese antiques and handicrafts. Goods of North Korean origin were similarly classified.

In enforcing the Comprehensive Certificate of Origin regulations, the Commerce and Industry Department directly supervises the raw material supply and the finished products of the factories; in some cases, it seals the goods after examination and keeps them under surveillance until they are exported. Severe legal and administrative penalties are slapped on manufacturers or dealers who are caught falsifying a Comprehensive Certificate of Origin. The colony government protects the validity of the certificates to insure trade relations with its biggest customer, and because it gives the colony a monopoly on certain goods for which Red China would otherwise have the market sewed up. The most vociferous critics of the Comprehensive Certificate of Origin are American tourists who recoil from it as if they had been handed two sets of income-tax demands for the same year.

With the road clear for industrial expansion, the response was overwhelming, and more than half the growth came in six light industries. Between 1948 and 1958, the six light-industry groups showed these increases in employment: garment-making, 20,000; metal products, 13,000; cotton spinning, 11,000; cotton weaving, 9,000; plastic wares, 8,000; and rubber footwear, 3,000.

At the end of 1961, registered and recorded industries employed a round total of 272,000 persons, with 42 percent of these workers concentrated in two categories; textile-making with 69,000, and garment-making with 45,000. Metal products were third in line with 28,000. Shipbuilding and ship-breaking employed 13,000. Plastics, non-existent until 1947, had separated into two major industries, plastic wares and plastic flowers, with each employing around 13,000 workers. Food manufacturing, printing and publishing, rubber products, machinery, electrical apparatus and chemicals were the other leaders. In the metal-products line, just one of its many specialized products, the manufacture of flashlight cases, employed more than 6,000 persons.

The success of Hong Kong's light industries is typified by three of its leaders in plastics, textiles and metal wares. The Three Ts—H. C. Ting, P. Y. Tang and John Tung—were prosperous Shanghai industrialists when the Chinese Communists closed in on them. Each one managed to reestablish himself in Hong Kong as the head of a major industry. Together, they represent one of Red China's unintentionally generous gifts to the colony—the exodus of capital and management skill. A whole new complex of tall, modern buildings in the North Point section of Hong Kong Island called Little Shanghai is a monument to this newly arrived capital.

H. C. Ting, managing director and principal owner of Kader Industrial Co., Ltd. at North Point, began as a battery salesman for a Shanghai factory, set up his own company, the Wei Ming Battery Works, in 1925, and began tinkering around in a laboratory to develop a long-lived battery. He picked up his chemistry as he went along and painstakingly dissected hundreds of messy cells until he evolved a really durable battery that sold well. He branched into flashlights, bulbs and carbon rods, survived the Japanese invasion of China and planned to try his luck in the plastics industry after the war. Foreign exchange limitations made it impossible to equip a plastics factory in Shanghai, so he sent a group of his employees to Hong Kong in 1947 with instructions to set up a plant.

The new factory was to include a cold-storage unit which could cool and store plastics and also make ice for sale. It was a dismal flop and Mr. Ting hurried down the following year to untangle the snarls. He soon discovered that he had, in effect, enrolled himself for a cram course in refrigeration engineering, but he learned enough to make the plant pay.

Today the North Point plant, greatly enlarged, employs 1,300 people and makes 400 different plastic items. Its four-story building of prestressed, reinforced concrete backs into a rocky hillside which is being blasted away to make room for a new ten-story plant. Mr. Ting trains all his own workers, pays them straight wages instead of the usual piece-work rates and hands out annual bonuses, in some instances, equal to ten months' pay.

Operating on the general premise that he'll try anything until he makes it work, Mr. Ting designs many of his own products, and if he can't find a machine to make it, designs that also. One machine molds a plastic automatic pistol and its bullets in a single operation; the model is so precisely fitted that it works as smoothly as the original gun. Other machines mold a pair of binoculars with one press, then equip it with accurate lenses stamped out of clear Styrene plastic. A plastic doll, including the eyes, is pressed out in seconds, but the mold has been carefully developed from a hand-made clay original that is reproduced first in plaster of Paris and then in polyester before the steel die is cut. Dressing the dolls keeps 100 girls busy at Kader sewing machines. The plant works three shifts daily, but Mr. Ting sleeps through one shift at his penthouse on the roof. His latest venture is transistor radios, jointly un-dertaken with a Japanese electrical appliance company.

"We can compete with anything except junk," Mr. Ting

said. "If Hong Kong turns out quality products at reasonable prices, we can gradually raise the living standards of our labor to the level of other countries. It can't be done overnight; they tried it in Red China and failed."

P. Y. Tang, head of the South Sea Textile Manufacturing Co. at Tsuen Wan, is an engineering graduate of the Massachusetts Institute of Technology and the largest producer of cotton yarn and grey cloth in the colony. His main plant covers nine acres along the waterfront and contains 45,000 spindles and 900 looms. Its employed force numbers 2,100.

Tsuen Wan, now an industrial center with more than 60,000 residents, was a village with a few huts and no roads when Mr. Tang erected a pilot plant there in 1948. He had brought 300 technicians and skilled workers, plus his own administrative experience as managing director of the gigantic Ching Foong Cotton Manufacturing Co. in Shanghai and other cities of China.

Experience was not enough; Hong Kong had practically nothing to help the mill get started—no cotton, power, spare parts, skilled labor or parallel industries, such as weaving and garment-making, that could use yarn and cloth. There was no local market and the humid climate quickly rusted the machinery.

Mr. Tang beat the rust problem and shaved his operating costs by keeping the machines in continuous use, running 8,500 hours a year, compared with 3,700 hours a year in German mills and 1,500 hours in English ones. He opened up new markets for his prolific output in Great Britain, the United States, Australia, Africa, and elsewhere. His early sales were made at a loss, but with his markets established and Red China knocked out of the market by the U.N. embargo, South Sea sales and profits soared.

The main plant is completely air-conditioned, reducing summer working temperatures by twenty degrees. The spindles and looms, imported from Japan, England, Switzerland and the United States, are the finest obtainable. Much of the carding, combing, and sizing machinery is fully automatic, tended by Chinese girls in their early twenties. Some of the girls appear to be prematurely grey, but it's nothing more than loose cotton that has settled on their black hair; all wear breathing masks to protect their lungs from floating cotton. Every phase of the operation is under strict quality control, preserving the uniform diameter of the yarn and testing its tensile strength.

The South Sea plant sometimes disconcerts visiting textile executives, who expect a Hong Kong textile mill to look like an over-extended cottage industry. What they find here, and in several other Hong Kong mills, is a streamlined efficiency equal to the best in the world.

The young men and women employees, most of them single, live in free dormitories near the plant, pay an average of 27 cents a day for meals and have a choice of Cantonese, Shanghai or Swatow cuisine. They have workmen's compensation, a barber shop with electric hair-dryers for the women, a vocational training program, and for high-performance workers, a lounge and recreation center. The plant is non-union, with a six-day, 48-hour week. Wages are slightly above the colony average for a registered factory, ranging from $1.38 to $2.25 a day.

Mr. Tang has been in the thick of the fight to protect the colony's textile industry from demands—especially clamorous in England and the United States—that its exports be reduced.

"I just can't see the wisdom of Western powers in restricting Hong Kong textile exports," he told David Lan, a reporter for *The China Mail*, a colony daily. "We have no hinterland or diversified industries to which refugees may turn from a threatened textile industry."

"From 1959 through 1961, total colony exports of cotton piece goods were less than 5 percent of Great Britain's production, and 0.53 percent of United States output," he stated.

"We are asking for no aid but only a fair chance to trade," he said.

John Tung, third of the alliterative industrial Taipans, has been connected with the colony's metalware industry since 1937. Like Mr. Tang, he was the son of a Chinese industrialist. His father started the I. Feng Enamelling Company in Shanghai shortly after World War I and established a Hong Kong branch in 1937. John, working part-time for his father while he attended the University of Shanghai, left both school and job and founded his own firm, the Freezinhot Bottle Co., to manufacture vacuum flasks. By 1940, he, too, set up a Hong Kong branch. When the Communists expropriated Shanghai industries, he moved to the colony to direct both the I. Feng and Freezinhot branches.

The I. Feng enterprise prospered, and in the familiar Hong Kong pattern, dozens of small operators rushed in to cut some of the pie. By 1956 there were approximately 30 of them in the field and Mr. Tung had to cut back his production. The marginal companies went broke in the glutted market, but I. Feng remained the largest in its line. Mr. Tung proceeded to build the Freezinhot bottles by handling all the manufacturing processes in his own plant, instead of the usual practice of contracting them out, and successfully invaded

Japanese markets in Africa, Latin America and Southeast Asia.

Like many other Hong Kong manufacturers, he set up subsidiary companies outside the colony. Bet-hedging is widely practiced among colony entrepreneurs; the economic climate is unpredictable and no one wants to be caught flat-footed. In the colony, Mr. Tung also runs a firebrick works, a marble plant and a trading company, shuttling daily between his various offices.

He takes a coolly realistic view of tomorrow's prospects, declaring that the market for enamelware and vacuum bottles in underdeveloped countries will drop when hot running water, electric percolators and refrigerators make his products less useful, or the countries develop their own industries to meet the need. He probably would not be offended if his potential competitors subscribed to this pessimistic outlook.

Mr. Tung's survival in the 1956 enamelware boom illustrates a recurring weakness in the colony's economy, the perennial, headlong dash to make a fast dollar. The urge is irresistible, with new industries coming over the horizon and eager money lying in wait for them. At the first sniff of profit, the money swarms into the latest bonanza, fresh companies pop up like dandelions and products flood the market. Older firms slash prices repeatedly to meet each competitive assault; presently, the bottom falls out and half the old and new companies disappear in a welter of bad debts. The frantic cycle has swept through the apparel, film, glove, plastic flower, and enamelware industries without losing any of its momentum or lure. It is often and justly deplored, but in Hong Kong it will always be difficult to find an investor panting to turn a slow dollar.

The race for a quick profit careens along at a perilous pace in the colony's building industry, where the investor in a large apartment or office building may get all his capital back within four years, or go broke in six months. The industry moved ahead at a moderate $25 million-a-year rate until about two years after the post-embargo manufacturing boom began. Then it took off, reaching a new record of $42,000,000 in 1959. In 1960 it shot up to $69,000,000, and held the steep angle of climb into 1961.

It is the building aspect of Hong Kong's industrial spurt that strikes every visitor at once. A skyscraper bank building and two hotels, of 600 and 1,000 rooms respectively, are going up in the central business district of Hong Kong Island. There is hardly a square block in the main business area where there is not at least one building under construction.

The transformation of the Tsim Sha Tsui section at the tip of Kowloon Peninsula is even more startling. In the 1920s, it was predominantly a quiet house-and-garden neighborhood strung along both sides of Nathan Road, the main north to south street. The Peninsula Hotel opened at the south end of Nathan Road in 1928 to become the new social center of the colony, and its Peninsula Court annex was added in 1957.

During the 1950s, Tsim Sha Tsui slowly became an area of small hotels and luxury shops catering to tourists. An epidemic of building fever swept over it in 1959, and the place will never be the same again. Three huge hotels—the Ambassador, Imperial and Park—opened in 1961 with a total of 1,025 rooms. Two years later, the 800-room President was to join the Kowloon tourist parade. Tall apartment buildings, reaching almost as high as their rents, and an assortment of compact luxury hotels, sprouted through the thick crust of tourists and shoppers. Guests at the top of the newly opened Imperial Hotel looked down on a scene of general devastation at the opposite side of Nathan Road; dozens of old structures being demolished to make way for larger and more expensive ones.

New hotels opening throughout the colony in 1963 will add 3,368 rooms, doubling its tourist capacity. Many of them will show the familiar marks of speculative building—undersized rooms, insufficient elevator service, thin walls and cracked masonry. The best hotels will stay the course, but the merely flashy ones may be pulled through the same wringer as the overly eager, overnight speculators in other industries.

The construction industry, which employs 160,000 people, roughly estimated, was also active in less speculative projects. From 1957 through 1961, it erected more than 200 factories, many of them on reclaimed land. Government construction on water-supply facilities, land reclamation, and resettlement estates ran just over $40,000,000 in 1960–61, and was scheduled to increase considerably in the next fiscal year.

All of the large new hotels in Hong Kong were built to serve a tourist trade which could scarcely have supported three of them in 1940. For well over a century, Hong Kong had about as much tourist appeal as the islands of Langerhans; and in its early days, the English used to sing a derisive song, "You can go to Hong Kong for Me." In the popular mind, it was associated with such disagreeable phenomena as rainstorms, typhoons, floods, pirates, malaria, bubonic plague, squalor and poisoners. Most of these scourges have disappeared, but it took travelers many years to forget them. People went to Hong Kong only on government or private business or because, being either rich or retired, they had been everywhere else and wanted to add one more odd-sounding place to their itinerary.

Distance alone was a formidable obstacle; by today's short-est air route, Hong Kong is 10,611 miles from New York and 7,286 miles from London. It was much farther by ship, and it took weeks to get there. Imperial Airways opened the first regular airline service from Europe in 1936, and Pan American World Airways started weekly transpacific flights in 1937. Early flights from New York or London still required a week, more or less, and although faster piston-engined planes gradually pared down the time, it took the introduc-tion of jet airliners in 1958 to cut the longest flights to approximately 24 hours.

The new Kai Tak Airport, whose 8,350-foot runway juts into Kowloon Bay on a strip of reclaimed land, opened on September 12, 1958, six weeks earlier than the first oceanic jet passenger service. Scheduled ocean liners and cruise ships continue to call at Hong Kong, but four-fifths of all tourists arrive by air at Kai Tak. More than 210,000 of them came in 1961, with Americans and residents of the British Common-wealth comprising the two largest groups. Not included in this total are the 132,000 members of the American armed forces who had shore leave in the colony during 1961. For many years they have been the largest group of colony vis-itors; liberal spenders and generally law-abiding.

After ignoring Hong Kong effortlessly for decades, Amer-icans had their attention drawn to it by a variety of stimu-lants. Hollywood motion pictures such as *Soldier of Fortune, Love Is a Many-Splendored Thing, The World of Suzie Wong,* and *Ferry to Hong Kong* were of varying artistic merit, but they all helped the tourist business. Television, ra-dio and film personalities—Arthur Godfrey, William Holden, Jack Paar, Ed Sullivan, and David Brinkley—presented docu-mentary reports on the colony. There was even a television adventure serial about Hong Kong, but with the exception of a few on-the-spot film clips spliced in for authenticity, it dealt with people, places and customs unknown to any colony resident.

Tourism stands next to the textile industry as a source of foreign exchange and it has created thousands of jobs for hotel and restaurant workers, entertainers, guides and shop clerks. Recognizing its economic value, the colony government set up the Hong Kong Tourist Association a few years ago. The association beams its Lorelei serenade to tourists overseas, but in its own yard, it functions as a watchdog. Its warning yip is brief: Don't flim-flam the tourists, or you'll kill a $120 million-a-year industry.

Transportation facilities in and out of the colony are equipped to handle any foreseeable increase in freight or passenger traffic during the next few years. Seventy-six shipping lines sail to 234 ports around the world. Nineteen airlines operate out of Kai Tak, with the four busiest—Cathay Pacific (chiefly regional), British Overseas Airways, Pan American and Japan Air Lines—averaging two or more arrivals and departures every day.

No one has the exact figures on how many people are employed in all the industries of the colony beyond the registered and recorded factories and including every category. But 1,200,000 have some sort of job, whether working at home, in factories, on farms, at sea or for the government. Government employs about 50,000.

There is no minimum wage. Most workers are paid by the day or on a piece-work basis. Normal daily wages of industrial workers are 50 cents to $1.30 for the unskilled, $1.20 to $1.70 for semiskilled, and $1.30 to $3.50 for skilled men. Women get 30 percent less than men. Overtime is at time and a quarter or time and a half, with the latter prevalent. Incentive pay is given for good performance and attendance. Some companies provide free or subsidized food to compensate workers for cost-of-living jumps. A bonus of one month's wages is paid by many companies just before the Chinese New Year.

As a rule the European firms and a few westernized Chinese firms provide a cost of living allowance on top of the basic wage. Yet in spite of rapid industrial expansion, inflation has been slight; the index rose only 22 points between 1947 and 1961. The eight-hour day and six-day, 48-hour week are observed by most European companies, but some Chinese companies have an 11-hour day. Women and all workers under eighteen are given a second rest day a week by law. Many big companies, especially those dealing in textiles, provide dormitories and free bedding for unmarried workers; some house the families of married workers, and the government encourages this practice by providing land for such quarters at half the market price. A few companies provide recreation rooms and free transportation to and from the job. Workmen's compensation insurance has been prescribed by law since 1953. Women, as well as children under fourteen years old, may not work between 8 P.M. and 7 A.M.

Hong Kong wages look tiny to an American worker who earns more in an hour than a colony factory hand receives in a day. But the chasm between the two standards of living is not so vast. The Hong Kong worker takes the bus, streetcar or ferryboat for less than two cents a ride; his lunch costs about ten cents, and his month's rent is under $5.00 if he lives in a resettlement estate, and below $23 a month if he occupies a low-income Housing Authority development unit.

There are 245 labor unions in the colony, but they lack bit-ing power in wage negotiations. Three have more than 10,000 members each: the seamen's union; the spinning, weaving and dyeing workers; and the motor transport workers. These three, with the unions of the seafarers, workers in Western-type employment, restaurant and café employees, government workers and teachers, represent 40 percent of all union membership. The unions split into a pro-Communist Federation and a pro-Nationalist Council. The pro-Red unions are strongest among seamen, public utilities, shipyards and textiles; the anti-Reds are most influential in the building trades, food and catering and numerous small industries. Only 25 of the 245 labor unions are free of political leadership. Collective bargaining is generally confined to the transport, printing, and enamelware industries, and to taxi drivers.

Most wages are set by agreement between the worker and his employer; the agreement is verbal and follows no uniform wage-scale. Family connections, references from friends, or the contracting system are used to get jobs. Except in the large shipyards and textile mills, the apprentice system is mostly a matter of observation and imitation. Several private trade schools train boys and girls in various jobs, and Hong Kong Technical College and Hong Kong University teach engineering, commerce and highly advanced technical specialties, with the university giving a full range of professional training. But when all are combined, they fall far short of the demand.

The majority of the colony's industrial workers impress both employers and outside observers as industrious, purposeful, capable and intelligent. They are unwilling to make bold, independent decisions, some employers complain. On the other hand, they are seldom encouraged to do so.

In the last few years, an increasing number of American

businessmen have found the risks and rewards of the colony's economy well worth their interest. The first American trading concern, Russell & Co., was established there in 1850, but the road was rocky, and Russell, along with several later Yankee traders, faded out of the picture before 1900. About a dozen American companies located agencies in Hong Kong in the early 1900s. Most notable of these was the International Banking Corp., which opened a Hong Kong branch in 1902; after a series of mergers and name changes it became a major branch of the First National City Bank of New York, occupying its own large building in the central financial district.

Except for First National City, Singer Sewing Machine Co., National Cash Register Co. and a few others, most of the American offices were agencies or area representatives until the last decade.

Anker B. Henningsen, a Montana-born businessman of Danish ancestry, came to Hong Kong from China, where his family had been in business since 1913. With his son A. P. Henningsen, he heads a group of companies that distribute Coca-Cola and other soft drinks, export and import women's wearing apparel, run a quality dress shop called Paquerette, Ltd., and act as agents for a number of American chemical, pharmaceutical and manufacturing companies. They employ 300 people.

The older Henningsen's father, a Danish immigrant to the United States, had built a prosperous produce business in the Northwest and later supplemented it by shipping eggs from China to the U. S. Eggs came in by the boatload until his competitors sabotaged the business by circulating the canard that the Chinese eggs were hundreds of years old. Mr. Henningsen turned then to Europe for his primary market, but his American produce operations took a beating in the 1919 to 1921 depression. A. B. went out to China in 1923 to start his own ice cream and frozen-drink-on-a-stick business. He had to install refrigeration units in all his retail outlets, working out of a central plant with 3,000 employees. In cold months, he packed and shipped eggs; in summer, he made and sold 125,000 frozen suckers a day. Sticks for the suckers were stamped out of Idaho pine planks, shipped from the U. S. in the form of heavy-weight packing crates to avoid lumber duty. It was no small item; the Shanghai plant used 250,000 board feet of Idaho pine a year.

In 1933 he set up a dairy business, imported 500 head of American cattle and a full line of equipment for a modern dairy farm. A few years later, Japanese bombers killed the entire herd. He was president of the American Association and the American Chamber of Commerce in Shanghai when he and 1,500 other Americans were interned by the invading Japanese. As head of the American business community, he was permitted to organize a hospital, school and food facilities for the prisoners. Repatriated to the United States in September, 1943, he operated a dried-egg plant for the Army during the rest of the war. He returned to China after the war, and ran produce and export companies until the Reds began to gain control of the country. Liquidating his interests in China, he came to Hong Kong and organized a soft-drink bottling company in 1948.

He and his son extended branches to Japan, Korea and Taiwan, but closed them down after a time, he said, because he could not find executive personnel capable and willing to run them. He expects Hong Kong to survive and prosper, despite the ever-present threat from Red China.

"Hong Kong is China's best source of foreign exchange,"

Mr. Henningsen says. "If the Reds took it over, the whole economy would collapse, just as it did in Shanghai. The Communists have mismanaged their food supply so badly that their people can't work. All they get to eat is a small rice ration, a few vegetables, very little fish and no meat at all. If people are underfed, they just die on the vine."

Robert J. Newton, another native of the American Northwest, has established his own prosperous business in the colony. Born in Salem, Oregon, he worked as a construction engineer in California, Hawaii and the Philippines. He made his first Hong Kong visit in the early 1930s, found it easy to do business with the people there and was deeply impressed by the skill of its workmen. He returned to the colony often in succeeding years.

He had made the building of boats his lifetime hobby, and was frequently praised for the quality of his craftsmanship. But it was not until the 1950s that he began to consider boat construction as a possible business. His two sons, Whitney and John, became his associates, with John heading a distributorship for Bireley's soft drinks. Whitney became the manager of American Marine, Ltd., the boat-building yard established by his father.

In 1958, the company set up operations in a tin-roofed shed that was not much larger than a two-car garage. The yard site was along the shore of an inlet on Clear Water Peninsula, nearly five miles due east of Kowloon. Well away from other industrial areas, it lay just across Junk Bay from the Chinese Nationalist refugee settlement at Rennie's Mill Camp.

American Marine, which produces pleasure boats for the American market, outgrew its corporate cradle in a few weeks; its present shed is 500 feet long and 300 feet wide, and will be doubled in area during 1962. The company turns out

40 to 50 yachts a year, selling from $7,000 to $70,000 each. Mr. Newton and his son are the only Americans in the company; all of their 300 workmen are Chinese.

Mr. Newton's basic assumption was that he could produce a sailboat, modified luxury junk, motor sailer, or power cruiser to the finest design specifications, ship it to the United States as deck cargo on a freighter, and still undersell American boat-builders by a fair margin. The idea appears to be sound. His yard crew is working on 30 boats at a time and expects to raise its annual output to 80 or 100 boats a year when the enlarged shed has been completed.

Wood for his boats comes from many countries—Sitka spruce, for spars, from the American Northwest; teak from Thailand; and other hardwoods from Borneo and mahogany planking from the Philippines. Engines and fittings come from the United States. The largest of his boats to date is a 59-foot motor sailer, and all are built to the specifications of American marine designers and architects such as Sparkman & Stephens, Inc. of New York, and William Lapworth of Los Angeles. It takes six to eight months to finish most boats.

One problem he has, Mr. Newton explains, is training Chinese workmen to use power tools. Ten years ago power equipment was a great rarity in the colony; now American Marine has 50 electric drills, planers, bandsaws and a bolt-threader. Some of his workmen had never seen a power tool before they were trained to use them at the boatyard. Whitney Newton's ability to speak Cantonese is helpful, but the instructor has to proceed with the utmost caution in introducing a greenhorn to a bandsaw.

American Marine builds a few modified junks, using American equipment and finishing them like yachts. The three masts of the typical Chinese junk are retained, but the rigging is simplified and the usual ponderous rudder is greatly reduced in size. They sell for $10,000 or more. The Newtons built one for Don the Beachcomber, Hollywood restaurant owner. Americans are often infatuated with the romantic outline of a large working junk, but they would soon go aground trying to handle its complicated sails.

American Marine follows the Chinese practice of paying one month's bonus to its workers at the New Year. Trucks carry the men to and from work. A barracks and mess hall accommodate those who live at the yard. The hamlet of Hang Hau, half-destroyed by fire years ago and still in ruins, was American Marine's only neighbor in 1958. Now there is a mill for cold-rolled steel and a ship-breaking shop, with the light-colored buildings of Haven of Hope Sanatorium arrayed along the hills of the opposite shore.

Mandarin Textiles, Ltd., best known in the United States for its Dynasty line of high-styled women's apparel, is also directed by an American, Linden E. Johnson. Mr. Johnson, who served with the U. S. armed forces in China during World War II, stayed on to become a Shanghai textile executive. When the Reds drove him out of China, he came to Hong Kong and founded Mandarin with a Chinese partner who was murdered by a fellow-Chinese in 1957. Mr. Johnson kept the business going, completed an eight-story plant in Kowloon, near Kai Tak, in 1958, and expanded it into one of the colony's finest tailoring and designing houses.

Mandarin, which makes the Empire line in cottons in addition to the Dynasty silks and brocades, employs up to 1,300 workers. It provides a recreation room, catered meals and classes in English for its work force. Most of its permanent staff are highly skilled people, like the young sewing-machine operator who stitches intricate rose and tea-leaf designs on quilted fabrics at high speed, working from memory with un-erring accuracy. The cutters, tailors, and pressers are ad-vanced craftsmen, trained by long apprenticeship.

Mandarin introduces about fifteen new silk and brocade patterns each year, originated by its own designer, Doris Saunders, with such names as Cherry Blossom, Ivory Blue, Sing Song and Garland. Its stockroom carries nearly 500 pat-terns, including as many as eight different color variations on a single pattern. Wives of visiting VIPs often tend to go hay-wire when exposed to this exciting inventory, and have had to be led or dragged away from the shelves. Most of the bro-cades are woven by the Fou Wah mills in Tsuen Wan. Fin-ished garments are packed in waterproof paper and special shipping boxes and sent to the U. S. by air express or sea freight.

Mandarin keeps its finger on the high-fashion pulse through its Dynasty Salon in the colony's Hotel Peninsula, but it also cagily remains in touch with a wider and less sophisticated market by noting what the American sailors buy at its service-men's outlet in Wanchai, where the fleet comes in.

Textiles have become the largest single factor in the col-ony's economy. Textile exports totaled $273.5 million in 1960, or 55 percent of the colony's entire domestic exports. In 1961, textiles constituted 52 percent of all exports. The in-dustry employs 42 percent of all the workers in registered and recorded industries. It has a capacity of 614,000 spindles and 18,700 looms.

All this is cause for rejoicing in Hong Kong textile circles, but to textile producers in England, the United States and Canada, it is a problem that becomes greater all the time. The United States absorbed 31 percent of the colony's textile ex-ports in 1960, and the British Isles were a close second with

26 percent. Textile exports to the United States took a sharp drop in 1961, while those to the British Isles showed only a slight decline.

There was much concern among Lancashire mill-owners when Hong Kong cottons began to hit the English market. American textile producers and textile union leaders joined in a protest that was echoed with lesser volume by the Canadian textile industry. In all three countries, textile men declared that if they had to compete with Hong Kong's low wage-scales, they would be driven to the wall.

American textile producers have their own special complaints against the Hong Kong industry. They point out that because of the existing price differential, Hong Kong can buy U. S. cotton at 8½ cents less per pound than American mills can, and that the colony has been stocking up heavily on it. In 1960, Hong Kong imported 55 percent of its raw cotton from the United States. The U. S. textile men say that while Japan's textile exports have been held down by a five-year quota limitation, Hong Kong has rushed in to sell America the items that Japan agreed not to sell.

The demand for restrictions on colony textile exports to the United States began in 1958. United States officials visited the colony in 1959 with a proposal for a voluntary cut in the exports. The Hong Kong garment manufacturers proposed a three-year quota arrangement, starting in July, 1960, to hold exports to the 1959 level, plus 15 percent on cotton blouses and blouse sets, shorts and trousers, sport shirts, brassieres and pajamas. American textile producers immediately rejected the proposal as far too generous to Hong Kong competitors.

During the negotiations, American importers placed huge orders with Hong Kong to get in ahead of the threatened limitations. When the agreement blew up, they found an interesting variety of reasons why they couldn't accept most of what they had ordered, such as late deliveries, and unsatisfactory quality. Exports to the U. S. dropped and the decline persisted into 1961.

In May, 1961, President Kennedy proposed an international textile conference to work out some agreeable way to control textile exports. The United States then suggested that Hong Kong cut its textile exports at least 30 percent below the levels of 1960. But the word "quota" had assumed a fearsome aspect in Hong Kong because of a textile agreement involving the colony, England, India and Pakistan. Hong Kong had agreed to limit its exports to the British Isles, provided that Pakistan and India would do the same. In 1961, the Hong Kong industry began to suspect that India and Pakistan might jump the traces, leaving the colony interests holding the bag.

A large section of the Hong Kong press is rabidly pro-textile industry, and every American move toward textile controls is headlined as a thrust at the heart of the colony's principal industry. Communist papers shoved their way into the act by crying that American restrictions would starve the refugee workers who left the People's Republic of China to escape that very fate.

After the July 1961 International Textile Conference at Geneva, the Hong Kong government, following long bilateral discussions with the U. S., agreed to limit its exports according to the Geneva Textile Agreement, with July 1960-June 1961 as the base year, and dividing the affected export items into 64 different categories. Starting date of the agreement was October 1, 1961.

Meanwhile, the United States Tariff Commission began to study the 8½-cents-a-pound cotton export differential at the direction of President Kennedy. Genuinely alarmed, Hong

Kong business groups hired Dean Acheson, lawyer and former American Secretary of State, to represent them before
the Commission and help to retain the price differential.

The textile volcano erupted again in March, 1962, when the
colony government, acting under the one-year agreement that
went into effect the previous October, banned eight categories
of textile exports to the United States. The Hong Kong *Tiger
Standard*, clamorous advocate of the textile interests, ex-
coriated the move as a prelude to economic ruin. Pande-
monium ran through the industry. The government ban was
lifted almost immediately. Prospects of a peaceful solution
seemed as poor as ever.

On September 6, 1962, the U.S. Tariff Commission voted
to retain the 8½-cent export differential and rejected a proposal to raise the duty on cotton imports. This action coaxed
the Hong Kong manufacturers out of their sulks, but it sent
the American textile-makers into a fresh tantrum.

Hong Kong's motion picture industry is one of the world's
most prolific, and least-known, producers of feature films.
More than 300 feature-length pictures were made in 1961 by
its six major studios and scores of independent producers who
rented working space from the big studios. All were in Cantonese or Mandarin, aimed at the Overseas Chinese market in
Taiwan, the Philippines, Southeast Asia and elsewhere. Mandarin features are generally based on heroic or historical
themes, with rich costuming and elaborate sets; each one
takes 35 to 40 days of shooting and costs around $40,000. A
few Mandarin films have contemporary stories. Cantonese
films, usually drawing on time-tested plots from Cantonese
opera, can be run off in 10 or 15 days for less than $20,000 and
are more popular than Mandarin with the Hong Kong fans.

As might be guessed from their shooting schedule, many of

these quickies are rubbish. But the quality of the Mandarin films has improved, and a few super-productions costing as much as $175,000 are made every year. Hong Kong films have won top honors at the East Asian Film Festival for the last four years.

The Shaw Brothers, Run Run Shaw and Run Me Shaw, bill themselves with typical cinematic restraint as The Greatest Purveyors of Entertainment in the Far East, and are the kings of the local industry. Late in 1961 they moved their Hong Kong organization into a modern and elaborate studio at Clearwater Bay in the New Territories. Its four sound stages were to be increased to six within a few months, and its employed force numbered several hundred, plus an equal number of low-paid extras.

Lin Dai, twenty-six-year-old beauty and box-office queen of the Shaw Brothers studio, took the 1961 best-actress Golden Harvest Award. As the highest-paid star, she earned $42,000 annually on a three-picture-a-year contract. A singer, actress and dancer, she is stunning by any standards, East or West, and the studio plans to release some of her best films in the American art-theater circuit. Thus far, their American audience has been restricted to Chinese-American viewers.

The Shaws, who also own studios in Malaya and a chain of 120 theaters in Southeast Asia, began operations in Hong Kong three years after Grandview Film Co. founded the local industry in 1933. After a slow start, the industry boomed in the early 1950s, overexpanded and crashed, leaving only four companies in the field by 1956. Pro-Nationalist studios such as Shaw Brothers have no market in Red China, but there are a number of Hong Kong film-makers who have a pro-Communist slant. Shaw's new studio can produce wide-screen pictures, overcoming one of the handicaps that has limited the growth of the industry in the colony. Generally speaking, there is still plenty of room for technical and artistic improvement.

The 1961 Hong Kong census reported a total of 337,000 women in all the employed forces, yet women have played a disproportionately small part in the direction of industry and public affairs until the last twenty years or so. It is not surprising that Chinese women were excluded from public life, since they had few rights outside their homes until the establishment of the Chinese Republic in 1911. But British women, presumably well-educated and qualified to take executive responsibilities, found few opportunities to do so. The fact that Queen Victoria ruled the colony for the first sixty years of its existence should have helped, but it didn't. What influence women had was unseen, and was exerted through their husbands or other men.

Even today there is not one woman in the top echelon of Hong Kong government, although women constitute about one-twelfth of the government's Class I and II administrative staff officers (more than a third of these women are Chinese).

In nongovernmental posts, there are about ten women conducting their own retail shops, chiefly in fashions, jewelry and objets d'art. Rosalind Henwood, an American, heads an air freight forwarding business.

There are about a dozen women of prominence in writing, advertising and publicity. Two of them, Mrs. Beatrice M. Church and Miss Elma Kelly, direct their own advertising and publicity agencies. Mrs. Church, a former Far Eastern correspondent for the *London Daily Mail*, survived Japanese air attacks and ship-sinkings during World War II, served in the SWANS, a women's service affiliated with the British Navy, and returned to Hong Kong to reestablish the pioneering advertising and publicity firm she had founded with her husband, Captain Charles Church. Captain Church, his health shattered by Japanese tortures during imprisonment at Singapore, died of the effects of his injuries in 1950. Mrs. Church assumed sole control of the business, the Advertising and Publicity Bureau, and has successfully operated it since then. Miss Kelly, a native of Melbourne, Australia, began her career as an analytical chemist. She also was a Japanese war prisoner before setting up her own agency, Cathay, Ltd., in Hong Kong.

There are about 20 women executives and administrators in private or semipublic health and welfare agencies. Women staff officers in government health and welfare work number approximately 150—by far the largest group of women in civil-service staff posts. The colony has a small number of women doctors, educators and lawyers, plus one architect, but most women professionals in these fields are government officers.

Women employed in art or cultural activities total about fifteen, including several Chinese movie actresses. Miss Aileen Woods, a colony resident for nearly forty years, is widely known for her Down Memory Lane program over Radio Hong Kong, which she conducted from 1947 to 1954. A Japanese prisoner in Hong Kong during the war, she subsisted on a semistarvation diet of rice, fish and boiled sweet-potato leaves; her weight fell to 81 pounds and many of her fellow prisoners died. Miss Woods, now seventy-five years old and in excellent health, was honored by a personal visit from Princess Alexandra of Kent during the Princess's tour of Hong Kong in November, 1961. She was awarded the Coronation Medal in 1953, and the Member of the British Empire in 1958. She still does occasional programs for Radio Hong Kong, a government agency, and is regarded as the unofficial dean of the colony's working women, having begun her career as a world-touring featured dancer in the *Ziegfeld Follies* and other shows more than fifty years ago.

In private business and professional activities, as in government staff positions, about one-third of the colony's career women are Chinese, and both groups of women have achieved much greater prestige and success than any previous generation of the colony's women. Among the Tanka fishing people of Hong Kong, women own most of the fishing junks. On Po Toi, a small island southeast of Hong Kong Island, a Chinese woman, who died in 1957, held the rank of village elder; as such, she was the arbiter of all local disputes, having an authority rarely given to women. Many women in the colony hope that the lady from Po Toi will become a trend-setter instead of a legend.

What are the prospects for Hong Kong industry and trade? Among the many persons who have weighed these prospects are three of the most influential men in the commercial life of the colony: Hugh Barton, chairman and managing director of Jardine, Matheson & Co.; Sir Michael Turner, chairman, general manager and a director of the Hongkong & Shanghai Banking Corp.; and John L. Marden, chairman of Wheelock, Marden & Co. A listing of their combined directorships would fill two closely printed pages, and it would be only a mild exaggeration to say that they and the companies they head are in everything of a business nature in the colony. Each man also holds an important position in the colony government; Sir Michael as an unofficial member of the Executive Council, Mr. Barton as an unofficial member of the Legislative Council, and Mr. Marden with unofficial membership in the Urban Council.

Mr. Barton heads one of the oldest and most respected business houses in Hong Kong, with financial or operational control of companies in such diverse lines as real estate, shipping, wharves, warehousing, insurance, utilities, textiles, transport, engineering, airlines and trading. Jardine's, as it is commonly called, was deeply engaged in the opium trade during the colony's early years, but has long since turned to other interests.

One of its recent investments, the Jardine Dyeing & Finishing Co., was established two years ago and now produces two million yards of high-quality cloth per month.

Barton believes that if the United States drops the 8½-cents-a-pound cotton export differential, most of the cloth produced in Hong Kong will not be able to compete in the world market. Of the 500 million yards of cloth produced annually by Hong Kong, a relatively small amount is exported to the United States.

However, Barton feels, removal of the 8½-cent differential would cripple the local industry's efforts to produce its cloth cheaply enough to compete in the markets of Southeast Asia and elsewhere.

"Many people urge the textile industry to accept tight controls of its exports, or they want our textile producers to diversify by going into new industries," he says. "But the imposition of such controls doesn't fit the character of Hong Kong, which has prospered because it is a free port with a minimum of controls.

"Of course it is easy to advise diversification, but what about the Shanghai textile industrialists who spent a lifetime becoming experts in the business? The Hong Kong textile industry is built on that knowledge, and it can't be reconverted to some other industry overnight," Barton states.

He feels that some degree of diversification is certainly desirable, but that Hong Kong cannot afford to drop its textile industry.

"There is a fresh Indonesian market for low-grade textiles produced here," he says. "And there are many good markets for Hong Kong's made-up cloth."

He points out that local industry in many lines was hit by a 1961 substantial rise in shipping costs and port charges. In turn, the shipping industry has taken a loss from the invasion of the dry-cargo field by the super-tankers originally built to ship oil. Freighters, tramp steamers, and ocean liners have all experienced a drop-off in profits because of this invasion, he declares. Many new nations, partly influenced by national pride and prestige, have launched their own shipping lines, further crowding and depressing the profit margins of existing lines.

"Industrial production and tourism are our two lungs," Barton says of Hong Kong's economy. "We not only have to maintain our present employment levels; we must also find jobs for thousands and thousands of young people in the next few years."

He cites one of the major discoveries of the 1961 census—that 40.8 percent of the total population of Hong Kong is under fifteen years of age—as evidence of the coming demand for new jobs.

Accustomed to economic upheavals, Jardine's has adapted itself to changed conditions by investing in growth industries, and by developing new industrial sites at Tsuen Wan, Kwun Tong and West Point. It is selling some of its land holdings to finance a six-year modernization of the wharf operations of the Hongkong and Kowloon Wharf & Godown Co. Its new international ship terminal in Kowloon, costing $7 to $8 million, will include a pier 1,200 feet long, and will have car parks, shopping areas and a bowling alley.

Sir Michael Turner, head of the Hongkong & Shanghai Bank, emphasizes that local industries, confronted with restrictions in their export markets, must seek new markets for their output.

"Our land and labor costs are rising," Sir Michael says. "But we must be able to compete with Japan, Formosa, and ultimately, Red China. Red China can ignore costs and flood our markets, as they did previously in shoes and textiles."

Sir Michael has a limited faith in the doctrine that the colony's market problems can be solved by diversification of its industries.

"Even diversification means that we'll encounter resistance in the new lines we enter." He believes that the colony's industries must maintain quality and raise it where possible, rather than lowering standards to compete with inferior products.

He says that Hong Kong has attracted investment capital from all over Southeast Asia because of its exceptional political stability, and because local industry was not disrupted by union work-stoppages. He cites the traditional Chinese dislike of regulation and regimentation as a factor inhibiting the expansion of union power.

"The shortage of land and water is still our greatest limitation," Sir Michael says. "Land development is very costly, and although the builder of an apartment house may recover his costs in one year, that is not possible in the construction of factories."

He notes that the colony has a serious problem of "under-employment," rather than unemployment. He adds that the colony's predominantly young population would necessitate a sharp increase in government spending for schools and hospitals. Like Mr. Barton, he recognizes that thousands of additional jobs must be ready for young people when they begin moving into the employment market.

He regards the preservation of Imperial Preference as vital to the colony in meeting Japanese competition, but he believes that Hong Kong will not be injured by the European Common Market if the colony's economic needs are recognized in the agreement.

Although the Hongkong & Shanghai Bank is commonly viewed as the incarnation of everything British, its founders included an American, two Parsees, two Germans and an Ottoman Jew. For many years it has been a leader in employing and training Portuguese office workers, accepting them on individual merit instead of drawing a rigidly British line. The bank celebrates its centennial in 1964.

John L. Marden is the chief executive of a company which dates from 1933 under its present title, but has corporate origins going back to the opening of the China trade. The Wheelock Marden companies have interests in shipping, shipbuilding, textiles, finance, aviation, land, insurance, merchandising and many other lines.

Among Hong Kong's industrial assets, Mr. Marden lists its freedom from controls, its political stability, its low income tax on individuals and corporations and its resistance to inflation.

It is his conviction that Hong Kong industry should concentrate on quality products, and those which require a high labor content. He cites transistor radios of the less complicated type as an example of the colony's high-labor products.

"I think we should emphasize that there is something more

at stake than profits," Marden says. "The colony is seeking to create 300,000 new jobs for the young people who will be coming on the job market soon; if we can do this without appealing for outside aid, then we've made a contribution to the economy of the entire free world."

In the past, he believes, colony industries just took orders as they came. Now, in his opinion, the industries must develop their own marketing facilities to discover what products are needed, and then work to meet these needs. He feels that there must be greater diversification if Hong Kong is to hold its place in the industrial world.

These three men, like practically every leader in its industrial and political community, are acutely conscious of the many hazards that Hong Kong faces.

And not one of them acts or speaks as though he were not solidly confident that Hong Kong will overcome its handicaps and external dangers and go on to greater prosperity.

CHAPTER FIVE

High Land, Low Water

"It is unfortunate that the space between the foot of the mountains and the edge of the sea is so very limited."

—HALL & BERNARD, *The Nemesis in China,* 1847

Hong Kong has always had more land and water than it could use, because most of the land is a hilly waste and most of the water is salty.

From the first years of the colony until today, the persisting shortage of usable land and fresh water has confronted every governor with a problem that he could neither solve nor ignore. They have all wrestled with it, none more vigorously than the governors of the last fifteen years, and the problem has become more costly, complex and acute than ever.

In any community, land and water problems are related to each other; in the peculiar circumstances of Hong Kong's climate, geography and population, they intersect at more points than Laocoön and the serpents.

Consider the governor's alternatives: If he stores the entire run-off of the summer rainy season in the reservoirs it will barely meet the minimum needs of the urban millions on Kowloon and Hong Kong Island, and it will cause the withering of the crops of farmers in the New Territories during the winter dry season. If he cuts the city supply, how can he meet the ever-increasing needs of the new industrial centers, like Tsuen Wan and Kwun Tong, that the government is building on land reclaimed from the sea?

The if's are endless: If he stops the reclamation program to reduce the demand for more water, real estate costs will climb so fast that local industries will price themselves out of the export market. If he builds all the reservoirs the colony needs, who will pay for them? If he doesn't, how can the fast-growing population of the colony survive? If the reservoirs displace more farmers, who will raise the food?

The present disposition of the colony government is to provide as much additional land and water as it can, and let the if's fall where they may. To that end, it has spent about $60 million on reclamation and $55 million to increase its water supply since World War II. Over the next decade, its further expenditures in these two areas may reach $300 million. Many projects have not yet been authorized, but much of the preliminary surveying has been done. With the need for them becoming more imperative as the colony's population continues to increase, it is not so much a question of if as of when.

Allocation of several hundred million dollars to correct deficiencies of the topography is none too large for the job that must be done. When one has noted that Hong Kong has a sheltered deep-water harbor (probably the bed of an old river that flowed from west to east), that one-seventh of its land is arable, and that its mines and quarries yield a modest amount of iron ore, building stone, kaolin clay, graphite, lead, wolfram and a few other minerals, one has exhausted the list of its terrestrial assets. Its liabilities are unlimited.

Three broken lines of perpendicular hills cut across the colony from northeast to southwest, with irregular spurs branching off haphazardly; two dozen peaks poke up from 1,000 to 3,140 feet. Eighty percent of the surface is either too steep for roads or buildings, too barren to grow anything but wiry grass or scrub, too swampy to walk through or so hacked up by erosion that it is worthless and an eyesore. The rest, except for farmland, is either in forest or packed with people in numbers ranging from 1,800 to 2,800 an acre. Rivers tumble from the high hills in all directions, but they are short and unreliable, mostly summer torrents and winter trickles.

Hong Kong's weather is impartially disrespectful toward annual averages, periodic tables and the population. Rainfall averages about 85 inches a year, with the rainy season extending from April through September. There have been long summer droughts and ruinous winter floods. On July 19, 1926, it rained nearly 4 inches in one hour and 21 inches in 24 hours.

Prevailing winds blow from the east in every month but June, and the colony's fishing settlements have been located to protect them from it. The protection avails nothing against typhoons, which usually form in the Caroline Islands, curve northwards over the Philippines and hit Hong Kong from all angles, principally during the June to October season, though there is no month which has not had at least one of them. Four out of five bypass the colony, but the fifth may inflict devastation on ships, boats and shoreline villages. It never snows and freezing temperatures are extremely rare, yet the high, year-round humidity can put a raw edge on cool wintry days and make summer clothing stickily uncomfortable. Except for flat farmland in the northwestern New Territories, topsoil is thin, highly acid and leaches badly during the rainy season.

This chronicle of drawbacks only tends to revive the question every British administrator since 1841 must have asked himself: Why did we ever settle this hump-backed wasteland? They have answered the question by a dogged and unremitting effort to make it a habitable place.

The first English traders had scarcely settled along the north shore of Hong Kong Island when it became evident that there was a shortage of suitable land. The slopes of Mt. Gough and Victoria Peak rose steeply behind Queen's Road, the only street along the shore. Holders of waterfront lots on the road extended them toward the harbor pretty much at random, giving them more level land but creating a jagged shoreline unprotected by any seawall. Several governors sought to build a straight and solid seawall, but the lot-holders balked at paying its cost.

Two poorly constructed seawalls, erected in piecemeal fashion, were wrecked by typhoons before the government was able to push through a unified seawall and reclamation scheme. By 1904, a massive seawall stretched along the island front for two miles, and Queen's Road stood two blocks inland from the harbor. Most of the colony's principal office buildings have been built on this reclaimed land.

Once the value of reclamation had been proved, the whole northern shore of the island was gradually faced with a seawall. Much of the Wanchai district rose from the sea in the 1920s and its new-found land was soon covered with tenements or bars and cabarets catering to the sailors' trade. Swamps became solid ground and promontories were swallowed up by the seven-mile-long reclamation.

Starting in 1867, a succession of seawall and land-fill projects altered the size and shape of the Kowloon Peninsula.

By the time of the Japanese invasion, a total of 1,425 acres, or more than two square miles, had been reclaimed. The gain was twofold, for it not only added level land, it absorbed all the fill from sites where obstructing hills had been cut down to make existing ground usable.

The foundation of the colony's tourist industry and air cargo business rests on land reclaimed from Kowloon Bay and converted into an international airport. Its name and its origin go back to 1918, when two real estate promoters, Sir Kai Ho Kai and Au Tak, organized the Kai Tak Land Development Co. to create building sites by filling in the northern end of Kowloon Bay. Homesites and an 800-foot-long airstrip were in use on the land by 1924, with Fowler's Flying School the first aviation tenant. Government took it over in 1930, improving and enlarging it in preparation for the first international flight, an Imperial Airways' weekly service to Penang started March 24, 1936, linking with the main route between England and Australia. Four other international airlines, including Pan American and Air France, joined the formation before the Japanese seized the field in 1941. The Japanese extended its area and built two concrete runways, but its buildings were bombed into rubble before the war ended.

Restored to full operations in 1947, Kai Tak handled the strangest one-way traffic boom in its history. In one month of 1949, 41,000 passengers were flown in from China to escape the advancing Communist armies. Mainland service ended a year later, and traffic declined to one-third of its former volume. The field itself, penned in by rocky peaks, had reached the limits of its development, and the largest four-engined ships were rapidly outgrowing it. For jets, it would be a cow pasture at the bottom of a canyon.

The Department of Civil Aviation, after concluding that nothing further could be done to expand the existing field, began casting around for alternate sites. Fourteen of them, including Stonecutters Island and Stanley Bay, were ruled out for excessive cost, inaccessibility, or risky topography before the experts decided to put the airport right next to the old one, on a strip of land that didn't then exist.

The government put up the money and the job of building a promontory 7,800 feet long and 800 feet wide that would point directly into Kowloon Bay began in 1956. A few hills would have to be knocked down to clear the approaches, but disposal of the dirt would be simple, since 20 million cubic yards of fill were needed to build the promontory. The new airport runway was to have a length of 8,350 feet, extending the full length of the reclaimed strip and well beyond its landward end.

Three thousand laborers, most of them hauling dirt by hand, worked nearly three years to lay down the man-made peninsula. Although it was near the old airport, it overcame the earlier field's approach limitations by being pointed straight at the 1,500-foot-wide harbor entrance of Lei Yue Mun, and at the opposite end, having the Kowloon hills truncated to permit another clear shot at the runway, depending on which direction best fitted weather conditions.

The new runway went into use in 1958, with the completion of the terminal coming several years later. Temporary terminal buildings bulged with incoming tourists, but they were moved through these buildings fairly well. Most colony residents are hardly aware of the arrival and departure of the huge jets, though they shake the earth with their thunder as

North from Victoria Peak. The colony government and main business section are chiefly based on Hong Kong Island, foreground. Kowloon Peninsula and the long runway of Kai Tak Airport lie at top center. The New Territories start with the mountains in the background, extend north to the Red China border. Hong Kong is one of the busiest seaports in the world.

Above: Hong Kong in a hurry. Queens Road Central, in the colony's commercial center, swarms with pedestrians in a typical noon-hour rush. *Below:* A Chinese funeral procession. Chief mourners ride in a rickshaw. Street bands, drummers, and cymbal players march with them. Firecrackers are exploded along the way to dispel evil spirits.

Many picturesque laddered streets, such as the one above, climb the slopes of Victoria Peak in the heavily populated Western District of Hong Kong Island. Passable only by foot or in sedan chair, they also serve as playgrounds for children and runs for dogs, cats, and chickens.

Above: Night view of Government House, executive mansion of Hong Kong's British Governor. Behind it are Victoria Peak and tiers of fine apartment buildings. *Below:* Billy Tingle, the colony's best known athletic instructor, demonstrates the game of cricket to young pupils at the Hong Kong Cricket Club.

In contrast to Hong Kong's many fashionable and modern houses and apartment buildings, thousands of tightly packed boats serve as floating homes in the mud flats of Aberdeen, on Hong Kong Island. Periodically they are damaged or destroyed by typhoon.

Bearded monsters like the one above adorn the prow of rowing shells which participate in Hong Kong's annual Dragon Boat Festival races, part of a colorful religious observance held annually in the late spring.

Workmen unload 800-pound hampers of vegetables from Red China at Lo Wu, where a railroad bridge crosses the Sham Chun River on the Hong Kong-China border. The Communist flag flies above guard post at the right.

A marine police inspector at Hong Kong hauls in a water-logged sampan used by six refugees in their escape from Red China. They spent three nights and two days in the leaky craft before a fishing junk picked them up near Lantau Island. Because of the overwhelming number of refugees arriving in Hong Kong police were forced to return the six to Red China.

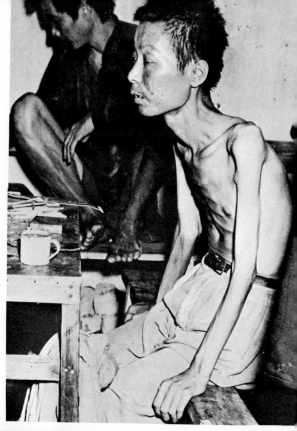

Above: This Hong Kong heroin addict has been reduced to near starvation by his craving for the drug. Drug addiction in the colony is closely related to crime and poor living conditions. *Below:* A hollowed-out wooden doll found in the home of a dope smuggler. The heroin cache, covered with a closely fitted lid, was difficult to detect.

Above: Girls at work in the vast spinning room of the South Sea Textile Manufacturing Co. at Tsuen Wan, Hong Kong, one of the world's most modern textile mills. *Below:* By contrast, a woman uses a primitive wooden plow to till a rice field in the New Territories, where power equipment is too large and too costly for the tiny farms.

Above: A carpenter at a Shau Kei Wan shipyard on Hong Kong Island uses an ancient bow type of drill in building a Chinese junk. *Below:* At another yard in Shau Kei Wan, a workman employs a portable electric power drill. Primitive and modern tools often are used side-by-side in the changing and expanding Hong Kong boat industry.

A young refugee Chinese girl paints artificial birds at the China Refugee Development Organization factory in Kowloon, where about 40,000 of these wire, paper and cotton birds are produced every month for sale overseas.

A welfare pioneer, Gus Borgeest established a farm colony on desolate Sunshine Island, Hong Kong, to teach refugees how to raise crops on marginal land. With him is his wife, Mona, and Ruth, one of their daughters.

A freighter moored to a Hong Kong harbor buoy off-loads its cargo into junks and lighters. There most cargo is handled in this way, rather than by transferring it directly to piers.

Fishing junks sail along Tolo Channel, one of the deep-water inlets in the Eastern New Territories of Hong Kong. The bleak hills are characteristic of the colony's predominately rocky, barren terrain.

Refugees from Red China collect tin, tar paper, scrap lumber and sacking for use in making their flimsy shelters. Multi-story concrete resettlement developments are gradually replacing such shacks in Hong Kong.

they pass over Kowloon. Kai Tak has become a full 24-hour airport. Its 200-foot-wide runway is stressed to take a maximum plane weight of 400,000 pounds, well above the limit of the heaviest airliners. From the air it looks like a super-highway lost at sea.

Opening of the new Kai Tak Airport brought the colony an additional gain by freeing 70 acres of the old field for industrial development.

Less than half a mile from the seaward end of Kai Tak, the first new town in the government's history is being built—Kwun Tong, an industrial, commercial and residential area along the northeastern shore of Kowloon Bay. A ten-year project of large extent, it required the removal of a whole range of hills. The spoil was then hauled to the bay and dumped behind a protecting seawall 2,477 feet long. The leveled hills and the land reclaimed from the sea will provide a 514-acre site, close to a square mile, for an industrial center whose population is expected to reach 300,000 within a few years.

Digging and filling began in 1955 and have proceeded with such speed that today, in order to get a panoramic view of the project, one has to go to a hill three quarters of a mile back from the seawall. Block after block of multi-storied factories stretch along the sea front, approximately eighty of them, several blocks deep in the industrial zone between the seawall and Kwun Tong Road, which cuts directly across the town. On the landward side of Kwun Tong Road, the commercial and recreational zones are beginning to take shape; behind them, the long files of resettlement estates housing 60,000 persons and various government-aided housing for another 15,000. Privately built houses are also being developed.

Kwun Tong has all the noisy, dusty confusion of any construction job in progress, but there are already 15,000 people working in its completed factories, making cotton yarn, furniture, garments, and other products. Most of the factories are humming and a few betray signs of hasty organization. One plant spent two years tinkering with stop-gap orders for simple novelties while its management tried to find some profitable use for a million dollars' worth of fine machinery standing idle under its roof.

Kwun Tong will never be a beauty spot because its main function is industrial. Nearly half its total area will be reserved for homes and commercial use, however. Proceeds from land sales are expected to repay the government for its $17 million investment in Kwun Tong.

Tsuen Wan, a second industrial town about eight miles northwest of Kwun Tong in the New Territories, has reclaimed around 70 acres from the sea. Gin Drinkers' Bay, an adjoining inlet used for ship-breaking, is being filled in to provide 400 more acres of industrial sites. No one knows the origin of its name but it no longer matters; this glass will soon be filled with earth. When completed, Tsuen Wan will be a town of about 175,000 people.

Specialized reclamation projects have been pushed ahead at many other spots. At North Point, on Hong Kong Island, 12,000 people live in tall apartments built on recently reclaimed land. The new City Hall opened in 1962 on reclaimed waterfront land in the Central District. Five blocks of the central waterfront, just west of the reclaimed land on which the Star Ferry's Hong Kong Island terminal sits, are being extended several hundred feet into the harbor for more building sites.

The principal land-fill operations have been restricted to the island and Kowloon Bay, except for Tseun Wan. The limitation has been human, rather than geographic; most urban workers can't afford to travel to outlying locations and they don't want to anyway. They plainly prefer the excitement, gossip and sociability of the crowded cities.

Nevertheless, central reclamation possibilities are running out, unless the government proposes to pave its entire harbor. As a more likely alternative, it sent engineers out in 1957 to study reclamation sites in the bays and shallow inlets of the New Territories. Five have been tentatively chosen that could be developed to create 3,000 more acres of land. The cost would come to more than $83 million, so there's no eagerness to tackle the project at once.

The never-ending task of providing more land for the colony's growing population would be meaningless without the assurance of an adequate water supply. At this stage in the colony's development, even when the work of increasing the water supply is proceeding on a scale no previous generation would have attempted, the builders and planners are not deluding themselves. They know that when they have completed the last unit of the reservoir system under construction, the needs of the colony will probably have outstripped its capacity. There were times in the past when some optimistic governor, presiding at the opening of a new dam or reservoir, fancied that the problem had been met. The next drought was sufficient to knock his hopeful predictions into a cocked hat.

Hong Kong has never been inclined to waste water. On the rare occasions when its people had a full supply, as in certain periods of 1958 and 1959, its maximum average consumption ran to about 88 million gallons a day for nearly 3,000,000 people. New York City, with just under 8,000,000 people, consumes about 1 billion 200 million gallons a day. Because of an unparalleled water-supply system, Americans are the world's champion water-wasters. An American will use 100 gallons a day, compared with 27 gallons per person in Hong Kong, and about 50 gallons per person in Great Britain.

There are compelling reasons why Hong Kong residents will not waste water. The colony, unlike New York City, cannot draw from a watershed covering several states. Except for a relatively small amount piped in from Red China since 1960, it has had to rely on surface water collected entirely from its 398¼ square miles of land area, which is about one-fourth larger than New York City. And it has to get the water while the getting is good; during the annual five-month dry season, the surface run-off averages only 600,000 gallons a day.

The colony may have been mistaken from the start about its potential water resources; even before it was established, sailing ships stopped regularly at Hong Kong Island to draw clear, sparkling water from its hillside springs. After the island was settled the springs soon fell short of needs, and five wells were sunk to tap new sources of supply. Their levels, too, sank as rapidly as the population rose. Governor Hercules Robinson expressed his concern over the dwindling supplies by offering $5,000 in 1859 to anyone who could design a reservoir system adequate for 85,000 residents. S. B. Rawling, civilian clerk-of-works for the Army Royal Engineers, took the prize with a plan to build a 2-million-gallon reservoir at Pok Fu Lam, on the slopes of Victoria Peak, and carry the water through a ten-inch pipe to tanks above Victoria City.

Completed in four years, Pok Fu Lam proved to be short of the need even then, for the population had risen to 125,000. Striving to catch up, the colony installed a much larger reservoir above Pok Fu Lam, linked it to a pair of supplementary reservoirs, and discovered that the demand was still in advance of supply. Before the end of the century, new reservoirs had been added at Tai Tam and Wong Nai Chung, and the water finally reached the eastern sections of the city. Filtration through sand beds was also incorporated into the system.

None of these efforts satisfied the popular needs for long. Completion of Tai Tam Tuk Reservoir in 1917 near the southeastern end of the island raised the storage capacity to 1 billion, 419 gallons and everyone thought the problem was solved at last. A series of punishing droughts killed that bright hope, and the building of the Aberdeen Reservoirs rounded out all the parts of the island that could be drained for storage. Two reservoirs on the Kowloon Peninsula were tied to the island with underwater pipelines, but this was done only after a spring drought in 1929 had dried up five of the island's six reservoirs, making it necessary to bring in water by ship from as far away as Shanghai.

The rain-gathering potential of the New Territories had been exploited by the 1930s with the construction of the Shek Li Pui and the Jubilee Reservoirs. When the Japanese arrived, they found 13 reservoirs with a storage capacity of 6 billion gallons. They let the mains deteriorate during their occupation of the colony, applying their own brand of water-rationing by cutting off all supply to entire sections of the colony whenever they chose to.

Following World War II, the government tried deep boring to reach underground water resources, but this turned out to be scarcely worth the effort. After years of surveying and study, engineers laid out the Tai Lam Chung Reservoir System, at the central western end of the New Territories. This called for construction of a two-section dam 2,300 feet long and 200 feet high. This gigantic main dam, built entirely of concrete, created a reservoir of 4 billion, 500 million gallons.

Twenty-three miles of "catchwaters," or concrete channels to trap run-off from the rains, funneled the surface water from 11,000 acres into the reservoir. It took eight years to construct, being completed in 1960 at a cost of almost $25 million.

None of these large dams served the needs of the hundreds of small villages in the New Territories, which still relied on wells and streams or threw up earth dams in hilly areas to form their own miniature reservoirs. After World War II the colony government and the Kadoorie Agricultural Aid Association, a private philanthropic body, furnished grants of cement to replace these crude and leaky installations with concrete dams and concrete-lined wells, plus pipes to carry the water into the villages.

Rice crops in the New Territories were dependent on their own irrigation systems, traditionally constructed of earth channels and dams. They were laid out with evident shrewdness to cover the greatest possible area, but the dams and channels had to be nursed along constantly to prevent leaking and to keep them from becoming choked with weeds. The government and the Kadoorie Association also furnished materials to replace these systems with concrete dams and channels. Nearly 600 dams and more than 220,000 feet of channels have been improved in this way since World War II.

When the Tai Lam Chung Reservoir was under construction, a very delicate balance of catchwaters and irrigation channels had to be worked out so that the reservoir collected all the excess summer rain not required for irrigation, but did not draw off the sparse winter rains which farmers had to have. The farmers' initial assumption when they saw the huge catchwater channels passing the farms on their way to the reservoir was that they were being robbed of water; it took considerable diplomacy and convincing proof to allay their suspicions.

Farmers who learned that their villages were about to be inundated by the big reservoir were even less happy. They rejected the government's proposal to move them to another rural area and insisted on moving, if move they must, to the developing industrial town of Tsuen Wan. They received the full market price for their farm property and were resettled in new houses at Tsuen Wan, with shop space they could rent to replace their farming income. A few holdouts threatened to stay in their old homes until the reservoir floated them to glory, but belatedly reversed themselves and walked out on dry land.

The Tai Lam Chung relocation was hardly concluded when the government found itself involved in an even knottier problem. Continuing demands for more water forced the construction of still another dam—Shek Pik, on Lantau Island. This was a remote part of the colony, much larger than Hong Kong Island, but completely without roads until 1957. A few government people visited the island regularly, but its isolated villages, with their square stone towers or "cannon houses," were more likely to regard all visitors as pirates until proved otherwise. Armed and alert, they holed up in the towers to defend themselves against marauders who still stage occasional raids in sparsely settled areas.

Two villages in southwestern Lantau, Shek Pik and Fan Pui, would have to be removed to make way for the new dam. Their people, having no knowledge of modern technology and no need for a dam, viewed the project with fear and hostility. The dam was not, in fact, being built for them; its collected water was to be carried by pipeline to Hong Kong

Island, Kowloon and Peng Chau. Fan Pui, the smaller village, had to be treated with diplomacy and compensated before its 62 people consented to move to another rural area on the island. Inhabitants of Shek Pik elected to move to Tsuen Wan, settling in new five-story blocks. The oldest inhabitant, an eighty-six-year-old woman, made the transfer with full official ceremony, her sedan chair borne by four policemen. The ancestral tablets and household gods also made the trip on the shoulder-poles of respectful bearers. Anything less than this diplomatic ritual would have made the entire relocation impossible.

Preliminary work on the Shek Pik Dam became a trail-blazing venture into unexplored territory. A ten-mile paved road had to be built along the edge of the sea from the sheltered harbor at Silver Mine Bay to the future dam site. Test borings at the foot of Shek Pik Valley where the dam was to cross disclosed that the ground was a porous mixture of gravel, boulders, and rotten granite down to 137 feet below the surface. Since the ground stood only 15 feet above sea level, seawater would be able to seep into the reservoir and the fresh water in the reservoir would escape beneath the dam, undermining it.

If a regular concrete dam were to be built on such ground, its foundations would have to go down at least 137 feet, a frightfully expensive procedure. Engineers produced a reasonable alternative by using the recently developed technique called grouting. In this process, a mixture of water, cement, and clay is pumped into porous ground under high pressure, sealing off the foundation without requiring excavation to bed rock. A series of tests established that this process was feasible for Shek Pik, and preparations to build an earth dam were made in 1958.

The dam was to be 2,300 feet long, with a maximum height of 180 feet. It would back up 5 billion, 400 million gallons; a third of the colony's total water storage. A ten-mile tunnel was to carry the water from the treatment works near the dam to Silver Mine Bay. From there it would be pumped under the sea in twin 30-inch-diameter pipelines to reach Hong Kong Island, eight miles east of Lantau. Fifteen miles of catchwaters were to drain about twelve square miles of land, aided by the fact that rainfall on Lantau Island is generally ten percent heavier than on Hong Kong Island and is more evenly distributed throughout the year.

One of the tunnels was delayed for a time by a peculiarly Chinese problem; its "fung shui" was regarded as injurious to a resident dragon. The fung shui, a very important consideration among local people, meant that any proposed change in the local landscape had to be undertaken with great care. It would never do to nip off the top of a hill that was shaped like a dragon, for that might blind the mythical beast and put a hex on the countryside. The thing to do was to hire a fung shui expert from a nearby village; for a suitable fee, he would propitiate the dragon and the work of dam-building could proceed.

In a more practical way, the engineers had to install concrete channels and pipelines to make certain that sufficient quantities of water were diverted to irrigate farms near the catchment area. Hillsides above the big catchwaters had to be faced with chunam, a mixture of straw, lime, clay and cement which keeps the hillside soil from washing into the catchwaters and clogging them.

By early 1962, the southwestern portion of Lantau was crisscrossed by deep catchwaters and the earth dam was rising at the foot of the valley, with its core of impermeable clay being made ready for a covering of ordinary clay and dirt. Up in the mountains at the head of the valley, Buddhist monks and nuns continued their quiet, contemplative existence in the Po Lin Monastery, almost untouched by the dam project. Even when a few more guests stayed overnight at the Po Lin hostel, the pattern of prayer and work did not change.

Construction of the dam, pipelines, tunnels, and catchwaters became an international venture, with French, English, American, and Hong Kong contractors sharing the work under supervision of government engineers. The entire $40 million job is to be completed late in 1963.

There were no claims that the completion of Shek Pik would give the colony all the water it required. The new dam on Lantau and the water pumped in from China would be helpful, but far short of indicated needs.

Two factors balanced each other in planning further exploitation of the colony's water resources. More reservoirs of the type already in use would displace more farmland than Hong Kong could afford to lose. But the introduction of grouting, the foundation technique successfully employed at Shek Pik, made it possible to consider reservoir sites which would have seemed ridiculously unsuitable a few years earlier. And these sites, it appeared, could be developed without invading farm areas.

In the late 1950s, engineers of the Public Works Department and two consulting firms directed their search for more water toward the thinly settled scrub country of the eastern New Territories. This part of the colony consists of two peninsulas with the irregular outline of an ink-blot, separated by the broad, ten-mile-long Tolo Channel. Both peninsulas are chopped into by dozens of deep bays, coves and inlets bordered by high, rocky hills. Hundreds of inshore fishermen ply the surrounding waters, but most of the region is too barren and mountainous for farming.

Survey engineers made two recommendations which startled laymen: (1) Build a 6,600-foot-long dam across the entrance of Plover Cove, a four-square-mile inlet from Tolo Channel, and cut it off from the sea. (2) Build a similar but much shorter dam to seal off Hebe Haven, an inlet about one-fourth as large as Plover Cove. When the dams were finished all that would be necessary would be to pump the seawater out of the inlets and let the rains fill them with fresh water. The two reservoirs would be enough to double the storage capacity of the colony's water-supply system.

These basic recommendations in further discussions evolved into an integrated scheme of tremendous size and complexity, covering the entire eastern half of the New Territories. It included a series of service reservoirs and pumping stations along a main pipeline extending from the Red China border to Kowloon. These would be linked to Plover Cove and Hebe Haven by another system of tunnels. Virtually all the surface rains in the eastern end of the New Territories would be fed through catchwaters into the two main reservoirs. Since Hebe Haven might collect more summer rain than it could hold, the excess water could be conveyed by tunnel to Plover Cove, with its much larger capacity. Even the water brought by pipeline from Red China would be fed into the integrated system. Three balancing reservoirs, to maintain a controlled and even flow of water, and two large new filtration plants, to purify the water before it made the last stage of its journey to urban consumers, were to become part of the system.

Many of the connecting pipelines were to be designed to convey water in either direction, making the utmost use of storage capacity. By these refinements of the original recommendations, the capacity of the integrated scheme would be raised to 100 million gallons a day when it came into full use.

The first stage of the gigantic new system had made remarkable progress by the early part of 1962. The Lion Rock Tunnel had already been begun by cutting through the side of a mountain to connect the filtration plant at Sha Tin with a pair of service reservoirs in Kowloon. The tunnel, 32 feet in diameter, will carry three pipelines, each four feet in diameter, and a two-lane, 24-foot-wide auto road three-fourths of a mile through Lion Rock Mountain. Excavation work on the Lion Rock Reservoirs, with a total capacity of 41 million gallons, had almost been completed. At the other end of the tunnel, at the Sha Tin filtration plant and pumping station, a hillside site as extensive as four football fields had been excavated and the spoil was being used to fill a shallow inlet. Construction of ten miles of tunnels and the 10-foot-high Lower Shing Mun Dam were well advanced.

Meanwhile, engineers were probing the soil structure at the entrance of Plover Cove. Working from barges in 35 feet of water, they bored down through 35 feet of soft clay, reaching to almost twice that depth before they found impermeable clay and rock to form the foundation for their earth-fill dam. When complete, the dam will extend 35 feet above the water and 70 feet below it, with grouting to provide a watertight foundation. The main section of the dam will cross the cove's wide entrance. Two shorter sections will close off side entrances to the cove.

The first stage of this integrated scheme will be rounded out in 1964. Both Hebe Haven and Plover Cove should be ready by 1970, though any completion dates beyond 1964 are likely to be elastic. At each stage, improvements are introduced and existing goals altered.

In addition to these broad-scale developments, the colony has taken immediate measures to conserve the present supply of fresh water by making it possible to use salt water for such purposes as flushing and fire-fighting. Since 1958, salt-water mains have been installed in four densely populated sections of Kowloon and two on Hong Kong Island. Fluoridation of the entire water supply began in March, 1961.

The possibility of distillation of seawater for producing a fresh-water supply has been examined by engineers, but thus far the outlook is discouraging; the cost remains far too high. There is even a faint, faraway hope that some day atomic energy may be employed to distill an unlimited supply of fresh water from the ocean at low cost.

If every phase of Hong Kong's integrated scheme is in operation by 1970, its water shortage may be over. Similarly, if all the reclamation projects now under consideration are brought to fulfillment in the next decade, there may be enough land to meet all ordinary requirements.

The determination of these requirements, however, will derive from the Department of Public Works only secondarily. The primary determinant will come from the Registry of Marriages.

Any recent visitor to the Central Marriage Registry would appreciate the difficulties in predicting the population of Hong Kong even five years hence; there the walls of two long corridors are so thickly papered with overlapping notices of marriage that not much more than the names and occupations of the prospective couples remain visible.

Neither land nor water is likely to become a surplus commodity in tomorrow's Hong Kong.

CHAPTER SIX

A New Day for Farms and Fisheries

"On our small and peculiar land area, it would be impossible to reach a high order of self-sufficiency in food production."

—W. J. BLACKIE, former Hong Kong Director of Agriculture, Fisheries & Forestry

For more than a thousand years men have wrested a precarious living from the farms and fishing grounds of the New Territories, yet they remained outside the economic and social orbit of Hong Kong until a few months after World War II.

Politically, the New Territories had been part of the British crown colony since 1898. Nevertheless, the people of this scrambled-egg land mass and the 235 islands around it had held their interest in its British rulers to the legal minimum. The British themselves, passing through the New Territories

on their way to the Fanling golf course or the Chinese border, viewed the region and its people with the fixed indiffer-
ence of a New York commuter rolling over the swampy
monotony of the Jersey meadows.

This reciprocal insularity broke down at last under the
pressure of two events which have touched and twisted the
lives of almost everyone in contemporary Hong Kong: the
Japanese Occupation of World War II and the rise of Communist China. To the people of the New Territories, the
Japanese interlude was an economic disaster; denuding their
forests, depleting their livestock and impoverishing their fishing fleet. Both the Japanese and the Communists drove thousands of refugees into the New Territories to compete with
resident farmers for scarce marginal land. The Communists
further disrupted things by closing the China market to New
Territories produce and by forcing colony fishermen to keep
twelve miles away from its coast and its islands.

The four main Chinese groups in the New Territories, the
Cantonese and Hakka farmers, and the Hoklo and Tanka fishermen, were no more severely shaken by all this than were
the British. When the Japanese and the Communists had done
their work, the British and the urban Chinese of Hong Kong
found themselves dependent as never before on the fish and
produce of the New Territories. The picturesque, faraway
people of the countryside had come into sudden, sharp focus
as instruments of the colony's survival.

No one seriously expects the farmers and fishermen of
Hong Kong to produce enough food to sustain more than
3,000,000 inhabitants, but the more they can bring to market,
the greater the colony's chances for survival.

The total area of farmland under cultivation has averaged
about 33,000 acres for many years, except for a sharp drop

during the Japanese occupation, but the size and nature of its yield have changed radically in the last fifteen years. The maximum farmland area cannot exceed much more than 40,-000 acres, and even then much of it would look more like a rock garden than a farm. American and European farmers would consider most of the colony land already under cultivation as unworthy of their time and effort.

In 1940, rice was the chief crop, occupying seven-tenths of all cultivated land in the colony. Since the war, rice has steadily lost acreage to vegetable-growing, and in spite of its greater productivity per acre through improved irrigation and a more judicious use of fertilizers, it has fallen far behind vegetables in cash value. Vegetable crops today yield almost three times as much money as rice; $7,614,000 for the 1960-61 vegetable crop, compared with $2,870,000 for rice. Vegetable production has more than quadrupled since 1947.

When the Japanese were driven from the colony in 1945, they had reduced the livestock population to 4,611 cattle, 659 water buffalo, 8,740 pigs and 31,000 poultry. A count at the end of 1960 showed 18,000 cattle, 2,000 water buffalo, 184,-000 pigs and 3,405,000 poultry. This tremendous increase stemmed directly from the expansion of the domestic market, but it was made possible by the colony government's postwar plunge into marketing cooperatives for farm and sea products, the introduction of private and public loans for farmers and fishermen at reasonable interest rates, and the application of scientific methods to every phase of the farming and fishing industries.

Agricultural production of every kind totaled $40,506,000 in 1960-61. In descending order of value, this included poultry (chiefly chickens), vegetables, pigs, rice, various animal products such as hides, hair and feathers, fresh milk, sweet potatoes and other field crops. Among other products of special interest are fruit (litchi, limes, tangerines, olives, etc.), pond fish (mullet and carp), export crops (water chestnuts, ginger, vegetable seeds, etc.) and such flowers as gladiolus, chrysanthemum, dahlia and carnation.

That $40,506,000 farm-income figure has a momentarily impressive ring until one sees how it is divided. The average vegetable farm is about two-thirds of an acre, and the average "paddy," or shallowly flooded unit of rice-growing land, usually runs to two acres, with an upward limit of five acres. There are several larger farms of 100 acres or more, but these are share-cropped by tenant farmers for exporters of special crops such as water chestnuts or ginger. The size of almost all other farms is dictated by the amount of hand labor one farm-owning family can perform; the only extra-human labor comes from the plow-pulling power of the dwarfish Brown Cattle and water buffalo. On these postage-stamp farms, tractors would be prohibitively expensive and as destructive as an army tank. Even a hand-operated power cultivator would be far too costly for a typical family farm.

By Western standards, any farm of less than two acres would barely qualify as a truck garden, but the Chinese of the New Territories cultivate the land with unique intensiveness. A fresh-water paddy produces at least two rice crops and often an additional "catch crop" of vegetables each year; six to eight crops are harvested annually on all-vegetable farms.

Farm income is as subdivided as the land. There are an estimated 30,000 farm families and a total of 250,000 persons who rely on farming for their living. The per capita income of the farming population therefore runs around $162 a year, or $13.50 a month, less the forty to sixty percent of crop value they must share with the landowner, leaving a meager net income of as little as $81 a year, or $6.75 a month. Things have been worse; in 1955 the annual per capita net income of farm people was about $30.

What the farm worker has, in one of the lowest-paid and most arduous jobs in the colony's industries, is a place to live, enough to eat and an almost irreducible minimum of money for clothing and other expenses. In thousands of cases, his lean resources are supplemented by remittances from his relatives overseas, but he could not have survived in the postwar economy without the basic reforms in marketing, credit and research that began in 1946. One expensive event such as a wedding ($200) or a funeral ($100) could keep a tenant farmer in debt for years to loan sharks who charged him interest of eight to thirty percent a month. In numerous instances, it still happens.

For generations Hong Kong farmers had lived in permanent bondage to the "laans," or middlemen, who controlled the marketing of farm and fishery products, paying the producers as little as possible and cutting themselves a thick slice of profit for the relatively simple process of taking the goods to market. They advanced money to farmers and fishermen at extraordinary usury rates, further tightening their stranglehold. The Japanese Occupation, by grinding the farm and fishing population into desperate poverty, unintentionally broke the grip of the laans.

When the British Military Administration took control in the fall of 1945, it acted decisively to save the primary industries. Two men, Father Thomas F. Ryan, Jesuit missionary and the colony's first Acting Superintendent of Agriculture, and Dr. G. A. C. Herklots, naturalist and author, were designated for the task.

Many years later, Father Ryan, who had long since returned to teaching at the Jesuit Wah Yan College on Hong Kong Island, said when asked about his 1945 assignment:

"I really knew very little about agriculture, but Dr. Herklots and I were asked to help with the vegetable and fish marketing. It was obvious that the laans were beginning again to take all the profits."

The Jesuit priest and the naturalist learned a lot about marketing in a hurry. The vegetable and fish marketing organizations they set up under government control ended the dominance of the laans, but not without some anguished howls from the displaced profiteers. For a standard ten percent commission, the vegetable marketing organization transported and sold all vegetables grown or imported into the colony at the government wholesale market in Kowloon. A Federation of Vegetable Marketing Cooperative Societies grew out of the original organizations. It extended credit to farmers and has progressed steadily toward ultimate control of the market by the co-op societies. As the co-ops take charge of organization work, three percent of the ten percent commission is refunded to them. The Vegetable Marketing Organization also distributes fertilizer in the form of matured nightsoil, i.e., human excrement treated to reduce its germ content.

The Fish Marketing Organization, established along the same general lines as the Vegetable Marketing Organization, controls the transport and wholesale marketing of marine fish, charging a six percent commission on sales. It created loan funds to help fishermen rehabilitate and mechanize their boats. Evolution of the Fish Marketing Organization toward a wholly cooperative set-up has been impeded by the fact that only fifteen percent of the fishermen can read or write, com-

pared with a colony-wide literacy rate of seventy-five percent. Living and working aboard their boats, fisher folk could
not attend school. This ancient pattern has been altered in the
last few years because more wives and children of fishermen
are living ashore. About 4,000 children of fishermen attend
schools on land, and there are special classes for adult fishermen.

Father Ryan and Dr. Herklots laid the foundation for the
first Department of Agriculture, Fisheries & Forestry, which
came into existence in 1950 after a series of preparatory steps
had been taken. Father Ryan initiated a survey of the colony's
primary industries and personally directed the renovation and
replanting of the Botanic Garden and other public park areas,
as well as the first postwar reforestation of the scalped hillsides in the reservoir catchment areas. In 1947, he relinquished
his colony post to become the Jesuit Superior in Hong Kong.
In recent years he has conducted a local radio program of
classical music as a sideline.

Long-term assistance to farmers came from another private
source in 1951: Horace and Lawrence Kadoorie, two Jewish
brothers who shared positions of prime importance in the
Hong Kong business community. Sir Elly Kadoorie was a
former official of the colony government and one of its early
business leaders. His two sons were members of a family
which came to Hong Kong from the Middle East in 1880 and
built a large fortune. The brothers were partners in the business house named for their father and directors of more than
thirty other companies. Both had earned reputations as
shrewd, tough businessmen; but Horace, the bachelor
brother, had acquired a special fame among ivory collectors
as the author of the seven-volume book, *The Art of Ivory
Sculpture in Cathay*.

The Kadoories, observing the general poverty of colony farmers and the even worse situation of the refugees who crowded into Hong Kong in the late 1940s, decided to do something to help these displaced persons get on their feet. Knowing the Chinese to be a predominantly agricultural people, they chose a form of help that would make impoverished farmers self-supporting; that of raising pigs donated by the Kadoories. Pig-raising is a fairly simple venture that makes good use of marginal land, and pork is always in demand at local markets.

Reaction to the idea was chilly; other businessmen considered it unworkable and farmers regarded it skeptically, looking for a catch in it. The Kadoorie brothers agreed to put it to a test, choosing 14 families with no farming experience for the experiment. The group included a handyman, a carpenter, a beggar, a semi-invalid and a stonebreaker. The Kadoories gave them cement, bamboo straws and a few hand tools and invited them to build their own pigsties.

"Every one of those families made good," Horace Kadoorie recalled in a 1961 interview. "Today they all have excellent farms. Their success in proving that you can really help people who are willing to help themselves was what convinced us we were on the right track."

The brothers, working independently at first, and then in close collaboration with the officials of the Department of Agriculture, have given various forms of assistance to over 300,000 people in 1,092 villages.

They functioned through two allied agencies, the Kadoorie Agricultural Aid Association, which makes outright gifts, and the Kadoorie Agricultural Aid Loan Fund, which makes interest-free loans. The two Kadoories and colony agricultural officials are jointly members of the boards of directors of the two institutions. The Association has donated the equivalent of $3 million-plus in agricultural gifts. The Fund, established by the Kadoories with an initial gift of $44,000, has been increased to $306,000 by the government. The J. E. Joseph Fund, another farm-loan fund, established in 1954, is also administered by the government; its initial capital of $79,000 is loaned at three percent interest.

In an economy like that of the United States, $3 million in gifts would disappear like a pebble in a lake, but with that amount the Kadoorie philanthropies have changed the face of the New Territories. The list of improvements is awe-inpiring, and it is no exaggeration to say one can hardly walk a mile anywhere in the rural district without seeing evidence of their eminently useful contributions.

They contributed junks and sampans to isolated villages, and then built 27 piers to accommodate them. Dirt paths were the only routes between many villages and farmers either walked or sloshed through the mud, sometimes using bicycles and carrying five or six members of the family or possibly a live pig lined up on the fenders and handlebars. The Kadoorie Association has provided 150 miles of concrete paths, six motor roads and 142 bridges to make the going easier.

Often villages depended on mountain springs for their drinking water, but these had an unfortunate habit of sinking back into the ground before they had served the thirsty villagers. The Association disciplined the vagrant waters with thirty miles of concrete channels, 293 dams, 400 wells, 51 sumps and 8 reservoirs. Rogue rivers and the invading sea had eaten away valuable farmland, and the Kadoorie Association produced restoratives with 29 seawalls, 30 retaining walls and a variety of culverts and floodgates. Odds and ends, helpful in diverse ways, ranged from rain shelters to compost pits, poultry sheds to outhouses.

Pigs were popular because, as Horace explained, "It's the only animal you can see expanding daily." Thousands were given away, and advice on caring for them was supplied by the agricultural stations.

One group that was the especial beneficiary of pig gifts were farm widows ranging from seventeen to ninety-six years of age. Horace, as the roving scout of the Kadoorie Association, had noticed that hundreds of women whose husbands had been killed by the Japanese or had died natural deaths had not only lost the family rice-winner, they lost the "face" or community status they enjoyed with their husbands. Custom frowned on their remarriage, so they could do little but linger disconsolately on the fringes of village life. The Kadoories talked it over and decided that a gift of pigs, cows, ducks or chickens would give these widows something to occupy themselves with and enable them to earn some money. In a period of two years 10,000 widows received these animals and enclosures for them. Feed they obtained through the Kadoorie Agriculture Aid Loan Fund. Blind and elderly women were able to care for flocks of chickens; younger ones received pigs and cows. The usual pig gift was six purebred Chinese sows from the Kadoorie Experimental and Extension Farm at Pak Ngau Shek; all pigs were inoculated against disease and the Agricultural Department specialists showed the widows how to care for the animals. Many women tripled their small incomes by breeding pigs and selling their offspring. As the owners of livestock, they became persons of consequence in their villages.

With the aid of government experts, the brothers bought

hundreds of foreign pedigreed pigs, and bred Berkshires, Yorkshires and middle whites with the local animals to produce a larger and hardier strain. Cows and water buffaloes, indispensable as draught animals, were distributed by drawing lots in the villages, and the drawings became lively public gatherings with soft drinks and cakes served all around. Gifts or loans financed the construction of numerous fish-breeding ponds, with the seed fish supplied gratis.

The 25,000 loans made through the Fund covered livestock, seeds and fertilizer, building materials, insecticides and spraying equipment, land development and other purposes. Over 95 percent of the loan applications are approved, and the repayment rate has remained very high.

Creating new land for farming has been an important part of Kadoorie efforts. Horace came upon a group of squatters who had been moved from the city to make room for a new road; he found them moping about forlornly on a rocky field which was the site of a cemetery from which the bodies had been removed. Horace suggested that they use the rocks to build pigsties, promising them the needed cement and two pigs for each sty. On his next visit he found many pigsties completed, but was temporarily baffled when the settlers asked him to buy for them a nearby hillside rock, fully 100 yards wide and stretching from the bottom of the hill to the top. He acquired the rock, and the settlers, working from the bottom upwards, covered it with terraced growing lands.

At Nim Shue Wan village, a hillside settlement along a steep shore, the Kadoorie Association built a seawall, mixed the sticky red earth of the hillside with beach sand, and produced a good soil for vegetable-growing which now supports 100 families in the area. At Pak Ngau Shek, the Kadoorie farm on the high slopes of Tai Mo Shan, highest (3,140 feet) mountain in the colony, the brothers began to experiment with plants and animals, chiefly because the land had been judged worthless for farmers. If they could make anything thrive there, they believed, it might teach them some way to utilize the colony's heavy proportion of wasteland. They had many failures, such as typhoons uprooting all their shallow-rooted peach trees, but they discovered that even trees and vegetables considered unsuitable for high lands did very well. Some vegetables, growing more slowly on the mountainsides, reached the market when lowland crops were less plentiful, and therefore brought better prices. The farm operated at a financial loss, but gave full value as an agricultural testing site.

The Kadoorie Agricultural Aid Association meets once every two weeks, considers 50 to 100 applications for help, and tries to assist about 15 new families every day. It has given away 7,000 pigs in less than three months. Many situations won't wait for committee meetings; some farmers in dire straits have walked up to Boulder Lodge, Horace's home at Castle Peak, to ask for help in the middle of the night. Horace, who often works a 13-hour day and spends Sundays roaming around the farm districts, is more flattered than annoyed by these occasional late-hour callers.

"Speed is of the essence in this work," he said. "When a typhoon heads this way, we assemble building materials for repair work and all the quick-growing seeds we can buy; then we're ready to help the farm people get back into operation and plant vegetables as soon as the flooding subsides."

Fire is often a total disaster to the rural poor, wrecking their homes and frequently killing their livestock. When an entire village was wiped out by fire in 1960, the Kadoories threw a round-the-clock emergency staff into a four-day rescue operation, providing new furniture, clothes, two months' food supply, extra cash, livestock, bicycles and rebuilding all the houses.

Hundreds of artificial limbs donated by Kadoorie Association have enabled crippled people to earn their living as farmers and fishermen. The Association doesn't scatter its benefits recklessly; all applicants are thoroughly investigated to discover whether they will work to improve themselves when they receive aid. When a man or woman receives a gift of livestock, he may not sell it for one year without Kadoorie Association consent; if disease or unavoidable accidents kill the stock, the Association replaces them free.

"Our idea has been to find out the wants of those in need," Horace said. "It is worth more than anything else."

The contributions of the Kadoorie brothers and the many other religious and philanthropic bodies working in the colony serve as a valuable supplement to the main task of directing and improving the primary industries. The principal responsibility lies with the Department of Agriculture and Forestry, and with the Department of Cooperative Development and Fisheries, which was separated from Agriculture and Forestry in 1961.

The Chinese farmers of the New Territories can grow a garden on the side of a rock—as Horace Kadoorie found out for himself—but they know little about scientific farming, and until the 1950s, there was no one to teach them. Now the Agriculture & Forestry Department conducts three-week general agricultural courses, followed by one-week specialized courses in paddy cultivation, pond-fish culture and other phases of farming. There are vocational courses, lectures to cooperatives, radio farming broadcasts, film shows, guided visits to experimental stations and an annual Agricultural Show at Yuen Long with prizes for the best farm products.

At the Sheung Shui Market Garden Experimental Station, only two miles from the Red China border, S. Y. Chan, an assistant agricultural officer, directs a five-acre center for testing every species of foreign and domestic vegetables and flowers he can lay his hands on. Chinese white cabbage, Taiwan radishes, sugar peas, chrysanthemums, 30 varieties of English and American tomatoes, chives, and corn each have their small test patch to show whether they can survive in Hong Kong's climate. Roses, for example, wilt and die in a few seasons, but the station is seeking new strains with greater durability. Unlike plants and flowers in most sections of the United States, the majority of Hong Kong vegetables and flowers grow best in winter, the local summers being too wet.

At Ta Kwu Ling Dryland Experimental Station, the problem is how to get some use out of the thousands of acres of former farmland abandoned because of poor soil or insufficient water. The station, started in 1956, made little progress at first. Then it added compost of manures and chemical fertilizers to the soil, and tried deep plowing to retain moisture in the earth. Large white local radishes as big as yams did well in this ground, and so did sweet potatoes. The department experts found that windbreaks of sugar cane helped to offset the drying effects of strong winds. Several types of fodder, including six varieties of grasses, were tried out in sample patches. Five of the station's eleven acres are devoted to improvement of local pig breeds by crossing them with exotic strains.

The Castle Peak Livestock Experimental Station, located in an area of badly eroded hills, is the chief center for artificial insemination of pigs. Semen from selected strains of Berkshire, middle white, and large white and improved local boars is injected into local sows, producing larger and hardier lit-ters. Various breeds of chickens are crossed to develop poultry which thrive under local conditions and are acceptable to Chinese tastes. A complete laboratory treats and experiments with every known disease of poultry, pigs and cattle. Pig semen is carried by bicycle, truck and helicopter to outlying sections of the New Territories to service local sows.

Artificial insemination of pigs, based on its highly successful use in Japan, has become increasingly important in Hong Kong, with more than 1,000 instances of its use in 1961.

In the northwestern lowlands near Yuen Long, the department has developed a fast-growing source of food in the fish-raising ponds. From the top of a small hill, Yu Yat-sum, fisheries officer, is able to point to a speckled, silvery expanse of such ponds, covering 700 acres in individual ponds from one to 10 acres each. Each acre produces about a ton of fish every year.

Mr. Yu explains that a five-acre pond, equipped with sluice gates and surrounded by dirt embankments, could be built for $2,700. Usually they are owned by a village or a co-op society. They are only five feet deep, but packed with 3,000 to 3,600 fry an acre, each about the length of a paper clip. The fish would all be crushed and battered if it were not for their superior adaptation—big head and silver carp cruise near the surface, grass carp favor the mid-levels, and grey mullet and mud carp gravitate to the bottom. Fed on rice bran, dry peanut cakes and soya bean meal, they fatten at a prodigious rate and are ready for the market within a year, selling at 21 to 30 cents a pound. For the pond owners, it's a net return of twenty percent per year. There are more than 1,000 acres of these ponds in the New Territories, and they are increasing at the rate of 60 acres a month.

The Chinese have their own strict ideas of what fresh fish

means; to them, the only fresh fish from a pond is a live one, so the carp and mullet travel to market in tubs, still alive. The job of Mr. Yu and other departmental experts is to see that the fish do not perish before their time because of diseases or excessive salinity in the pond water.

The Tai Lung Forestry and Crop Experimental Station concentrates on the expansion of the colony's forests, which almost disappeared during World War II. Here the six-inch seedlings of Chinese pine, eucalyptus, China fir and other species are placed in polythene tubes and covered with soil by patient Hakka women who do the work by hand. After a few months in the shade and a brief maturing period in full sunlight, the polythene tube is removed and the tree is planted on a hillside in one of the reservoir catchment areas. Spaced about six feet apart on all sides, they go in at the rate of 2,500 an acre. Tai Lung produces 1,500,000 of these plantings each year. A month after they are placed on the hillsides, their progress is checked by an inspector; if more than twenty percent have died, the area is replanted. A second check is made a year later.

Four main forest areas stretching across the New Territories from Tolo Harbor to Lantau Island now total more than 11,500 acres. In ten years some of the lean China pines have shot up to 30 feet high. The overworked forestry staff has been so busy planting trees and keeping a close watch on forest fires that it has had little time for the next stage of the reforestation, which is thinning overcrowded areas. Other complications confront them when a firebreak is cut through the hillside forests; the cutover strip erodes quickly in the summer rainstorms, damaging the tree plantations and sending silt into the reservoirs.

If forestry is the youngest of Hong Kong's primary industries, fishing is indisputably the oldest, and for many centuries, the largest primary income producer. Until fairly recent times, fishermen were inclined to demonstrate their versatility and supplement their income by piracy. Fast, steel-hulled naval ships with long-range guns have taken much of the lure out of part-time piracy, especially for the crews of slow-moving junks, and the fisher folk have become a law-abiding group. Today they number around 86,000 and catch approximately $10 million worth of fish every year. Not included in their ranks are the keepers of fish ponds, who are regarded as farmers, or those who live on boats but earn their living by hauling cargo, running water-taxis or selling merchandise from their boats.

The fishing people, chiefly Tanka but including other Chinese like the Hoklo and Hakka, are concentrated at Aberdeen and Shau Kei Wan on Hong Kong Island and seven settlements in the New Territories. By environment and preference, they are deeply conservative, disinclined to mix in the affairs of landlubbers. Nevertheless, the irresistible winds of change which have swept through the colony since World War II have shaken them loose from their traditional moorings.

Like the farmers, they were able to free themselves from the iron grip of the laans when the Fish Marketing Organization put the middlemen out of business. The Fish Marketing Organization gave them a fair return on their catch, established cheap credit to improve their boats and equipment, provided boats and trucks to get their fish to the five wholesale markets and founded schools for their children. CARE and other relief organizations came to their aid. The Fisheries Division offered classes in navigation, modern seamanship and boat design, marine engineering and the use of up-to-date

fishing equipment, with classes being adapted to the fishermen's working schedules. A fisheries research unit from Hong
Kong University became a regular part of the departmental
organization. The 240-ton otter trawler *Cape St. Mary*
cruised the fishing grounds from the Gulf of Tong King, west
of Hainan Island, to Taiwan in the east, gathering data on
ocean currents, water temperatures and depths and the feeding habits of fish. A fishing master was appointed and careful
studies were made of pearl- and edible-oyster culture.

All these are routine procedures in present-day fishing
centers, but they were virtually unknown in Hong Kong until 1946. Since then, despite harassment and inshore fishing
restrictions enforced by Red China, the tonnage and market
value of the annual catch have almost tripled.

Red China has maintained a certain disinterestedness in
its mistreatment of fishermen. During the last five years the
Communists demanded so great a share of the fish caught by
their own people that thousands of their fishing boats never
returned. Some sailed far out in the China Sea, then turned
back toward Hong Kong and became refugees; others slipped
through Chinese shore patrols at night and defected to the
British colony. Between 1957 and 1962, the new arrivals
swelled the colony fishing fleet from 6,000 to the present
10,550 units.

The most radical change in the colony's fleet, however, has
come from within. The Chinese junk, famous throughout
the world as the symbol of Hong Kong, has dropped its picturesque sails; more than 4,000 of them now churn along under Diesel power. The Chinese junk is as diverse in its size,
shape and function as the infinitely varied Chinese people.
There are sixteen different classes of junks in Hong Kong
alone, and none of them closely resembles a junk from any

other part of China. They are single-, double- and triple-masted; they are little craft 25 feet long or lumbering giants of 100 foot length. To a colony fisheries expert, "junk" is only a loose generic term; he immediately classifies it according to the job it is designed for, as a long-liner (four classes by size), seiner (two main types, depending on the net it uses), trawler (four main types, depending on the kind of trawling it does), gill-netters, fish-collecting junks and several miscellaneous varieties.

Since the British came to Hong Kong, the junks operating in local waters have borrowed design features from European ships. The big fishing junks of Hong Kong, with their high stern, horizontal rails and the large, perforated rudder pivoting in a deep, vertical groove on the stern, resemble no other junks in the world. Like junks from all parts of China, and even the boats of ancient Egypt, they have an oculus, or painted image of the human eye, on their bow. In fishing junks, the center of the eye is directed downward so that it can keep a close watch on the fish; trading junks have the eye aimed higher so that it can scan the distant horizon. The bow eyes of the old-fashioned sailing junks no longer have much to look forward to. The deep-sea trawlers, operating as far as 250 miles out, are all mechanized. The sailing junks operate closer to shore, but the cargo-carrying junks in Victoria harbor are predominantly mechanized. To anyone who has crossed the harbor recently it is obvious that the sails are disappearing at an alarming rate.

The fishermen who live and work on junks instead of viewing them abstractly from a distance have not yet formed a Committee for the Preservation of the Romantic Junk. After approaching mechanization with reluctance and suspicion in 1948, they became convinced that the big sailing junk is through. Motorized junks can reach the distant fishing grounds much faster, they catch a lion's share of the fish, and they return to market far ahead of sail competition. Because of their greater speed and stability, they can venture out in the typhoon season when sail craft are obliged to stick closer to shore. Within ten years, fishing authorities say, the sailing junk will have become virtually extinct.

It has been proposed that the Hong Kong Tourist Association hire a couple of junks to sail up and down the harbor for the sole delectation of tourists, but no official action has been taken. Tourists can travel 40 miles west to Macao where the harbor is still crowded with sailing junks. Here the sails persist only because the Macao fishing industry lacks the low-interest loans available to Hong Kong fishermen through the Fish Marketing Organization and the fishing co-ops. Without such credit, very few fishermen could afford Diesel engines or other motor-driven equipment. In Hong Kong, even the little 4-horsepower engines of sampans are bought on credit.

Now that progress has reached the fishing fleet, it will not be satisfied until it changes everything. Under the direction of such knowledgeable men as Jack Cater, co-op and fisheries commissioner, Lieutenant Commander K. Stather, fishing master, and Wing-Hong Cheung, craft technician on modern junk design, the whole junk-building industry is being turned upside down.

For centuries, the junk has been built without plans or templates, with the designers proceeding entirely by habit and skill. This is relatively easy in building a 15-foot sampan, but when it is extended to 100-ton vessels of 90-foot length it becomes both art and architecture. The size of the investment, by local standards, is staggering: $40,000 for a large trawler and its mechanized equipment, and around $7,000 for a mechanized 40-footer.

There are nearly 100 junk-building yards in the colony, but no more than ten of these are capable of building a junk from blueprints. The fisheries department is conducting boat-design classes in three major fishing centers, Aberdeen, Shau Kei Wan and Cheung Chau, and training builders to read plans. The classes are held at night to avoid conflict with working hours, and the courses are for three months.

The junk-building yards present a vivid picture of a civilization in transition. At one yard, a workman is laboriously breaming the hull of a sampan—killing marine borers by passing bundles of burning hay beside and beneath it—and a workman or two in an adjoining yard are covering the hull of another boat with anti-fouling paint. The object of the two operations is identical, but the anti-fouling paint protects the wood about four times as long as breaming and takes no longer to apply. On the port side of an 86-foot trawler, a Chinese carpenter is using a half-inch electric power drill; on the starboard, another man is drilling holes with a steel bit spun by a leather thong with its ends fixed to a wooden bow.

Lu Pan, the Celestial master builder who transmitted the secrets of carpentry and shipbuilding to mankind, is honored with a tiny shrine in an obscure corner of every yard. Joss sticks are lighted before a statuette of this practical divinity, and his birthday observance on the 13th day of the Sixth Moon is a holiday in the shipyards. Lu Pan has not yet betrayed any overt sign of annoyance at the invasion of his domain by power tools and Diesel engines.

The timber that is cut for these all-wooden ships is tough and durable—China fir, teak, and various hardwoods chiefly from Borneo, like billian, kapor and yacal. The planks are hewn at mills near the yards, and bent to fit the curvature of the hull. The curving is accomplished by heating the center of the plank with a small fire and weighting its ends with heavy stones to set the curve. The 3-inch-thick planks are secured to the upright framing members with 14-inch steel spikes, and the main stringer, just below deck level, is fastened with threaded bolts. Despite the general disarray of the open yards and the lack of precise plans, the junk almost invariably turns out to be a nicely dovetailed, exactly balanced boat, good for twenty or thirty years of service in the rough weather of the China Sea.

The long-liner ranks as the giant of the junk fleet, having an over-all length between 80 and 100 feet. Junks of this class fish from 20 to 60 miles south of the colony, cruising above a vast expanse of underwater flats where depths seldom exceed 90 feet and the muddy bottom makes other kinds of fishing unfeasible.

A typical long-liner under construction at the Yee Hop Shipyard in Shau Kei Wan has a 90-foot length and the elephantine stern characteristic of its class. Its high poop carries bunks for 16 men, with additional bunks located forward and a total crew capacity of 57 men, sandwiched in with no more than a yard of clearance between upper and lower bunks. Eight sampans can be stowed along its deck and lowered over the side when the fishing grounds are reached. Despite its traditional outline, it has Diesel engines, twin-screw propellors and a 20-ton fishhold lined with modern insulation material.

Costing about $36,000 with full equipment, one long-liner, for example, was ordered by Hai Lee Chan, a Shau Kei Wan fisherman who already owned another like it, plus two smaller junks. During the two and one-half months that 35 carpenters required to complete it, Mrs. Chan and her twelve-year-old daughter remained on or around the junk to keep a watchful eye on its construction. A long-liner of this kind may put out as many as 100,000 hooks on lines attached to its bow and stern or strung out by its covey of sampans. A single trip to the fishing grounds may keep it at sea for a week or more and bring a ten-ton catch of golden thread, shark and lizard fish.

Comparable in size but differing completely in design are two deep-sea trawlers built at the Kwong Lee Cheung Shipyard in Kowloon. These are sister ships, 86 feet long, and the first ones of their size that faithfully followed the modern specifications laid down by Mr. Cheung and the Fisheries Department. They were the first big trawlers constructed according to written plans and framed around modern templates or patterns in Hong Kong.

As they neared completion late in 1961, the twin wooden trawlers of 100 tons each looked more like dismasted clipper ships than junks. The old type of high poop had been cut down and crew quarters moved forward. The fat, bulging stern had been slimmed down to improve the streamline, and the traditional rudder-slot was gone. The deck was level and uncluttered, with far more working space than older junks provided. The outline of the hull was slim and graceful, giving more longitudinal stability than the tub-bottomed junk. The free-swinging tiller and massive wooden rudder had been replaced by a ship's wheel and a much smaller rudder of steel that turned on a metal shaft. Powered winches would be welded to their decks. Mechanized and streamlined, the new trawlers could deliver more speed than a motorized trawler of conventional shape, and require less fuel to do it.

When the two partners who had ordered the trawlers,

fishermen Lee Loy Shing and Cheng Chung Kay, smilingly greeted visitors to the yard, pointing out the features of their new ships with considerable pride, it was evident that they regarded the old-style junk as an expensive antique. Mechanization has already proved itself; although mechanized boats number less than half the fishing fleet, they take 80 percent of the catch. Many fishermen are beginning to believe that modern ship design is as important to the future of Hong Kong's fishing fleet as mechanization.

Steel-hulled trawlers of the Japanese "bull" type are already being used by the fishing companies in the colony. One dozen of them operate in the Gulf of Tong King, near Hainan Island. However, they are much too costly for most fishing families.

Colony fishing methods are as varied as the boats used. The deep-sea trawlers, generally working in pairs, drag a huge bag-shaped net along the sea bottom, gathering in horsehead and red snapper, or red goatfish and golden thread. Purse-seiners, working in pairs and fairly close to shore, stretch a big net between them at night and use a bright light to lure such smaller fish as anchovies and carangoid into the net. The Pa T'eng seiners set gill nets along the bottom for yellow croaker, and drift nets for white pomfret and mackerel. Other types include gill-netters, shrimp beam-trawlers, and three smaller classes of long-liners. About twenty kinds of fish form most of the catch, and among these are conger pike, big eyes, grouper, young barracuda and red sea bream.

The ship carpenters of Hong Kong are far above average ability, so much so that the Chinese Communists have attempted, without notable success, to induce them to build junks in China. Demand for their skills has, however, raised their wages about one-third in the last two years.

The fishermen have had their rigid conservatism shattered by the changes around them. In spite of their usual illiteracy, they have learned the rules of navigation at fisheries department schools. More advanced classes have qualified for licenses as engineers, pilots, navigators and boat-builders. For the first time they have lodged their families on shore, with the wives becoming used to housekeeping and the children attending schools.

Many Westerners, seeing this upheaval in the fine, free life of the fisherman, deplore the passing of the old ways. The fishermen, always quicker at grabbing for prosperity than in clinging to romantic illusions, are moving forward at top speed without a thought to their suddenly disappearing past.

CHAPTER SEVEN

Crime, Power and Corruption

"We have absolutely no doubt from the evidence and statistics we have studied that corruption exists on a scale which justifies the strongest counter-measures."

—HONG KONG ADVISORY COMMITTEE ON CORRUPTION,
January, 1962

The British crown colony of Hong Kong came into existence under circumstances bearing less resemblance to the majesty of British law and order than they did to a territorial dispute between the Capone and O'Banion mobs during the Chicago of the 1920s. Its founding fathers were dope peddlers whose ability to bribe Chinese customs officials made the traders rich and goaded the Chinese Emperor into a war that cost him the loss of a worthless island called Hong Kong.

The Rev. George Smith, an English missionary who visited the colony during its first five years, approached the place with the exalted conviction that his country had "been honoured by God as the chosen instrument for diffusing the pure light of Protestant Christianity throughout the world." He went ashore to discover a polyglot Gehenna with no market for the Word.

"The lowest dregs of native society flock to the British settlement in the hope of gain or plunder," he wrote. "There are but faint prospects at present of any other than either a migratory or a predatory race being attracted to Hong Kong, who, when their hopes of gain or pilfering vanish, without hesitation or difficulty remove elsewhere."

The Rev. Smith was no more favorably disposed toward his fellow countrymen. He felt the British rulers were too harsh with the Chinese, permitting the general population to be exploited by a few Mandarins. As for the merchants and traders, he regarded their behavior as setting a bad example for the Chinese. Saving souls in Hong Kong, he decided, demanded more miracles than he had at his disposal, and with considerable relief, he transferred his missionary efforts to the more congenial atmosphere of South China.

Other missionaries accepted the long odds against grappling successfully with the devil in Hong Kong, but the struggle left many of them disheartened. When the merchants and sailors were not engaged in the opium traffic, they frequently busied themselves by purchasing Chinese mistresses from the Tanka boat people. Many of the Eurasians of South China were the issue of this type of transaction.

Law enforcement in the colony was a farce. The few Europeans who could be induced to join the underpaid police force were the scourings of the Empire, remittance men or wastrels who accepted the jobs because they did not dare go home to England.

Householders, disgusted with the ineptness of the police,

hired private watchmen who went about at night beating bamboo drums to advertise their presence. This noisy custom was later forbidden, and burglary, highway robbery and harbor piracy increased. Sir John F. Davis, the colony's second governor, tried to persuade property owners to improve police protection by paying more taxes for it, but the merchants demurred, setting a precedent which was applied to many proposed improvements in years to come. The attitude seemed to be: Progress is fine, provided one doesn't have to pay for it. Sir John attempted to keep track of known criminals by obliging every colony resident to register, but was forced to abandon the idea when the Chinese staged a three-month general strike in protest.

Piracy, smuggling, opium-smoking, prostitution, semislave trading in contract laborers, gambling, and graft flourished for many years, resisting the sporadic attacks of a succession of governors. In 1858, for the first and last time, an exceptional balance was achieved. Licenses for the sale of liquor, the favorite Western vice, and revenue from opium, the leading weakness of the Chinese, each brought 10,000 pounds of income to the colony government.

Under such powerful governors as Sir Richard Graves Macdonnell (1866-72) and Sir Arthur E. Kennedy (1872-77), the colony made significant advances in the control of piracy and urban crime. The quality of police protection improved and both men won the applause of local merchants by their Draconic policy of branding, flogging and deporting lawbreakers. The Chinese Emperor and the liberal elements in the British Parliament disapproved of the severity applied but did not intervene to stop it.

The Chinese government never ceased its opposition to the

smuggling of opium from Hong Kong, although many of its venal officials shared in the profits of the traffic. For two decades, from the mid-1860s to the mid-1880s, China attempted to enforce a blockade against smuggled salt and opium, but opium continued to represent almost half its total imports.

A joint Sino-British commission agreed to place some limitation on the trade in 1886, but the British zeal for enforcement was diluted by the desire for continuing profits. Even after controls were repeatedly tightened in the early 1900s, the returns held steady; in 1906, the opium trade was valued at 5 million pounds and yielded $2 million in colony revenue. Unfavorable world opinion gradually narrowed the trade, but the nonmedical sale and use of the drug was not entirely banned until World War II.

In the last several decades, the Hong Kong Police Department has outgrown its disreputable origins and has become an efficient law-enforcement organization. Nevertheless, the image of the colony that persists in the imagination of many Westerners who have never been there is a cesspool of iniquity such as the one that horrified the Rev. Smith.

Just how wicked and criminal is today's Hong Kong?

A layman's comparison of the crime rates of the United States and Hong Kong for the year 1960, as published by the Federal Bureau of Investigation and the Hong Kong Police Department respectively, gives an objective picture of their relative lawlessness.

Both sets of figures are for predominantly urban areas, covering ten of the most comparable categories of crime. The figures give the actual number of crimes per one million population. Because of inherent differences in the manner of classifying and reporting crimes, a margin of error of ten percent should be allowed in their interpretation.

1960—CRIME RATES PER 1 MILLION POPULATION

CRIME CATEGORY	UNITED STATES	HONG KONG
Murder	55	8
Rape	74	50
Serious Assault	645	178
Burglary	1,358	157
Larceny	2,785	2,562
Forgery	234	60
Prostitution	319	527
Narcotics	289	4,677
Drunkenness	16,375	257
Robbery	361	30

Such statistics are always subject to many different inter-
pretations, which will not be made here. But they confirm one
impression shared by virtually everyone who has spent many
nights (either at home or on the streets) in both New York
City and Hong Kong: You're a lot safer in Hong Kong.

The most glaring disparity between the rates is, of course,
in the comparative number of arrests for drunkenness. The
American rate is more than 60 times higher than that of Hong
Kong, and it is a safe inference that a fair share of the colony
arrests for drunkenness are made among Europeans and
Americans, who comprise less than two percent of the population. Hundreds of thousands of Chinese in Hong Kong
drink beer, wine or hard liquor, but a Chinese drunk in public is a rarity.

In major crimes of violence—murder, rape, serious assault
and robbery—America has a much higher crime rate. With
the stated allowance for error, the United States and Hong
Kong could be considered about equally inclined toward larceny—a legal term which covers the more popular forms of
stealing. Stealing automobiles, however, has not really caught

on in the colony; there is practically no place to hide a car after stealing it. Bicycle theft is more common there.

Prostitution is one of the two categories in which Hong Kong has a higher rate than America. A highly intelligent missionary who has dealt with the problem for many years had this succinct comment:

"The problem hinges on two factors; the British Army Garrison and the fact that Hong Kong is a recreation port for the United States Navy. Remove these and the problem vanishes."

For a variety of realistic reasons, this missionary does not expect the problem to vanish, though the police and the clergy, working from different directions, are doing their best to reduce its incidence. Both groups recognize poverty as one major cause of prostitution that can be fought with education and better jobs.

The comparative rates of narcotics offenses in the United States and Hong Kong indicate that such crime is sixteen times more prevalent in the colony than in America. They also confirm a fact recognized by every law-enforcement unit in Hong Kong: Drugs are the No. 1 colony crime problem. By government estimates, there are no less than 150,000, and perhaps as many as 250,000 drug addicts in the colony. In the entire United States there are between 45,000 and 60,-000 drug addicts.

The gravity of the colony's narcotics problem is best illustrated by the type of addiction practiced there. Almost all addicts use either opium or heroin, with heroin users three times more numerous than opium addicts. The trend toward heroin has grown more powerful every year since World War II, because the tight postwar laws against opium drove the drug sellers to a much more potent narcotic and one that could be smuggled more easily. Heroin is a second cousin to opium, being derived from morphine, which, in turn, has been extracted from opium.

Heroin, commonly called "the living death," is from 30 to 80 times stronger than opium. An opium smoker may go along for years, suffering no more physical damage than a heavy drinker; a heroin addict, who may be hooked in as short a time as two weeks, sinks into physical, mental and moral ruin within a few months.

A peculiar kind of economic injustice operates among drug addicts, who are most often found among the poorest segments of the colony's Chinese population. Even in the years when the British traded openly and without compunction in opium, they almost never became addicted to it, and today a British addict in Hong Kong is an extreme rarity. A number of young Americans living or visiting in the colony have picked up the habit, probably under the impression that they are defying conventions. They, at least, can afford the price of the rope with which they hang themselves. This is not so for the Chinese addict, whose habit costs him an average of $193 a year (HK $1,100), or much more than he can earn in a similar period. Unless he has saved enough money to keep him going until the drugs kill him, he turns to various kinds of crime to support his habit.

Opium-smoking is a cumbersome process requiring a bulky pipe, pots of the drug, a lamp to heat it and scrapers to clean the pipe. Smoking produces a strong odor which makes a pipe session vulnerable to police detection and arrest. There are no opium dens in Hong Kong; the usual term is opium divan, implying an elegance seldom encountered in the addicts' squalid hangouts.

Heroin, odorless and requiring no bulky apparatus, is taken

in various ways. "Chasing the dragon" is done by mixing heroin granules and base powder in folded tinfoil, then heating it over a flame and inhaling the fumes through a tube of rolled paper or bamboo. When a matchbox cover is substituted for the tube, the method is called "playing the mouth organ." A third technique involves the placing of heroin granules in the tip of a cigarette, which is lit and held in an upright position while the smoker draws on it; this is known as "firing the ack-ack gun." Needle injection, and the smoking or swallowing of pills made by mixing heroin with other ingredients are additional methods.

The opium poppy may only be grown illegally in Hong Kong, but the few farmers who attempt to raise it in isolated valleys have produced hardly enough for their own use. Practically all of it comes in by ships and planes in the form of raw opium or morphine, which can be converted to heroin within the colony. On ships, the drugs are hidden in the least accessible parts of the vessel or concealed in cargo shipments; they can also be dumped overside in a waterproof container with a float and marker as the ship nears the harbor, to be picked up by small, fast boats which land them in sparsely settled areas. Variations of the same methods are used by incoming planes, with a prearranged airdrop sometimes being employed.

With thousands of ships and planes arriving and departing every year, the chances of stopping all narcotics smuggling are practically nil. A complete search of every arrival would be physically impossible, and even in cases where the police or the Preventive Service of the Commerce and Industry Department have been tipped off to an incoming shipment, it may take a full day to locate the hiding place. The drugs may be packed inside a cable drum, buried in bales of waste, concealed in double-bottomed baskets, cached inside the bodies of dolls or surrounded by bundles of firewood; the hiding places are as inexhaustible as the cleverness of the smugglers.

Where do the narcotics come from? Harry J. Anslinger, United States Commissioner of Narcotics from 1930 to 1962, had been telling the world for at least a decade that Red China was the chief source of supply. Anslinger said the Chinese Communists were up to their necks in the traffic because it brought them the foreign exchange they desperately needed and simultaneously undermined the morale of the West by spreading drug addiction among its people.

Not one official in the British crown colony accepted Mr. Anslinger's thesis for a minute. Hong Kong Police Commissioner Henry W. E. Heath, the Secretariat for Chinese Affairs, and the Preventive Service of the Commerce and Industry Department unanimously declared that there was absolutely no evidence that any large amount of the drugs smuggled into the colony came from Red China. American customs officials in Hong Kong were inclined to sustain the British view.

Anslinger had named Yunnan Province in southwestern China as the leading opium-growing area. Colony officials will concede that some opium may be grown in Yunnan, but they believe that a much greater share is cultivated in northwest Laos, northern Thailand and the Shan States of eastern Burma. These four areas are so close to one another that the difference between the two hypotheses is more political than geographic.

Regardless of which field the poppy comes from, colony officials have found that more than half the opium seized upon entering Hong Kong has arrived on ships and planes that made their last previous stop at Bangkok, Thailand. It is presumed that few drugs arrived bearing the name and address of the manufacturer or the stamp giving the country of origin.

In 1960, the colony's antinarcotics units set what they believe to be a world record for drug seizures, grabbing 39 shipments that included 3,626 pounds of opium, 153 pounds of morphine, 337 pounds of morphine hydrochloride, 5 pounds of heroin and 155 pounds of barbitone. On November 30, 1960, the Preventive Service captured 1,078 pounds of raw opium hidden in bundles of hollowed-out teakwood on a newly arrived ship. Less than two weeks later they discovered another vessel trying the same trick and made a haul of 769 pounds of raw opium, 16 pounds of prepared opium, 45½ pounds of morphine and 293 pounds of morphine hydrochloride. There were 50 seizures in 1961, putting a further serious crimp in the smuggling racket.

Feeling persecuted and hurt, many smugglers shifted their base of operations to Singapore. Even so, it was not an unqualified triumph for Hong Kong's antinarcotics force; by pinching off the drug supply they forced its market price sky-high, and desperate addicts began stealing and robbing to pay for their dope.

Halting the manufacture of heroin within the colony is as difficult as catching dope smugglers. A heroin "factory" requires little space and can be set up in some obscure corner of the New Territories or lodged in an expensive top-floor apartment on Hong Kong Island; the profit margin is so great that production costs are but a small obstacle. Enforcement costs are almost as steep. In 1959, the Preventive Service trebled its manpower. In February, 1961, maximum penalties for drug manufacturing were raised from a fine of $8,750 and ten years in prison to a $17,500 fine and life imprisonment.

Almost two-thirds of all prisoners in Hong Kong jails are drug addicts, but the jailing of addicts, however necessary to protect society, offers no cure for addiction. The colony government has sought to meet this phase of the problem by setting up a narcotics rehabilitation center at Tai Lam Chung Prison and a voluntary treatment section in the government hospital at Castle Peak.

Dr. Alberto M. Rodrigues, a colony-born physician of Portuguese ancestry and an unofficial member of the Hong Kong Legislative Council, became chairman of a voluntary committee formed in 1959 to help drug addicts. With government approval, his committee took over Shek Kwu Island near Lantau in 1960 to establish a center where about 500 addicts could be accommodated if they volunteered for treatment. The island was chosen because it was isolated, and with proper security measures, could keep the addict entirely away from drugs until medical and nursing care had put him back on his feet. Gus Borgeest, the refugee rehabilitation pioneer who established a welfare center on Sunshine Island, helped in the early planning of Shek Kwu Chau, which began operations during 1962.

Sir Sik-nin Chau, who has served on both the Executive and Legislative Councils, headed an antinarcotics publicity campaign which was solidly backed by the British and Chinese newspapers. The Kaifong associations joined in the drive with lectures and leaflet-distribution among the Chinese community. The public was urged to report any information about narcotics sales or divans, but the response was slow and timid; many ordinary citizens were obviously afraid of beatings and reprisals by the Triad gangs engaged in drug-peddling. Others hung back in obedience to a deep-seated Chinese tradition of not sticking your neck out by reporting on the other fellow's dirty work. Some headway has been made against this attitude, but the general feeling of the drive's publicity people is that their campaign must be sustained for years to overcome it.

Hong Kong's drug problem is unlike that of New York City, where drug addiction among teen-agers is cause for grave concern. Few Chinese youngsters seem to be attracted to the habit. It is the middle-aged, the unemployed, and most of all, the desperately poor who chase the dragon for a brief sensation of well-being, ease and warmth that is succeeded by a crushing letdown, physical collapse and eventual death. Abrupt withdrawal of the drugs is like an earthquake from within, causing cramps, vomiting, excruciating bodily pain and pathological restlessness. Only a gradual withdrawal under close medical supervision will bring about a cure, and even that carries no guarantee if the rehabilitated addict is turned back to joblessness and squalor.

Much of the drug traffic into Hong Kong is not intended for local consumption, but for reexport to America and Europe. The crossroads position of Hong Kong on international air and shipping routes makes it particularly advantageous to this trade, and internal enforcement is insufficient to cope with it. To bolster their defenses against this traffic, colony drug-suppression officials depend on close coordination with police in Southeast Asia, with the World Health Organization Committee on Drugs Liable to Produce Addiction, and the Commission on Narcotic Drugs of the United Nations Economic and Social Council. The colony police force has opened its own sub-bureau of Interpol (International Criminal Police Organization) to strengthen its offensive against international drug peddlers.

One oddity of the colony's widespread drug addiction is

that it is seldom apparent to the average visitor; he may spend weeks there without seeing a single identifiable drug victim. Trained observers can often spot an addict by his dazed expression or emaciated appearance, but even in these cases they need further evidence to verify the appraisal. Dragon-chasers don't charge through the streets like rogue elephants—not in the colony, at any rate—they stay hidden and comatose in their squatter shacks or divans.

Police find the Triad gangs perennially active in the sale of narcotics, just as they are in pimpery, extortion and shakedown rackets. Congested areas such as Yau Ma Tei and Sham Shui Po have the highest crime rates and the largest Triad membership. Only about five percent of the 500,000 Triad members are engaged in major crimes, yet the threat of vengeance from this militant minority is generally sufficient to keep the other members silent and submissive. The mere implication of Triad backing, in a threatening letter sent to a rich Chinese, usually produces cash to pay off the letter writer, although police have recently had more success in persuading prospective victims of these menaces to contact them instead of paying off. Kidnapings are rare, though at least one case made the headlines in 1961.

The makeup of the police department closely reflects both the hierarchy and the numerical grouping of the colony's population. The line force of uniformed men and detectives in all grades totaled 8,333 in 1961. Nine-tenths were Chinese and less than 500 were British, with less than 200 Pakistanis and a handful of Portuguese. The top 50 administrative posts were almost solidly British, however. The force also includes a civilian staff of 1,400.

For the purposes of the ordinary citizen, a colony cop is a Chinese cop, for these are the only officers he sees regularly.

Taken as a group, they are an alert-looking, smartly uniformed body, predominantly young, slim and athletic. Day or
night, they appear to be very much on the job, and the world-
wide complaint that a cop is never there when you need him
seems peculiarly inapplicable to Hong Kong. The Chinese
officer quite obviously is proud of his job, but the swaggering
bully-boy pose is alien to his nature.

A few Chinese officers, like police in all other cities, go bad.
When they are drummed out of the force, it is generally for
shaking down a hawker or a merchant. More serious cases involve the protection of gambling, prostitution, after-hour
bars, or even collaboration with Triad gangsters who split
their protection money with the man on the beat. Once in a
great while a case like that of Assistant Superintendent John
Chao-ko Tsang crops up, with a high-ranking Chinese officer
involved in spying for a foreign government—Communist
China, in this instance. But such is the exception and does not
change one lesson the British rulers have learned in 120 years
of hiring almost every kind of recruit from a Scotsman to a
Sikh; that of them all, the rank-and-file Chinese cop is the
finest the colony has ever had.

The command structure of the police department, which is
highly centralized under an all-British top administration, is
reflected in almost every branch of the colony government.
There are approximately 15,000 natives of the British Isles in
the colony, excluding members of the armed forces and their
families, and they occupy virtually all of the top government
posts.

A number of writers have expressed the view that Hong
Kong is actually controlled by about twenty persons, and
while this could be criticized as extreme—and certainly impossible to prove—it could just as well be said that it is con-

trolled by not more than ten persons: The governor; the colonial secretary; the financial secretary; the director of Public Works; the managing director of Jardine, Matheson & Co. (the most powerful and longest-established business house); the general manager of the Hongkong & Shanghai Bank (the leading financial institution); the two most influential Chinese members of the Executive and Legislative Councils; and the most prominent Portuguese and Indian member of the Executive or Legislative Council. Perhaps the best way to test this top-ten theory would be to try running something in opposition to these ten, and no one has ventured that yet.

There is no important elective office in Hong Kong, no widely qualified electorate and no open agitation for universal suffrage. Nor is there any sign of a forcibly suppressed yearning for democratic rule on the part of the general population. The Communists, of course, loudly profess their love of elective government, but the British and a majority of the Chinese construe this to mean the entering wedge for Red China to annex the colony. This is an old-fashioned colonial autocracy, completely dominated by a small minority at the top, but even without a vote it appears to enjoy more confidence from its subjects than do the Reds on the mainland of China.

The greatest strength of the colony government is that in spite of its pin-point degree of representation, it can rule in an orderly and efficient manner without the excesses of tyranny or dictatorship. For ultimately, it is not the governing few but the law that rules in Hong Kong.

The Hong Kong government is a subsidiary of the British Crown. It gets its orders from the Colonial Office and they are carried out by the governor and two advisory bodies, the Executive and Legislative Councils. The governor is the head of both councils. Five persons have seats in both councils by virtue of their office—the commander of British forces in the colony, the colonial secretary, the attorney general, the secretary for Chinese affairs, and the financial secretary. In addition, one colony official is nominated to the Executive Council, and four other government officials are nominated for the Legislative Council. The governor goes outside the official family to nominate six unofficial members of the Executive Council and eight unofficial members of the Legislative Council. Altogether, there are 31 places in this policy-making hierarchy. Since several of its members hold two jobs in this selective directorate, there are at present a total of 23 men participating in top-level government.

The governor must consult with the Executive Council on all important matters, but he decides what must be done. If he takes action against the express advice of his Executive Council, he owes a full explanation for doing so to the Colonial Secretary. The governor makes the laws with the advice and consent of the Legislative Council, and he must have its approval for all public spending. British common law, adapted where necessary to local conditions and Chinese customs, is the legal code of Hong Kong.

Thus the colony presents a unique governmental phenomenon. Approximately ten to twenty English-speaking men holding undisputed sway over 3,300,000 subjects, of whom not one in ten understands the language of his rulers and hardly fifty percent can claim Hong Kong as their birthplace.

By all visible signs, the colony is one of the best-run governments in the Far East. Its roads are paved and traffic moves in an orderly way in spite of the highest vehicle concentration per mile of road anywhere in the world. The same order prevails in the incessant shuttling of harbor vessels. Public transportation is swift, frequent and generally on schedule. Poverty and privation are everywhere, but starvation is virtually non-existent. Business and trade thrive and unemployment is low. Wages seem minuscule when compared with American standards, yet are higher than in most of the countries of Asia. A majority of its people are indifferent to the government, but they are not afraid of it. When something has to be done, there are people at the top with the resolution and the intelligence to do it without trampling human rights.

Is Hong Kong's autocracy, therefore, a model for the world? On the contrary, there is hardly another place where its practices would be applicable. Hong Kong's exasperating uniqueness has defied even the efforts of the Colonial Office to make it conform to British government practices.

With all its efficiency, however, Hong Kong has the weaknesses of its governmental structure and its political environment. Because of its extreme centralization, its almost ingrown character in relation to its constituents, it is often out of touch with the people it governs. Enormous barriers of language and culture block its view, and graft and corruption threaten it from every angle. In Asia, graft is the deadliest enemy of every form of government which pretends to deal justly with its citizens, and Hong Kong is not invulnerable to its attack.

From the earliest days of the colony, the Chinese people who emigrated there were fugitives from restraint and oppression. Many of them were outright fugitives from justice. Whatever their virtues or vices, they had found existence under the government of their homeland so intolerable that they willingly submitted to the rule of an alien people they neither trusted nor admired. From centuries of bitter experience in China, they believed that no government was to be trusted. The secret of survival was to avoid all open defiance of governments and to go on living within the framework of one's family and clan as though the government did not exist. One did not cheat the other members of his clan, because retribution could be swift and terrible. Relations with civil rulers were not an ethical compact; they were a battle of wits, a stubborn struggle for self-preservation in which the cunning of the individual was the only weapon against the greed and power of the state.

How much more applicable these lessons were when those rulers were foreign devils who did not speak one's language! One did not rebel against the headstrong foreigners and their military superiority; he obeyed them in externals, so far as it was necessary to escape reprisals, and went on quietly building his own internal mechanisms of graft like a busy termite in an unsuspecting household. If the people of the household mistook the termites for industrious but harmless little ants, it was all the easier for him.

The metaphor need not be done to death, for it is no longer as apposite as it once was. But there is no question that graft and corruption continue to eat away at the structure of the colony government. In a hundred casual conversations with a hundred different colony residents—English, Chinese, American, Portuguese, governmental and nongovernmental —the visitor will almost never hear that the ruling powers have railroaded some poor devil off to jail without cause, swindled him out of his property to benefit the state, or hounded the populace into semistarvation with unbearable taxation. If these evils exist, they are neither frequent enough nor sufficiently conspicuous to engage people's passions.

But on the subject of graft—the innumerable, small nicks taken from merchants, builders, and the ordinary citizen seeking any type of official favor or permit—the floodgates of complaint are wide open. Much of this is generalized, un-

proved, even irresponsible, operating at about the same intel-
lectual level as a taxi-driver's jeremiad. Nevertheless, there is
a core of solid complaint that cannot be ignored.

Within the colony government, there is a large segment that
bridles at the least intimation of official graft. The motto of
this segment is: Don't rock the boat. We know we're not per-
fect, they seem to be saying, but don't go around kicking over
beehives, or the first thing we know, the Colonial Office will
be down on our heads with all kinds of inquiries, full-dress
investigations and a fearful flap. We'll all be sacked, sent home
in disgrace, and it won't change one thing for the better. So
let's keep quiet, muddle along as best we can and try to eliminate the grafters quietly, one at a time. We're really not a
bad lot of chaps, you know.

Fortunately, some of the colony's chief officers do not sub-
scribe to the theory that corruption can be defeated by a public pretense that it does not exist.

Something like a civic shock-wave was recorded in Hong
Kong on January 11, 1962, when Chief Justice Michael Hogan
opened the Supreme Court Assizes by coming to grips with
the issue of corruption.

"No one would claim we are entirely immune from this
evil," Sir Michael said. He noted that the heavy penalties prescribed for corruption offenses must be enforced without re-
course to "the surreptitious whisper in the corridor; the accusation made behind his (the accused's) back; or the anonymous
letter. If such methods should come to be accepted, then we
would have another evil just as bad, if not worse, than corruption."

The Chief Justice proceeded to put his finger on one of the
main obstacles to the exposure of corruption:

"There is a reluctance to come forward and give information; to come, if necessary, into court and face the possibility of a cross-examination, attacking character, credit and the power of recollection—in fact a reluctance to pay the price that the rule of law demands."

He contrasted this attitude with the recent case of a Mr. Tong, who captured and held on to a sneak-thief despite six stab wounds, and asked:

"Does this mean that physical courage is more plentiful than moral courage in Hong Kong today?"

He reached the heart of the matter with the observation that a citizen will be very slow to come forward with a complaint against an official if he knows that perhaps tomorrow or the next day or the day after, he has got to come and ask that official, or some colleague of that official, or somebody apparently identified with him in interest, for a concession, or a privilege, or some act of consideration.

It is only when men have clearly defined rights, he continued, that they enjoy the security to challenge the abuse of power and the ability to choke off corruption. If an official can grant or withhold permission "without the necessity of giving public reasons for the decision," the Chief Justice declared, "you immediately create an opening for corruption or the suspicion of it."

The Chief Justice's address, particularly in its allusion to "closed-door" decisions and a lack of moral sense in the community, produced headlines and editorials in the local press and acute twinges of discomfort among those who either benefited by corruption or feared any public admission that it existed. In itself, the address was neither an exposé nor an indictment, but its delivery by the brilliant and articulate Chief Justice in one of the most solemn ceremonies of the governmental year rang a clear warning from the citadel: If the corrupters were haled before the courts, they could expect no easy-going tolerance for their misdeeds.

During the previous July, Governor Black had moved to correct one weakness peculiar to Hong Kong. Because of the Chinese tradition that personal contact with the government is to be avoided, many residents were reluctant to approach an official for such routine information as where to apply for an identity card or how to locate a lost pet. If they plucked up the courage to ask a question, they assumed that some fee, to be paid either above or below the table, would be exacted for any answer given. The situation offered a happy hunting ground for grafters, either those on the government payroll who dealt with the general public or the self-appointed private "fixers" who directed the applicant to a particular official for a small fee. Sometimes the fixer and the official were in cahoots and sheared the lamb at both ends of his journey.

Why it took the colony 120 years to plug this rat hole is a baffling question. It was done at last by creating a Public Enquiry Service with an all-Chinese staff capable of speaking virtually any local dialect and of supplying direct and accurate answers to every kind of question about the government and its functions. Coming under the general authority of the Secretariat for Chinese Affairs, it is headed by Paul K. C. Tsui, a native of Hong Kong and a colony administrative officer since 1948. Controller Tsui spent months roaming the colony, talking to editors, listening to gossip in goldsmiths' shops and to the complaints people dictated to sidewalk letter-writers or expressed to housing and tenancy offices.

When he felt that he had gained some idea of the questions and problems on people's minds, Mr. Tsui sought the answers to them from the appropriate departments. He then assembled a small staff, compiled and cross-indexed a vast store of information in readily accessible form, and established an office in the entrance hall of the Central Government Offices, West Wing, on July 3, 1961. There his three information officers, who had expected to have to handle 80 requests for information a day, found them streaming in at the rate of about 135 a day. Early in 1962, a similar office had to be opened in Kowloon to meet the same demand. When the Chinese people were satisfied that they could get specific, friendly answers to their problems without having to pay a fee, they were both amazed and grateful.

Mr. Tsui, taking a tip from the operators of goldsmiths' shops, put his staff on hard chairs and the public on soft chairs, permitting them to talk comfortably across a low counter in a pleasant, informal atmosphere. At times it takes an agitated inquirer fifteen minutes to blow off steam before he can get around to stating what it is he really wants to know, but the staff will patiently wait him out. A married woman about thirty years of age appears to represent the favorite official type of most questioners, although they like also to have an older male official handy as a corroborating reference. Queries in English are handled as efficiently as are those in Chinese.

Once the news of this service reaches all colony residents —many English and Chinese had still not heard of it in 1962 —one of the most prevalent forms of petty graft and ill-will toward government will have been eliminated.

Chief Justice Hogan's attack on "closed-door" decisions and official impropriety was followed a week later by the sixth report of the Advisory Committee on Corruption, composed of a five-man body appointed by Governor Black from the membership of the Executive and Legislative Councils.

The report found the highest susceptibility to corruption among the departments dealing directly with the general public—police, public works, urban services, commerce and industry and refugee resettlement. Inspection services of all kinds, it said, showed the greatest vulnerability to graft.

So far the report only echoes a truism known to every municipal administration; that when the government comes to bear on some individual's right to perform a particular function, usually for money, a few gold coins in an inspector's pocket will often expedite a favorable decision.

The Advisory Committee on Corruption has recommended clearly defined, simple licensing procedures and the introduction of bilingual (Chinese and English) application forms and explanatory booklets. A corollary recommendation that all new government employees receive a pamphlet detailing the penalties for corruption has already been accepted.

The Committee called for legislation that would require a public servant to explain exactly how he came to be in possession of any property that was not in keeping with his income, and to face a penalty if his explanation did not hold. They also sought a law giving the courts the power to seize any money involved in a corruption charge, plus a recommendation for stiffer punishments against corruption.

The report urged that the names of officials convicted of corruption be made public, and that figures showing the total number of officials dismissed be published at certain intervals. At present, there are numerous angry cries that when a crooked British official is caught and sacked, he is spirited out of the colony without a word about it; whereas a Chinese official fired for a similar offense receives unrelenting publicity and back-handed treatment that implies, "Well, what else can you expect from these Orientals?"

The Anti-Corruption Branch of the police department is now the chief agency responsible for detecting corruption in all departments of government. The Committee has invited direct reports of corruption from the public, some of which have led to the prosecution and firing of several officials. During the first eleven months of 1961, the police department received an additional 422 complaints charging corruption. Americans are usually surprised to find that the colony's police department is charged with detecting corruption in other government departments. In America it is done the other way around; other government departments seem to be investigating the police force for signs of corruption.

Generally unsubstantiated but endlessly repeated to visitors, are the popular charges that the police are shaking down shop-keepers and peddlers, or that building inspectors are blinded by gold when a builder is detected extending a structure over a sidewalk in violation of local codes and ordinances.

The report, last of the series issued by the Committee, suggested that it would be desirable to hold the givers of bribes equally guilty with the civil servants who accepted them. This is a sticky issue in any community, despite the unassailability of its ethical position. If it were rigidly enforced, it would infringe the freedom of speech of many prominent persons who deplore dishonesty in government, because it would put them in jail.

The Advisory Committee has also warned civil servants to deal only with the applicants in person, or with professional representatives in order to exclude corrupt middlemen from all transactions. This warning is especially appropriate in Hong Kong, where a middleman with no discernible function except his ability to collect a fee will attempt to worm himself into every business deal.

All of the Committee's recommendations are made directly

to the governor, who in turn discusses them with the Colonial Office before taking action.

Colony newspapers have printed long excerpts from all the reports, and the *China Mail* declared that they simply said what the newspaper had been publishing for two years.

What Chief Justice Hogan and the Committee have jointly accomplished is to raise an issue of critical importance in the survival of the colony government. Whether it will be resolved as decisively as it has been faced may require months and years to answer.

CHAPTER EIGHT

Two Worlds in One House

"Care must be taken not to confound the habits and institutions of the Chinese with what prevails in other parts of the world."

—BRITISH HOUSE OF LORDS (circa 1880)

Hong Kong has furnished the Sino-British answer to a universal question: What's in it for me? Its progress from the earliest days has been more powerfully influenced by the lure of gold than by the Golden Rule, with its British and Chinese residents having little in common except their human nature and an equal dedication to the maximum profit in the minimum time.

"They don't even speak the same language!" is a convenient expression of the ultimate separation between peoples, but while it is true that nine-tenths of Hong Kong's Chinese do not speak English, the linguistic gap is only one of the many chasms that stand between them and their British rulers.

The British traders and fighting men who muscled their

way into possession of Hong Kong Island in 1841 were looked
upon with fear and loathing by the Chinese governing class,
who considered them gun-toting barbarian brawlers. To the
English, the Chinese seemed a docile subspecies of humanity.
It has taken most of the intervening 121 years to convince a
majority of both sides that the initial judgments may have been
wrong.

The differences between nineteenth century Chinese and
European civilizations were wide. Europeans, when they
thought about religion at all, worshipped one God in a variety
of antagonistic churches; the Chinese worshipped hundreds of
gods, sometimes subscribing to several contradictory creeds
simultaneously, without apparent conflict. Europeans were
monogamous by law and custom; the Chinese, without odium,
could be as polygamous as their means would allow.

None of these theological or moral disparities weighed
heavily on the English while they were securing a foothold
in China and building the opium trade. On the contrary, when
they noted the willingness with which Chinese customs officials accepted their bribes, they felt they had established a
kind of moral bond with the East. These people, whatever
their eccentricities, were ready to do business in the accepted
Western way.

When the British settled down to the business of governing
their new colony, they collided at every turn with the language barrier. Except for a few conscientious missionaries
and a minuscule number of lay scholars, the British were
wholly ignorant of Cantonese, the prevailing Hong Kong
tongue, and they were loftily disinclined to learn it. The ex-
tremes to which this arrogant insularity sometimes went were
demonstrated by Governor Samuel George Bonham (1848-
1854), who denied promotions to those subordinates who

learned Chinese; he felt that the language was injurious to the mind, robbing it of common sense. In other respects, Governor Bonham was not so benighted as his linguistic convictions would indicate. Nor was he alone in his attitude toward the Chinese people; Governor Hercules Robinson (1859-1865) once wrote that it was his constant endeavor to "preserve the European and American community from the injury and inconvenience of intermixture" with the Chinese population.

Since all government business was (and continues to be) conducted in English, British officials frequently had to rely on Portuguese interpreters who had moved to Hong Kong from Macao. The Portuguese, facile linguists and unburdened by delusions of racial superiority, filled the role admirably. But in the colony courts, the simple task of swearing a witness in presented obstacles even to the best interpreters. Having never sworn an oath in the English fashion, the Chinese viewed it as just one more instance of outlandish mumbo-jumbo. At first the English tried cutting off a rooster's head as a testament of the witness's intention to tell the truth; then an earthenware bowl was broken to signify the same thing. A yellow paper inscribed with oaths or the name of the witness was burned in court as another form of swearing-in. Governor Bonham instituted a direct oral affirmation in 1852, but the complications that ensued must have intensified his conviction that the Chinese language was an insult to logic. If a defendant were asked, "Do you plead guilty?" the question was rendered in colloquial Cantonese as "You yes or no not guilty?" If the respondent answered "Yes, I am not guilty," it could mean either "Not Guilty" or "Guilty." Somehow the oaths were sworn, but not without a certain despair among the court attendants.

Although the European community seldom concerned itself with Chinese customs, it managed to raise a considerable storm over their "places of convenience" during the 1860s. These creations of the colony's Chinese merchants were a sort of employee-retirement plan which consisted of taking one's elderly or ailing workers to a crude shelter located on the north slope of Victoria Peak. There the faithful employee was rewarded for his long service by being given a quantity of drinking water and a coffin and left to die; if he were blessed with friends, they might visit him at this place, offer him an occasional scrap of food or a fresh ration of drinking water, and finally bury him. Often he died alone and without proper burial. This was too much, even for European opium traders, and Governor Richard Macdonnell stilled their protests by offering a free site for a Chinese hospital at Possession Point. This replacement of the terrible "dying-houses" was financed by the wealthier Chinese for their destitute countrymen. It became the first of the Tung Wah Chinese hospitals, now greatly expanded and modernized. The inevitable outcry that provision of the simplest medical care for the destitute would cause these facilities to be jammed by hordes of undeserving poor was raised—as it still is today—and proved false.

Sanitary conditions among the Chinese were horrible when the British arrived and remained so for the rest of the nineteenth century. The colony government made many attempts to improve them, but it was regularly stymied by the tenement dwellers who opposed any form of health inspection as an invasion of privacy, and by landlords who resented any proposal which threatened their profit margins. During the bubonic plague epidemics of the 1890s, the government provided a special plague burial-ground and offered the families of the dead quantities of lime to render the bodies of the victims noninfectious. The Chinese responded by abandoning their dead in the streets or throwing them in shallow graves; the donated lime was sold to building contractors.

The surviving tenements of the Western District of Hong Kong Island are still a shock to visiting Westerners. Still, their dark, dirty and overcrowded condition is a distinct improvement upon the disease-ridden pestholes of the last century. Sanitary inspectors, no longer detested and attacked by the population, can go anywhere and they carry full police powers for enforcing corrective action. The Chinese, never any fonder of dirt than the English, have been converted to the belief that the once-hated British methods can help them to achieve cleanliness.

Because of their tenuous contact with the Chinese residents of the colony, the British rulers tended to deal with them through intermediaries. This function was at first performed by the Mandarins, or members of the Chinese official class, who were as willing to gouge their countrymen for the British as they had been to do it for the Emperor; provided, of course, that they were able to deduct their usual cut. Governor Arthur Kennedy (1872-1877), who was the first to invite the Chinese to receptions at Government House, relied on the committee of the Man Mo Temple to control Chinese affairs.

Man Mo Temple, an ancient building still standing on Hollywood Road in the congested Western District, was a mixture of Buddhist and Taoist elements. Its leaders were Kennedy's very potent allies, all working secretly to control Chinese affairs, acting as commercial arbitrators, negotiating the sale of official titles, and welcoming visiting Mandarins. Man Mo Temple, now administered by the Tung Wah Hospital committee, remained a respectable institution, but a number of other temples sprang up to challenge its influence.

In numerous cases the so-called temples were nothing more than a sanctimonious swindle. Privately promoted as a business speculation, they solicited funds from the public with fraudulent claims of divine or political influence. Abuses of this sort became so flagrant that the colony government, after long delay, enacted the Chinese Temples Ordinance in 1928, which provided for registration of the temples and an accounting of their funds to the Secretariat for Chinese Affairs. Certain long-established temples were exempt from various provisions of the Ordinance, but the founding of temples as a private business venture was forbidden. Surplus funds of the existing temples—the amount remaining after all maintenance and operating costs had been met—were transferred to a general Chinese charities fund.

The Chinese Mui Tsai custom, that of selling young girls as servants, troubled British and Chinese relations in Hong Kong for half a century. From ancient times, Chinese families had purchased little girls from impoverished parents and put them to work as household drudges. The colony officials raised their first strong objections to the practice in 1878, condemning it as thinly disguised slavery. Speaking of slavery, the Chinese retorted, what about the licensed brothels where 80 percent of the inmates had been sold into prostitution?

A committee appointed by Governor John Pope Hennessy (1877-1882) found that hundreds of the Mui Tsai, when they had outgrown their household enslavement, were being resold as prostitutes for shipment to Singapore, California and Australia. A species of Caucasian scum who lived in the colony were active partners in the trade. Governor Hennessy and Chief Justice John Smale forwarded the committee's reports to the British House of Lords with urgent recommendations for tight corrective laws. The Lords, suddenly revealing an unsuspected concern for the integrity of Chinese customs, killed most of the proposed reforms.

Establishment of the Po Leung Kuk, or Society for the Protection of Virtue, helped to limit the kidnaping of women and girls, but the institution of Mui Tsai was to persist well into the twentieth century. The English eventually outlawed licensed brothels after decades of criticism from many countries.

Covert prostitution continues at a brisk pace in Hong Kong today, with sailors favoring the Wanchai district and the bars of the Tsim Sha Tsui section of Kowloon. The Chinese are more inclined to patronize the western areas of Hong Kong Island. The dance hall and cabaret girls of Wanchai, whose ranks include some spectacularly beautiful women, charge their eager patrons about four dollars an hour for the privilege of dancing with them, sharing a plate of melon seeds and drinking tea. The cabarets are murky dens, furnished in Chinese warehouse modern, with a third-rate jazz band dragging the tempo along in the semidarkness. There is no guarantee of intimacies—emphatically not on the premises—and the prospective suitor is obliged to continue shelling out his money for repeated visits until the girl decides whether he has the kind of bankroll she could care for. If he is too repulsive to her, not even that will do.

A cabaret girl can earn $300 a month or more, or about five times as much as a schoolteacher earns. Few of these girls speak English, but this ability has never been regarded as a prerequisite. Apart from the moral considerations of the job, its competitive aspects are becoming more intense all the time. Bar girls, who have little respect for the traditional preliminaries, may bestow their favors on five customers while the cabaret charmers are fencing with one.

The singsong girls, formerly held in great esteem as entertainers and prostitutes, have almost disappeared from the
colony. Many of them were Mui Tsai who had been trained
to sing seemingly interminable Cantonese songs in a falsetto
voice for their tea-shop patrons, accompanying themselves on
a kind of horizontal stringed instrument which they tapped
with padded hammers. In the later evening, they moved about
from one businessmen's club to another in the West Point section of the island. Not all were prostitutes, and there is still
at least one tea shop along Queen's Road Central where entertainment is confined to music. Westerners who hear their music often find themselves thinking of older days.

Considering the fact that Hong Kong is a world seaport,
the rate of venereal infection is surprisingly low. To a greater
extent than in most Western cities, poverty is a basic cause of
prostitution, but here too sheer laziness, greed and stupidity
play their part in the provision of recruits. As usual, the greatest profits from the trade go to its protectors—Triad gangsters and corrupt policemen.

The entire subject of the status and treatment of women
has provided a continual source of animosity and disagreement
throughout the colony's history. The rich Chinese Taipans,
with their numerous wives and mistresses lodged in separate
establishments, have remained the envy of many a Western
man who could not emulate them without violating the laws
of the colony and placing himself beyond the pale of polite
Western society.

Since the founding of the Chinese Republic in 1911, well-
educated Chinese women have not looked happily on polygamy. Their convictions were solidified and shared by millions
of other Chinese wives when Red China tightened the marriage laws, making monogamy not only legal but practically

mandatory. These improvements in the status of Chinese women have not gone unnoticed in Hong Kong, where a British, Christian, monogamous community finds itself in the embarrassing position of tolerating plural marriage among its Chinese subjects long after the institution has been outlawed in China.

There is nothing in this thorny problem which lends itself to edicts and sweeping judgments. It is charged with the most delicate emotional considerations, involving not only the legality of existing marriages, the legitimacy of offspring and the fundamental rights of women, but also the division of property and the inheritance of estates. Colony officials are aware that the work of solving it must be approached with the greatest subtlety.

To begin with, there are six kinds of marriages to be considered, all with different premises. Two are classified as Chinese Modern Marriages; those contracted in Hong Kong under Nationalist China laws, and those contracted in China or any other place outside the colony under the same Nationalist laws. Marriages contracted under Chinese custom as it existed and was recognized in 1843 are Chinese Customary Marriages. Marriages under the colony's laws, Christian or otherwise, are called Registry Marriages. There are also Reputed Marriages, which is the colony designation for common-law marriages, and, finally, a group called Foreign Marriages, which includes all those contracted outside the colony under foreign laws, particularly those performed and registered in Red China under its monogamous marriage law. Thus, the usually simple question, "Are you married?" when fully answered in Hong Kong, may take a considerable amount of the inquirer's time.

Chinese Customary Marriages, still popular in the colony,

are generally recognized as valid, but there is no single defi-
nition which covers them. There are any number of ancient
prescriptions for them which contradict one another, but
they are alike in that they follow the accepted rites and ceremonies of the families of the bride and groom. Chinese women
with a modern consciousness of their rights have no affection
for such unions, since they permit a husband to divorce his
wife for any reason and give her no right to leave him if she
really feels inclined to do so. Furthermore, and this is an
equally sore point, it permits the husband to take concubines,
though the notion that a wife might adopt a similar polygamy
is quite inconceivable.

Chinese Modern Marriages in the colony far outnumber all
other types—more than 200,000, by an official estimate—although Registry Marriages have recently gained in number.
All that is required to make them valid is an open ceremony
witnessed by two persons. The Nationalist laws applicable to
such unions give the man no legal right to acquire a concubine, despite the fact that some husbands in the colony find it
convenient to pretend they do. The "extra" girls are naturally
flattered to be told they are concubines (i.e., secondary wives
with full domestic rights), rather than mistresses with no legal
or social standing.

In everyday relationships with the courts and the government, Chinese Modern Marriages are recognized as respectable unions. None the less, they have no legal validity when
contracted in Hong Kong, for they are neither entered at the
Marriage Registry nor are they celebrated according to "the
personal law and religion of the parties," as colony laws require.

Reputed Marriages are, in many respects, exactly like common-law marriages in the United States: two people live to-

gether, sometimes have children and are regarded by themselves and their friends as married, unless they should grow weary of each other and part. In Hong Kong, however, a concubine is sometimes added, making the institution look something like a house of cards with an annex. Foreign Marriages, or unions contracted abroad and according to the laws of the country where the couple formerly lived, present few legal obstacles. If they were married in Red China, and the marriage was registered there, the union is monogamous; when the couple move to Hong Kong, their marriage has the same standing as that of an American or European couple living in the colony.

The complications arising from this matrimonial disparity have been the subject of intensive study since World War II. In earlier days, the marital customs of the Chinese community were of little interest to the British. One did not associate with the Chinese unless it was required for the purposes of political window-dressing. But the glacial snobbery of old colonialism suffered a disrespectful mauling during World War II from which it has never quite recovered. At that time the Chinese penetrated all but the tightest circles of Hong Kong society, and hundreds of British and Chinese intermarried without loss of "face" in either group. This last was the boldest departure, for while it was true that outcasts of both races had intermarried since the founding of the colony, a socially acceptable member of either race who attempted it was snubbed by both English and Chinese.

British-Chinese intermarriages are monogamous, and in spite of the inevitable interference of aunts, uncles and cousins, have generally worked out better than either race would have expected them to two decades ago. Of themselves, these mixed marriages are not a social issue in the colony, but they have indirectly breached the barrier between the two racial communities. Marriage laws of all sorts have become the concern of the entire colony population.

The 1948 Committee on Chinese Law and Custom defined many of the marital contradictions which persist to this day. Then, as now, one of the most vexing questions was the legal status of the "secondary wife" or concubine sanctioned by Chinese Customary Marriages. The English meaning of "concubine," connoting a mistress or secret paramour, was not applicable to the Chinese concubine; she joined her husband's household, with or without the principal wife's consent, and it was his obligation to support her. Her children were legitimate, but her husband could divorce her more readily than he could his principal wife.

But what were the rights of real and pseudo-concubines? Could they and their children be discarded without support? To what extent might they challenge the rights of the real wife? The 1948 Committee produced no definitive answers to these questions, nor did it urge any precipitate action to change the status of concubines. It did recommend that after a certain date, the taking of new concubines be declared illegal.

Sir Man Kam Lo, a Chinese member of the Hong Kong Executive Council, subsequently wrote a dissent to the 1948 report, saying that he believed the concubine should be allowed to remain in cases where the principal wife was ill or unable to bear children. As he noted, the birth of a male heir is of the greatest importance to the succession of a Chinese family. Very few families, he felt, would regard an adopted son as a suitable heir.

Arthur Ridehalgh, former Attorney General, and John C. McDouall, Secretary for Chinese Affairs, made a detailed study of Chinese marriages in the colony in 1960 and submitted a variety of recommendations intended to clear up some of the ambiguities and contradictions.

It was their proposal that the government set a definite date for outlawing Chinese Modern Marriages and to validate all marriages of this type which had been previously contracted as monogamous unions, provided that neither spouse was lawfully married to anyone else. The so-called concubines of husbands who had been parties to a Chinese Modern Marriage would receive no further legal recognition, and in fact they had never been entitled to any.

Regarding Chinese Customary Marriages, the study favored the recording of these marriages to establish their validity, and the banning of all future marriages in which either partner is under sixteen years of age. As to Reputed Marriages, the study advocated remarriage of the couples under colony law with the right to back-date the marriage to the time they had begun to live together.

The Ridehalgh-McDouall report also favored several changes in the divorce laws. One change would permit a principal wife in a Chinese Customary Marriage to get a divorce with maintenance until her death or remarriage if the husband, after a date to be set by law, acquired a concubine without the principal wife's consent or knowledge. Another recommendation, after a date set by law, would bar divorce in a Chinese Customary Marriage without the free consent of both parties.

The study warned against any all-out banning of concubines in Chinese Customary Marriages, but supported gradual restriction of the right to take concubines. As for mistresses in other types of marriages who posed as legal concubines, the study urged the government to expose the practice as a popular fallacy with no lawful basis. It also gave its backing to laws which granted a legal concubine full rights to seek a divorce and obtain maintenance for her children, and legislation which empowered a principal wife to sue a husband for divorce and support of herself and children.

Other recommendations proposed added protection of the rights of wives in Chinese Modern Marriages against infringement by pseudo-concubines, and legal provision to assure the support of illegitimate children.

All these findings are still being weighed by the colony government and quick action on them is unlikely. To a large degree, the proposed changes in marriage laws represent a new offensive in the long war for women's rights, and it might be noted that the women of this century have compiled an impressive list of victories in this regard. With enough nagging and prodding, they should be able to carry the day in Hong Kong too.

In the discussion of such pervasive issues as the difference between Chinese and British marriage customs, it is convenient to view the Chinese as a single group of people constituting 98.2 percent of the colony's population. Since 95 percent of the population speak Cantonese, it would seem to follow that Hong Kong is a homogeneous community, except for a light top-dressing of "foreign devils." But this superficial impression is as wide of the mark as the saying "All Chinese look alike."

There are scholars who object to the word Chinese as the description of one people, arguing quite persuasively that there are so many racial strains in China that no single label adequately describes them. The point is drawn a bit fine for the majority of Western observers, yet anyone who spends a few weeks in Hong Kong will begin to appreciate the racial diversity of the Chinese people.

By the unverified judgment of the eye, the colony's Chinese people are two or three inches shorter than the American of average height, and noticeably taller than the average Japanese or Filipino. But that is perhaps the limit of any valid comparison between Americans and Chinese as far as appearance goes.

The Chinese one sees on the street range from jockey-sized runts to towering giants; from tiny women weighing perhaps 90 pounds to queenly six-footers; from the palest of white skins to a deep walnut brown. Many have features which seem more Slavic or Polish than anything classifiable as Chinese. There are almond eyes and pop eyes; slit eyes and bug-eyes. Noses tend to be a little less prominent and less sharply defined than European noses, but exceptions occur. The bloated red nose of the dedicated drinker never shows itself, except on a Caucasian face. Dark hair is almost universal and bald heads less common than in an American crowd. Pudgy types occur with some regularity, but tremendously fat people are rarely seen.

About half the people who live in the urban areas were born in the colony and most of their ancestors came from Kwangtung, the Chinese Province immediately north of the Hong Kong border. Kwangtung was also the birthplace of the majority of the recent refugees from Red China. Eight-tenths of the city-dwellers speak the dialect of Cantonese used in Canton City, where the British traders were based before Hong Kong became a colony. This dialect and others closely related to it are the *lingua franca* of the colony's urban Chinese, but there are 96 Cantonese dialects in existence, many

of them unintelligible to users of the Canton City dialect.
The babble of urban tongues includes Hoklo, Sze Yap and
Hakka, all from different parts of Kwangtung, Shanghainese
(chiefly heard at North Point and Hung Hom in the colony),
Chiuchow (in the Western District), Fukienese (at North
Point) and Kuoyu, or Mandarin (near Hong Kong Uni-
versity and at Rennie's Mill Camp).

In the New Territories, where even a Westerner can detect differences of dress and custom, the Cantonese hold most
of the flat, fertile farmland and speak a dialect which puzzles
city Cantonese. Ancestors of the Cantonese farmers have lived
in the New Territories for nine centuries. The Hakka people,
whose women may be identified immediately by their broad-
brimmed straw hats with a hanging fringe of thin black
cloth, settled the same area at about the time of the earliest
Cantonese, but were pushed into the less desirable farmland
and generally dominated by the Cantonese. They fought each
other intermittently for centuries, but the feud has died down
and they now share several villages peacefully, frequently
intermarry, and restrict their warfare to husband-wife
squabbles. The Hakkas of the eastern New Territories operate their own single-masted, high-hull boats for hauling
farm produce and ferrying passengers.

The Hoklos, a smaller group with a knack for handling
light, fast boats, once lived entirely on boats and worked as
shrimp fishermen. They moved ashore many years ago and
now have their chief settlements on Cheung Chau and Peng
Chau, a few miles west of Hong Kong Island.

By the testimony of historians, the Tanka people, who dom-
inate the colony's fishing industry, are the oldest surviving
group in Hong Kong. Antedating the Chinese, they lived in
the area when the Cantonese came along to push them off the

land and generally treat them like despised inferiors. They lived entirely on boats, and when the British traders arrived, the Tanka had no compunctions about dealing with them in defiance of the Chinese Emperor's orders. Over 90 percent of them speak Cantonese, with a small number speaking Hoklo and other dialects. Hardy and conservative, they avoid city ways, live on their junks and sampans and follow their own distinctive festivals and religious ceremonies. Since World War II they have begun to send their children to schools ashore and to become more directly involved in the economic life of the colony.

World War II provided a turning point in the fortunes of those boat people who operated cargo lighters in the harbor. Heartily disliking the Japanese, they used false-bottomed boats to secrete food stolen from their cargoes and then distributed it among the half-starved population ashore. They were the only residents permitted to eat in the large hotel restaurants like those at the luxurious Peninsula in Kowloon. Most of them, wholly unfamiliar with chairs, ate by squatting on the chair-seats as they had squatted on deck while eating at sea. Nowadays, they are more sophisticated, and in spite of their non-Chinese origin, as intensely Chinese as any group in the colony.

Because of the floodtide of tourists which has swept into Hong Kong in the last few years, it has become a conversational bromide to say that the influx will soon destroy its colorful Chinese community. To accept such a doctrine is to overestimate the impact of tourism and underrate the resistance of the Chinese.

The Hong Kong tourist is a highly localized phenomenon. Except for a fast motor tour through the main roads of the New Territories and a short whirl around Hong Kong Island, he rarely wanders more than a mile from the island and Kowloon terminals of the Star Ferry. He shops, gawks, eats at a few restaurants which are more tourist-oriented than Oriental, and is gone, leaving nothing but the click of the shopkeepers' abacuses to mark his passage.

It may seem incongruous to characterize nearly one-fourth of the human race as clannish, but it is undeniable that the Chinese, no matter where they have lived, have retained their home ties, customs and culture. They are rock-ribbed individualists rather than nationalists, but when they live abroad, whether in Hong Kong or the Chinatowns of San Francisco and New York, they remain distinctly and unalterably Chinese. In Singapore and Manila they are resented for their commercial shrewdness and their stubborn insistence on remaining Chinese. If their next-door neighbors can't change them, what reason is there to believe that the tourists of Hong Kong can do so?

There are certain comic aspects to the relations of the British and Chinese in Hong Kong. Living side-by-side for 121 years, they have told each other—sometimes directly, more often by implication—"You can't change me!" To a large extent, they have both held out, like a silent couple eating at opposite ends of a long dinner table. Lately the table has been contracting, but the prospects of a cozy twosome are still somewhat distant.

Meanwhile, the Chinese go on living by their own calendar, celebrating festivals and family events according to their traditions, and following their ancient religions. The rural people cling to their belief in fung shui (literally, wind and water), a form of geomancy which guides them in locating their houses and burial places on the particular site most pleasing to the living and the dead. On the other hand, the old superstitious fear of Western medicine has been overcome; in the 1961 Hong Kong cholera outbreak, 80 percent of the population flocked to government centers for inoculations.

Neither the British, the Nationalist Republic, nor the Chinese Communists—all of whom favor the 12-month Western calendar—have been able to wean the colony's Chinese people from their ancient lunar calendar. The old calendar was supposedly devised in 2254 B.C. by astrologers working under the orders of Emperor Yao, who wanted it to serve as a crop-planting guide for his predominantly agricultural subjects. It is the gauge by which all festivals are set and varies in length from 354 to 385 days. The years proceed in cycles of twelve, each being named for a particular animal such as the rat, rabbit, rooster and horse until the twelfth animal is reached and the cycle repeats. Each year is subdivided into 24 solar "joints and breaths," which being based on close observation of weather and the growing season, tick off the seasonal changes with remarkable accuracy.

Because of its variable length and its nonconformity to Western ideas of what a calendar should look like, the Chinese calendar causes endless confusion for foreigners. Most of them cling firmly to the Gregorian calendar and keep a close eye on the colony's newspapers to learn when the next festival is due. The religious significance of the festival means nothing to them and it does not need to; the ceremonies and celebrations attending the day are so animated and colorful that they can be enjoyed for their spectacle alone.

Chinese New Year, generally occurring between the middle of January and the third week of February, is celebrated on the first three days of the First Moon. It marks the beginning of spring, and gives the Chinese population sufficient time to recover from the shock of seeing the Westerners

booze it up on New Year's Eve. Chinese employees receive a
bonus of an extra month's pay, the shops close and firecrackers, permitted by colony law for a two-day period, keep
up an unending cannonade. A tourist wandering into the up-
roar feels like a dude in a frontier saloon; everybody seems to
be shooting at his feet.

Red papers lettered with gold are stuck on boats and the
doors of shops and houses inviting the lucky spirits to lend a
hand. The fearful din of the firecrackers is a pointed hint to
malicious spirits, advising them to get out fast. All debts are
paid, finances permitting, and the past year's feuds and
grudges are wiped out, so far as human nature will allow.

The heart of the observance takes place in the home, with
all members of the family dining together on the last night of
the old year and the children receiving "lucky" money in red
envelopes to assure them of safe passage through the coming
year. After dinner, everyone adjourns to the courtyard where
branches of sesame, fir and cypress have been strewn; these
are stepped on and burned as a symbol of the departing year.
Firecrackers are set off to discourage the prowlings of the
Skin Tiger, a kind of reverse-action Robin Hood who steals
the cakes of the poor to give them to the rich; as the Skin
Tiger views it, the poor have lived off the wealthy all year,
so isn't it time to square accounts?

A lighted lamp is placed before the shrine of the Kitchen
God, who is expected back from his trip to divine headquarters. Every door is sealed and locked until 5 A.M. the next day,
when the entire household gets up to see the master of the
house reopen the doors, remove the seals and extend a welcome to the New Year. Incense sticks are lighted, Heaven,
Earth and the family ancestors are honored and the Kitchen
God, now returned from his journey, is properly greeted.

New Year's Day is the occasion for a complete family re-union, with outsiders being excluded. No meat is eaten, since the use of a knife on this day would imply cutting off a friend-ship, and no sweeping is done, for a broom might sweep away good luck. Later, gifts are exchanged, with baskets of food being rated as thoroughly acceptable. The season's greetings —"Kung Hei Fat Choy"—ring out everywhere.

In Hong Kong, a local newspaper and the radio promote a Fat Choy Drive to provide a New Year's feast for even the poorest families. When the family phase of the celebration is over, there is a day for visiting friends, and with true Chinese practicality, a final day to worship the God of Wealth, mak-ing certain that he does everything divinely possible in the year ahead to boost the family's fortunes. In former days it was customary to prolong the observance for fifteen days or more, but the demands of modern business limit it to three or four days in most instances.

The birthday of Kuan Yin, the Buddhist Goddess of Mercy, is celebrated on the 19th day of the Second Moon, and she is regarded with such affection that practically all of the Taoist temples honor her as well. Legend describes her as the young-est daughter of an ancient prince who attempted to force her into marriage to perpetuate the family line. She objected, was murdered by her father in some ambiguous fashion and de-scended to Hell, where by sheer charm she transformed the place into a paradise. Returned to earth, she found her father dying of a skin disease and cut off parts of her own body to preserve his unworthy hide. Women are especially devoted to her, bearing birthday gifts of food, paper clothing, chickens and roast pig to her image in the temples. Until the thirteenth century, Kuan Yin was often represented as a male divinity, probably with the connivance of early defenders of male prerogatives, but she has become exclusively female since then, for only as a woman could she possess an ear sympathetically attuned to the troubles of mortal women.

The Ching Ming Festival, occurring toward the end of the Second Moon or at the beginning of the Third Moon (late March or early April in our calendar), provides an occasion to honor one's ancestors. The worship of ancestors is the keystone of Chinese religious beliefs, as well as the strongest link binding them together as a single people. Its profound influence on every phase of Chinese life is seldom fully appreciated by foreigners, who regard it as morbid, backward-looking and intellectually sterile. But even foreigners in Hong Kong share some of the Ching Ming spirit by using the day to tidy up the graves of their own departed and place flowers by the headstones.

The Chinese do no cooking and eat no hot food on the day preceding Ching Ming, acting in deference to a long-gone official who was accidentally burned to death by his dunder-headed confreres. Women and children wear a sprig of willow on the day itself to safeguard themselves against the posthumous horror of returning to this life in the form of dogs. The family visits its ancestral graves, makes any needed repairs and sets out a feast for the dead. Paper replicas of money and clothing are burned to let the deceased know that their interests are being looked after, and a little diversionary fire is lighted nearby to distract evil spirits and keep them from butting into the main sacrifice. Having made its gesture of feeding the dead, the family then falls to and eats the feast itself.

Because land is scarce in the colony, graves are rented only for a limited period. Six or seven years after a member of the family has died, his survivors obtain an exhumation permit and visit the grave on Ching Ming to dig up his coffin. The bones are removed from the coffin, carefully sorted and cleaned with sandpaper, and packed into an earthenware urn with the skull on top. The undertaker, accompanied by members of the family, then removes the urn to a hillside site in the New Territories, selecting a location with a favorable fung shui, where the deceased presumably will be able to enjoy a pleasant view.

Chinese coffins are a massive, rough-hewn product, resembling a four-leaf clover in outline; if they are still in sound condition after their first tenant is evicted, they may be resold at a discount for rehabilitation and put to use again.

Many Occidentals would pale at the thought of sandpapering and reassembling the last of Aunt Matilda, but the Chinese entertain no such qualms. They take a calm and realistic view of death, handling the bones of the dead with complete respect, but without morbidity or gloom. Ching Ming is a time of remembrance rather than lamentation.

T'ien Hou, the Taoist Queen of Heaven, celebrates her birthday on the 23d day of the Third Moon. For the boat people, it is the most important festival of the year; T'ien Hou is their chief patron, keeping her benign eye on such matters as a good catch and fair weather. Her shrines are in the cabin of every junk, and her 24 temples stand in every village that overlooks the sea. In her earthly days, the story goes, she was a fisherman's daughter. Once she fell into a trance while her parents were far out at sea. Dreaming that a storm was about to drown them, she roused herself and pointed directly at their boat. It was the only one in the fleet to return safely.

Her ship-saving talents led directly to her deification, and she has since acquired two invaluable assistants, Thousand-Mile Eyes and Fair-Wind Ears. Her principal temple is at Joss

House Bay on Tung Lung Island, about two miles east of Hong Kong Island. On her birthday, an all-day ferry service brings her worshippers from the main island, and the boat people arrive in sea-trains of junks towed by a launch, flying dozens of flags and Happy-Birthday banners. Every boat is packed to the gunwales with men, women and children jostling one another as they reach for sweet cakes, tea and soft drinks. At Joss House Bay, the passengers swarm ashore as if the boats were about to sink and climb a wide granite stairway to the temple. Incense sticks are lighted, roasted animals and red eggs are placed before the Goddess and a small contribution is handed to the temple attendant.

Bursting firecrackers, lion dances and processions enliven the celebration until the men of the various fishing guilds wind it up with a hot scramble for "the luck," a bamboo projectile with a number inside. It drops into the crowd like a bride's bouquet, but the free-for-all that follows is no place for a bridesmaid. The winning team makes the year's luck and gets possession of an elaborate portable shrine to the Queen of Heaven. Rich and poor, humble and great join without class distinction in having a gossipy, boisterous holiday.

The people of Cheung Chau feel obliged to say a kind word for all the animals and fish who were executed to feed mankind during the past year, and this debt is squared by the four-day Bun Festival on their dumbbell-shaped island. Its date is set by lot, and usually falls in the last few days of the Third Moon or the first ten days of the Fourth Moon. No animals are killed and no fish are caught during the festival. Troupes of actors are imported to perform in an enormous temporary theater, with its roof of coarse matting supported on a bamboo framework tied together with rattan strips. Daily and nightly presentations of Cantonese Opera are put on with the performers in elaborate costumes, shrilling their lines above the tireless clamor of cymbals.

The festival centerpiece consists of a triple-peaked bun mountain, or conical framework covered with varicolored buns from its base to its 60-foot summit. As soon as it is completed, it is covered with a tarpaulin to protect the buns until the climactic ceremony on the final day of the festival.

The various guilds on the islands compete in a long procession which passes under floral arches on the village streets. The perennial feature of the procession is a series of tableaux enacted by children on platforms borne on the shoulders of several men. The subjects are mythological, and by the ingenious use of a well-concealed steel framework, make a mere toddler appear to be dancing nimbly on the tip of a fiddle held by a child standing beneath the dancer. It's all an amiable fake, understood as such by the crowd, but executed with such aplomb by the children that it never fails to delight the spectators. Images of Gods and Goddesses are also carried in the line of march, with lion dancers and clowns to add further excitement. A mass for the recently departed fish and animals is celebrated on the final night, and their hungry souls are permitted to take a few ghostly nips at the bun mountain. An officiating priest decides when they've had enough, takes a careful look around to see that no latecomers from the Great Beyond have been neglected, and signals the slavering bystanders to pitch in. The young men of the island scramble up the bunny slopes in a mad dash for the topmost bun, but there are thousands of edibles at all levels, so no climber need go hungry.

The Dragon Boat Festival, coming on the fifth day of the Fifth Moon (late May to late June), probably attracts more attention from the foreign population than any other Chinese celebration. It is hotly competitive, pitting large teams of rowers against each other in all-day races at Aberdeen, Kennedy Town, Tai Po and elsewhere. The individual heats are short, close together and accompanied by loud cheers and the booming of the pace-setting drums in every boat. A carved dragon's head ornaments the bow and the stern is a simulated dragon's tail; in between lies 80 to 100 feet of low, fairly narrow hull, with the rowers flailing away in a fast circular stroke. The crews, who train for three or four weeks before the annual races, also keep the boats in shape, and one European crew that includes a number of government employees competes at Tai Po.

It was a government employee who gave rise to the festival in the fourth century, B.C. He was the honest Chu Yuan, an official who tried to persuade the Chinese Emperor to correct the corruption of his court; when his pleas were ignored, he drowned himself by leaping into the Nih Loh River. A group of sympathetic villagers rowed out to the site and cast silk-wrapped dumplings into the water, hoping to attract his wandering spirit, or in another version of the legend, to lure the fish away and protect his body from their attack. The bow man of today's Dragon Boats preserves the tradition by casting rice cakes or dumplings wrapped with bamboo leaves from his craft. The principles of cleanliness exemplified by Chu Yuan are practiced a few days in advance of the races, when every family cleans house and sets off firecrackers to stampede lurking cockroaches into panicky flight. The races themselves exercise a purifying influence, for most of the rowers are thoroughly drenched by the splashing paddles.

The Mid-Autumn Festival, celebrated on the 15th day of the Eighth Moon, belongs entirely to women, and is marked by them in the privacy of the home. The feminine principle in nature is in the ascendant and the moon, which is considered a female deity, is at the apogee. A table is set in the courtyard, and the moon is offered gifts of tea, food, burning incense and the seed of the water calthrop. The service takes place at night, illuminated by lanterns and moonlight, and includes a prayer to the honored satellite, who is also quizzed about the matrimonial prospects of her devotees. Fruit and moon cakes are essential to the feast that follows, and as always, fire-crackers are exploded. Wealthier households may set up a midnight moon-viewing party, with a banquet and a group of blind musicians singing an ode to the moon. These blind musicians, numbering about 100 in all, have their own colony at the west end of Hong Kong Island and earn about $12 for a party booking. Recorders and lutes are their usual intruments, giving their music a quaint Elizabethan flavor.

Ancestral graves are visited for the second time each year on the ninth day of the Ninth Moon; summer weeds and grass are cleared away and sacrifices of money and clothing are offered to keep the deceased wealthy and warm through the coming winter. The date coincides with that of the Cheung Yung Festival, when it is said to be lucky to climb to a high place. Burial urns rest fairly high on the hillsides, so it is easy to combine both celebrations and top them off with a picnic in the open.

On Cheung Yung, thousands of Chinese ride up Victoria Peak on the tram, buying toys and other presents for the children at improvised stalls along the way. Picnickers cover the top of every hill in the colony. Kite-flyers observe the day by the curious sport of kite-fighting, which involves manipulating one kite so that it knocks another out of the sky or snaps its string. The hill-climbing custom supposedly began when a Chinese father of long ago saved his family from a plague by taking them into the mountains.

A veritable regiment of gods, ghosts and spirits—some beneficent, some wicked—have their special observances during the year. Buddhist and Taoist deities have a tendency to overlap, just as followers of Taoism may be equally ardent Buddhists. Once the two religions battled and persecuted each other like the religions of the West, but they have long since settled down to peaceful coexistence. There is no reliable count of their membership in Hong Kong, though the Buddhists claim around 500,000 adherents. An unspecified, but probably small number of Chinese are Buddhists, Taoists and Christians simultaneously, or at least they consider themselves so.

Confucianism also has its following in the colony, but its places of worship are generally merged with Buddhist and Taoist temples.

Roman Catholic and Protestant missionaries have been at work in Hong Kong from its beginning as a colony, founding schools and caring for the poor. Neither group made much headway in attracting converts until the late 1940s, perhaps because of the ironbound Chinese resistance to every form of foreign influence. But the Communist regime on the mainland has proved a stimulant to Christianity in Hong Kong.

The well-financed and highly effective work of Protestant churches, particularly among refugees from Red China, has won them many converts, and the number of Protestant parishes has greatly increased in the last few years. Anglicans, Methodists, Baptists, Presbyterians, Lutherans and other denominations have made substantial gains.

The number of Roman Catholics, who are equally active in educational and welfare fields, has grown from 43,000 in 1951 to 180,000 in 1962. They are currently making about 15,000 converts a year, and 12,000 of these are adults. Some of their mission priests, who have found conversions much more difficult to achieve in Japan, believe that the terror and hopelessness of life under the Chinese Communists have turned many Chinese refugees to Christianity. Enrollment in Catholic schools of the colony is well over 100,000, and two-thirds of their enrollment is non-Catholic. Like every other Christian group in the colony, the Catholics have given help without drawing denominational lines.

The Portuguese, of whom there are about 2,000 in Hong Kong, are the descendants of former Macao settlers who arrived with the first wave of British traders, acting as their interpreters. They were adaptable, quick with figures and gifted linguists, establishing themselves as clerk-interpreters in business and financial houses. A few invested wisely in land and became millionaires. In more recent years, they have turned to professional work, becoming lawyers, doctors and engineers. Starting with J. P. Braga in 1929, the Portuguese community has had several representatives on the Executive and Legislative Councils. Its present outstanding leaders, in addition to professional people, include exchange brokers, importers and exporters and manufacturers' agents.

A second wave of Portuguese came to the colony from Macao after World War II, hoping to discover the business opportunities denied by the sleepy, static little overseas province of Portugal. But they faced stiff competition from young Chinese women who had entered office work and had received superior English education in the colony schools. Few had been to college and they lacked the drive demanded by the rough-and-tumble economy of Hong Kong; before long, most of the new arrivals moved on to Canada, Brazil or the United States.

Indians, including Parsees, Bhohras, Khwojas, Sindhis and Sikhs, came to Hong Kong in the early days as traders, soldiers and policemen. Today they are primarily merchants and traders, although there are still a few Indian and Pakistani residents who preserve their uniformed role as policemen, soldiers, or private guards for banks and financial houses. The Indian community is about the same size as the Portuguese—between 2,000 and 3,000—and like it, has produced a few top-level government officials, doctors and lawyers, and millionaire merchants.

Americans are still a very small minority, but they have money and a keen appetite to make more. If they also have ability, they fit smoothly into the competitive economy of the colony. The importance of American aid, both private and public, in caring for the colony's refugees is deeply appreciated by both the government and the Chinese population, and the effect is only slightly marred when some Yankee tourist tries to give the impression that it all came out of his personal funds. Such tourists, it may be noted, are exceptional.

Despite their historical background of anticolonial insurrection, Americans have been well received in Hong Kong during most of its existence. It was once said that a young Hong Kong Englishman could not marry outside the charmed circle of the British Isles, Canada or Australia unless he chose an American girl; otherwise, he would lose his social position and probably his job. This has not been true for some years now, but it leaves a lingering question in the minds of some Americans: Why did they include us rebels?

Another question that occurs to almost every American

who has seen the colony is: How do 15,000 British run this place? (Actually, there are about 33,000 people from all parts of the British Commonwealth living in Hong Kong, but the ruling group comes from the British Isles and barely exceeds 15,000.) It is evident from the most perfunctory glance around the streets that the British do run Hong Kong; autocratically, efficiently, firmly, sometimes unimaginatively, never with any pretense of popular rule, but almost always with strict justice. There is contained corruption, but less of it than anywhere else in the Far East. At times an unwonted conviction of Britannic righteousness roils the overseas visitor. This reaction is often encountered in one type of American who insists he does not want to run the world, and means he wants it run his way—by somebody else.

Americans are quite surprised when they strike the unexpected vein of iron that lies under the polished surface of British manners. These British are tough people; disciplined, well-educated, capable of decision and resolute action. Because they possess these qualities to a degree unexcelled and perhaps unmatched by any other country in the world, the British in Hong Kong are a corporal's guard commanding an army.

But one might pause here to consider the young American woman who stood at the rail of an excursion boat in Hong Kong harbor, looking wistfully up at Government House, the seat of majesty.

"If only they were a little more lovable!" she said.

CHAPTER NINE

Rambling around the Colony

"The journey of a thousand miles commences with a single step."
—CHINESE PROVERB

At the upper terminus of the Peak Tram, two-thirds of the way up Victoria Peak, a narrow promenade called Lugard Road winds around the mountain until its name changes to Harlech Road and then continues along the south face of the mountain to return to the Peak Tram terminus. By strolling along this route on a fine clear day, a visitor can see the whole of Hong Kong stretching out in all directions.

Often the view is cut off by thick jungle growth, stretching over the road like the green arches of a natural cathedral. But there are narrow gaps and occasional wide, treeless spaces where the stroller can look up the rocky slopes to discover the mansions of the Taipans, jutting through the tangled trees. Rococo palaces of pink, yellow, and dazzling white stand isolated from one another and the life of the community by the intertwining trees that hide their approach roads. Their isolation is fortified by barbed-wire fences, warning signs and snarling watchdogs. The only uninvited guest that breaches these barriers is the heavy mist that envelops the Peak above the fog line for six months of the year, covering furniture and clothes with green mold unless drying closets and dehumidifiers are kept in full operation.

Once the British held exclusive title to the foggy heights; in the days before auto roads were built to the top, they chartered the Peak Tram to carry their party guests to its upper end, where they were met by sedan chairs which took them the rest of the way. Now Chinese millionaires share the majesty and the mist of the Peak, and there are tall apartment buildings for more exalted government employees and prosperous civilians.

To tourists and Taipans, the heights of Victoria Peak offer a matchless view of the harbor. The distant deep-blue water crinkles in the wind as the sun glints on its surface. Dozens of ferryboats point their arrowhead wakes at Hong Kong Island and Kowloon, or head outward for the coasts and islands of the New Territories. An American aircraft carrier rides at anchor off Wanchai with its escort vessels near at hand.

West of Kowloon Peninsula, a triple line of cargo ships turn lazily around their anchor buoys; each one having enough room to make a full circle without touching another ship. Six rows of junks and sampans, each row lashed to the sides of a freighter while they transfer its cargo, move in unison with the freighter's slow swing, looking like a gargantuan, improvised raft. Unattached junks duck in and out, anywhere and everywhere, clearly with the special blessings of T'ien Hou, for they rarely collide.

North of the harbor, beyond the wedge-shaped outline of Kowloon, past the Kai Tak airstrip that cuts through Kowloon Bay like the white streak of a torpedo, is Hong Kong's "Great Wall"—a line of hills that looms jagged and forbidding across the southern fringe of the New Territories. These are the "nine dragons" from which Kowloon got its name, but they are difficult to single out, except for unmistakable ones like Lion Rock and Kowloon Peak, because they are so tightly packed together.

Even Ti Ping, the Sung Emperor who was prodded into naming them the Nine Dragons, complained that he could find only eight, until an obliging courtier reminded him that the dragon is the symbol of the Emperor, thus making him the ninth peak. Ti Ping, quite young at the time, was placated by this rationalization.

Due west of Victoria Peak, small islands string out like steppingstones until the eye stops at the ridge-backed mass of Lantau, largest island in the colony and nearly twice the size of Hong Kong Island. Some of the defeated followers of Ti Ping are reported to have settled there after the death of their Emperor, but until a few years ago it was a barren and remote isle, inhabited only by a few thousand farmers and fishermen and a few monasteries.

Halfway down the western slope of Victoria Peak, a small mound of earth thrusts itself against the mountainside. Dong Kingman, the Chinese-American watercolorist who grew up in the crowded tenements at the foot of the Peak, recalls that he and his young friends used to watch that mound with considerable apprehension. From where they stood, it looked exactly like a turtle climbing the mountain. The Chinese consider it to be a real turtle, and believe that when the turtle reaches the summit of the Peak, Hong Kong will sink into the sea. Dong and his fellow-watchers made regular checks to see that the turtle hadn't stolen an overnight march on them.

The most beautiful side of Hong Kong Island lies to the south and east of Victoria Peak, with forested hillsides and a green valley that slopes down to Pok Fu Lam, the colony's first reservoir. Lamma Island, a favorite digging ground for colony archaeologists, looms large to the south.

When visitors grow squint-eyed from the panoramic view, they often wind up their excursion by stopping at the little restaurant near the Peak Tram terminus to eat a sandwich or some Chinese small cakes. Spirits revived, they linger on the breezy terrace to watch the sun go down beyond Lantau.

The Peak Tram is almost as famous as Victoria Peak, and needs no endorsement except to note that its fares are very low and that it hasn't had an accident since 1888. In eight minutes, the tram carries its passengers down to the edge of the Central District, where they may catch a bus or a taxi.

Government House and the Botanic Garden are just across Garden Road from the lower end of the Peak Tram. Looking like a Franciscan Mission of early California with its white walls and square tower, Government House is the private residence of the colony governor. The sightseer may look around the outside, and with luck, see all hands snap to when the governor's black sedan enters or leaves the circular driveway, displaying red crowns at front and rear instead of license plates. The English manage their official exits and entrances with great style, and everything moves precisely on time.

The Botanic Garden is a kind of split-level Eden planted with thousands of subtropical plants and flowers. Its small zoo and aviary are popular with children, and the bird collection is a bright splash of brilliant colors. Small signs in English and Chinese identify the plants and animals. A good deal of family snapshot-taking goes on around the fountain at the lower end of the garden. It might be a scene in New York's Central Park, except that Chinese children are better behaved.

Albert Path, a serpentine walk shaded by tropical shrubbery, winds down from the Botanic Garden past Government House to Ice House Street and the rear of the First National City Bank. Ice House Street continues downward a couple of blocks to the West Wing of the Central Government offices at Queen's Road Central.

On Battery Path, directly in front of the West Wing, a lampshade stand operates on what is obviously government property. It's all quite official; the owner has a permit from the Department of Public Works. Sin Hoi, late father of the present owner, Sin Hung, had sold lampshades on the site for thirteen years before the West Wing was built in 1954. Lady Maurine Grantham, wife of the former governor, was a frequent shopper at the stand, and when she saw it threatened with displacement by the government offices, she put in a word for Sin Hoi. His son now runs it under the grand name of The Magnific Company, selling lampshades and small china animals.

One block north on Ice House Street and a block east on Des Voeux Road is Statue Square, where parked cars outnumber the statues 200 to 1. This area is more than the center of the colony's financial institutions; it is an ideal cross-section of colony architecture. The honeycomb-and-gingerbread design of the Hong Kong Club is typical of what most of the colony's buildings looked like in 1890, as is the Prince's Building on the opposite side of the square.

Post-World War II buildings like Union House, two blocks west along the waterfront, represent a kind of "no nonsense modern"—big, plain and blocky. The tower of the Bank of

China, just east of the Hongkong and Shanghai Bank, rises massively above its old established neighbor. The Red Chinese operate it now and many of its upper offices are vacant; the bank itself is a quiet institution with fewer guards than most local banks have. The Chartered Bank, on the other side of the Hongkong and Shanghai Bank, is the newest, tallest and most curious of the three moneyed giants, with a fortresslike tower and a green façade that resembles a vast electronic switchboard.

The Hongkong and Shanghai building, older than either of the banks beside it, surpasses them in architectural distinction, with its bold vertical lines and its solid central tower surrounded by lower wrap-around structures and crowned by a ziggurat roof that tapers upward like a truncated pyramid. It looks like a building that nothing could push over, which seems the right emphasis for a bank.

Directly south of the Hong Kong Club lie three and a half acres of the most valuable land in the colony, all of it laid out in cricket fields except for a small corner occupied by the building of the Hong Kong Cricket Club. If the land were for sale, bidding would start at about $175 a square foot; but the British would as soon sell the playing fields of Eton. Cricket is an integral part of life under the Union Jack. Most Americans find it too strenuous, even as a spectator sport; they often become exhausted by the effort of trying to figure it out.

If a visitor drops by the Cricket Club on any Saturday morning between October and April, he can scarcely find the cricketers for the red-and-white-capped youngsters bounding about in various sectors of the field, playing a dozen different games without apparent confusion. All the players are from four to twelve years old; mostly boys, with a few girls here and there. It is the weekly workout of the Tingle Athletic Association, one of the colony's honored institutions. Billy Tingle, an ex-boxer and lifetime physical culture instructor, has taught 50,000 children to kick, throw, catch, swim and master the rudiments of cricket, soccer, rugby and basketball. Billy is a short, compactly built man about sixty, who speaks softly but accepts no back talk; discipline is as much a part of the job as athletic skill, he believes.

Parents are permitted to look on from the grandstand while Billy and his nine assistants put 350 children through a three-hour workout. These are "upper-class" boys and girls, but Billy also conducts classes among the shack dwellers in Wanchai. The colony's schools, with 700,000 pupils, often resort to three daily shifts to accommodate them. Very few schools can afford any physical training program.

At the seaward end of Statue Square, the government has remedied a deficiency of many years by erecting a City Hall, a five-unit complex with a 12-story tower, concert hall, theater, banquet hall, library, museum, art gallery and municipal offices. Architecturally, it is modern, rectangular and unadorned, in sharp contrast to the curlicues of the Hong Kong Club next door. Part of the hall was opened in 1962, with the rest planned for completion in 1963. Sir Malcolm Sargent and the London Philharmonic Orchestra launched the concert hall with suitable fanfare, presumably ending the long, lean era in which visiting artists had to go from one private hall to another, hoping that music lovers would find them.

The Star Ferry terminal, right beside City Hall at the waterfront, is the tie that binds Kowloon and Hong Kong Island together. Every day, 100,000 commuters cross the harbor on these spotless new boats at a first-class fare of 3½ cents or second-class at less than 2 cents. The ferry stops running at 1:30 A.M. on most nights, and for the late prowler it's a "walla

walla" and a 50-cent trip on this rolling, pitching, cross-harbor motor launch. Walla-walla is the Cantonese equivalent of "yak-yak," and memorializes the endless bickering over fares that the launch owners indulged in before a flat rate was set by the government. Sir Lancelot, the Calypso King who plays many Hong Kong engagements, was trapped on one of these wallowing tubs and composed a "Walla Walla Calypso," celebrating "the rockin' and the rollin' and the quakin' and the shakin' " they inflict on night owls.

Walla-wallas and sightseeing boats operate from the Queen's Pier in Hong Kong and the Public Pier in Kowloon, both less than a block east of the Star Ferry terminals. There is more of the flavor of the old days at Blake Pier, a few hundred feet west of the Star Ferry terminal on the Hong Kong side. Private yachts and mailboats discharge there, and there's always a bustle of arrivals and departures. But the colony's reclamation scheme will before long swallow up Blake Pier and its works. The General Post Office, a moldering antique opposite Blake Pier, is also to be replaced soon; until it goes, it is a handy place to mail packages or to buy Hong Kong government publications.

Wyndham Street, which runs south off Queen's Road Central, is the last resting place of another antique, the sedan chair, which was the favored conveyance when roads were too steep or too rough for rickshaws. Of the four registered sedan chairs left in the colony, two are generally parked there, waiting patiently for a fare. A few of the older Chinese residents still use them, but Europeans have grown chair-shy, possibly worried about what kind of picture they present while riding between two poor fellows panting along in the traces. And well they might be.

A line of rickshaws also parks along Wyndham Street, but

their business is better than that of the sedan chairs. Tourists and many Chinese continue to hire them; tourists enjoy the picturesque novelty and the Chinese find them practical for funeral processions or for hauling packages too large to carry on a bus or tram without causing a riot. Police report 866 registered rickshaws, with the number declining each year. Many people shun them as degrading and inhumane; others are unwilling to risk their lives by weaving through motor traffic in such a flimsy craft. Rickshaw drivers, subjected to alternate sweating and cooling, are particularly vulnerable to tuberculosis.

The alleys and side streets of the Central District are a source of wonder and surprise to tourists. Pedder Lane, branching off Pedder Street directly opposite the Gloucester Hotel, is lined with open-air cobblers. Hundreds of shoes, mended and unmended, are racked behind the repair stands, and the cobblers are as busy as Kris Kringle's toy-builders on December 23d. Shoeshine Alley, a short section of Theater Lane which runs from the west end of Pedder Lane to Des Voeux Road Central, has ten to a dozen shoeshine boys stationed along the pavement. Customers stand in the alley with richshaws and motorbikes brushing their coattails while they get shoeshines.

Shoeshine Alley is no silent workshop; a steady stream of walla-walla flies back and forth among the boys, and if a passing pedestrian pauses or glances in their direction, several boys pounce on him, demanding his patronage. The moment he selects one lad for the job, the others shower the winner with Cantonese insults and heckle him while he works. The victim pays no attention; it's an accepted professional hazard. Besides, the boy is too busy studying the customer, trying to decide whether he's an American. Americans are easy marks;

always willing to pay three times the going rate. With an American, the canny lad can simply say "thanks" and pocket twice as much change as he's entitled to. Fifty cents Hong Kong or 8½ cents American is a generous rate, but few Yankee tourists seem conscious of the local scale.

For the tourist whose curiosity extends beyond the Central District, one of the major departure points is the Hongkong and Yaumati Vehicular Ferry Pier, four blocks west of Pedder Street, at Connaught Road and in front of the Fire Brigade Building. Several different passengers ferry lines and the Kowloon truck-and-auto ferry use the pier. The paved area at the pier entrance is the main depot for bus routes to all parts of Hong Kong Island.

Until the new Hang Seng Bank building was erected, the Li Po Chun Chambers was the tallest building on the western fringe of the Central District. The Foreign Correspondents' Club of Hong Kong occupies the penthouse of the building, named for its owner, seventy-five-year-old Li Po Chun, eighth son of Li Sing, late multimillionaire merchant who was a founder of the Tung Wah Hospital. Li Sing, one of the most colorful of Hong Kong's early Taipans, once donated $100,-000 for a flood-control project at San Wui, his native village in Kwangtung Province. About a century ago, when a foreign ship carrying thousands of Chinese to California struck a rock near Hong Kong, he chartered a steamer, stocked it with food and sent it to the rescue, saving everyone aboard the stranded vessel.

The Central Market, a bare concrete building located a block south of the Vehicular Ferry Pier, offers every kind of meat, vegetable, fish or fowl eaten by the people of Hong Kong. Everything is fresh, because Chinese customers reject any sort of tired produce. It exudes a wide range of smells, with fish out-smelling all the rest. An inexperienced shopper must move cautiously or he may be sideswiped by a hog carcass as it bounces along on a man's shoulders en route from a delivery truck to one of the meat stands.

Visitors who grow tired of walking may increase their range by riding the Hong Kong Tramway. Its green, double-decked streetcars cover the full length of the island waterfront. First-class passengers sit on the upper deck, where the fare is 3½ cents. Starting from the Central District, the car marked "Kennedy Town" goes the farthest west, and the Shau Kei Wan car runs to the eastern extremity of the line.

The trolley tourist may hop off the car at any corner that interests him. In the evening, the street market beside the Macao Ferry Pier on the western waterfront presents a pavement-level carnival. Merchandise is spread out on the asphalt paving—combs, flashlights, toys, food and clothing—with gasoline lanterns lighting the scene. Several spaces are reserved for pitchmen who, though they speak in Cantonese, are obviously delivering a spiel about products guaranteed to double the customer's life-span, make him an eternal delight to women and quadruple his earning power—all at prices so low it would be folly not to snap them up.

The tram shuts down around midnight, but there is hardly an hour of day or night when street stands are not open. Families run most of them, with each member taking his turn at waiting on trade. Children are on the streets all night—sometimes because they have no place else to go. The 1961 census turned up thousands of families who rented a bedspace for eight hours a day, sharing it with two other families entitled to the same eight-hour shift. When one family is asleep in the cubicle, the other two are either working or wandering the streets. Visitors must walk carefully in the Western District at night, not for fear of attack, but to avoid sidewalk sleepers.

During racing days of the October to May season at Happy Valley Jockey Club, every tram is packed. Not far from the jockey club on the tram line is Victoria Park, finest of the colony's public recreation grounds. A statue of Queen Victoria overlooks the park, honoring the royal matron who treated the acquisition of Hong Kong as a family joke. The Causeway Bay Typhoon Shelter raises a forest of masts and spars at the seaward edge of the park.

Happy Valley, studded with schools, sports arenas, cemeteries and hospitals, comes down to the waterfront at Wanchai. The tightly packed tenements of Wanchai have refugee shacks on their rooftops and rows of sailors' bars and cabarets at street level. When night comes on, subsidized intimacy is available on every street corner, but the eleven movie theaters in the area are less expensive.

North Point, the next waterfront community east of Wanchai, is the "Little Shanghai" that boomed after 1949, when refugee industrialists from Shanghai established factories there. It has a prospering night life zone along King's Road, and introduced "key clubs" to the colony. These were semiprivate bar-and-girl flats to which the member gained admission by paying $50 to $100 for a key. The clubs spread to the Central District and Kowloon before police raids began to hit them. A number survive, drawing their clientele from open-handed tourists and tired but hopeful businessmen. In contrast to these nocturnal playpens, some of the best new housing projects line the North Point waterfront.

To the east of North Point, the towering cranes of the Tai Koo Dockyards jut up along the shore. Shau Kei Wan, at the end of the tram line, is a fishing and junk-building center.

Tram lines don't serve the towns and resorts on the south side of the island; to reach these, the tourist must take buses, taxis or guided tours.

The south shore town of Aberdeen is important to the colony as a fishing and marketing center, but visitors will remember it for its floating sampan population and its floating seafood restaurants, the Sea Palace and the Tai Pak Fong. The latter, decorated with unsparing flamboyance, are dazzlingly outlined in lights after dark. Fish dinners are netted from large tanks at the rear of the restaurants. The service is as much a part of show business as it is of the food trade. Both branches are represented on the dinner check.

There are two ways for the visitor to reach the floating restaurants. The first is to take a taxi across the island to Aberdeen, then hail a girl-powered sampan for a short trip across the harbor. Another thoroughly luxurious way is to board the 110-foot luxury cruiser *Wan Fu* any evening at Queen's Pier or the Kowloon Public Pier, making the entire trip by sea around the west end of the island. The *Wan Fu*, a modern, Diesel-powered ship, is a fully rigged brigantine built along the lines of the early opium-trade escort vessels, with 18 simulated gun-ports on its sides. It makes the evening cruise to Aberdeen, stops for dinner at the Sea Palace, and returns to town about midnight. Cost of the meal and trip totals $10. Its skipper, Mike Morris, is a former Marine Police Inspector.

Aberdeen is on the regular itinerary of the daytime round-the-island automobile tours which take four hours. A car meets the traveler at the top of the Peak Tram, winds down the mountainsides to Happy Valley and includes a stop at Tiger Balm Gardens, the fantastic creation of Aw Boon Haw. The late Mr. Aw made his fortune by selling Tiger Balm— an "infallible" cure for every form of psychosomatic ill. He has furnished his gardens free-style, throwing in everything from folklore to scenes from the Buddhist Hell. There is even a 165-foot pagoda, which has repaid its cost a dozen times by its use on Hong Kong travel posters. The whole place is living proof of the swathe a Chinese millionaire can cut when he feels like splurging. Texans seem tame by comparison.

Mr. Aw's tastes were no more extravagant than those of Mr. Eu, who built two medieval castles on Hong Kong island —Eucliffe and Euston. Eucliffe is at Repulse Bay, a summer resort and the next stop on the island motor tour. The legend of Mr. Eu has several versions, but they generally agree that he was a Chinese who, several decades ago, settled in Malaya with his mother. When the two struck hard times, Mr. Eu felt that his fellow-Chinese were indifferent to the family's difficulties, and he vowed never to help other Chinese or to return to China—an extraordinary act for any Chinese. He indentured himself as a miner, saved enough to buy his freedom, and married a woman who owned a small grocery store. The couple pooled their earnings to buy an abandoned tin mine where he had formerly worked. Either he knew something or played a hunch, because the mine yielded rich quantities of ore that made him a millionaire.

But his mother never reconciled herself to his anti-Chinese vow and hired a fung shui expert who reported that the real trouble stemmed from the Eu family tomb, which faced south, away from China, influencing her son to turn his back on his homeland. The tomb was realigned to face north, and

Mr. Eu relaxed his anti-Chinese prejudices sufficiently to return to Hong Kong—if not to China.

He began erecting two enormous stone castles, acting on a Chinese belief that he would live as long as its building continued. Mr. Eu has passed on, but his castles survive. When completed, Eucliffe was crammed with European suits of armor and several upstairs rooms were hung with oil paintings of nudes. Euston, at 755 Bonham Road, on the northern slope of Victoria Peak, is a seven-storied anachronism. Its twin towers and mullioned windows give no evidence of Chinese design, but they may represent the Chinese reply to functional architecture.

Repulse Bay, with a curving beach and the luxurious Repulse Bay Hotel, is the colony's best-known summer resort. Like the upper Peak area, or Shek-O and Stanley in the southeast part of the island, it has many wealthy residents and large homes.

The auto tour passes Deep Water Bay Golf Club—one of several golf courses in Hong Kong—and the Dairy Farm, a major source of the colony's fresh milk. Queen Mary Hospital lies along the route near the west end of the island; an outstanding institution that emphasizes the scarcity of first-class hospitals in the colony. There are less than 10,000 hospital beds for 3,300,000 people, and the majority of the hospitals are overcrowded, understaffed, antiquated and well below first-class standards of care. The colony government is in the midst of a campaign to raise the capacity and standards of its hospitals, however. More than 1,000 beds are to be added by the end of 1963, but Hong Kong will remain well below English and American norms of hospital care.

Nevertheless, Hong Kong has made substantial medical progress during the last decade. Tuberculosis causes about eight times more deaths than all other infectious diseases, but the T.B. death rate has been reduced from 158.8 per 100,000 population in 1952 to 60.1 deaths per 100,000 in 1961.

Hong Kong University and the Chinese business section of the Western District are the last sightseeing attractions of the motor tour before it returns to the center of town. A motor trip around the island costs $7, plus the price of meals for the tourist and his driver-guide.

The Western District is seldom included on tourist maps of Hong Kong Island; the assumption seems to be that if a traveler ventures beyond the Central District, he will instantly be swallowed up by the earth. This assumption is twaddle. Jan Jan's Map of Hong Kong, sold at bus and ferry terminals, gives an excellent layout of the Western District, but even without its help, a sightseer may visit a number of places in the Western District without getting lost.

Pottinger Street, in the section running south off Queen's Road Central, has a lively array of ribbon, button and zipper stands. Cochrane Street, parallel to Pottinger and one block west of it, has a few stores selling silk "dragons" (actually, lions' heads). Such dragons, made to order, may cost as much as several hundred dollars each, and at least three weeks are required to fashion a large one.

These dragons, priced according to their overall length and elaborateness of detail, weave through the streets on Chinese holidays operated by a line of men marching under the flexible silk-covered framework.

Wing On Street, a dark narrow alley between Queen's Road Central and Des Voeux Road, is hemmed in on both sides by dozens of stands selling cotton and wool yard-goods. Everything is open to the street, and there is no charge for inspecting the bewildering assortment of cloth and color.

Goldsmiths' shops are strung along Queen's Road Central in the vicinity of the Kwong On Bank at Gilman's Bazaar. They stock every kind of gold jewelry—a particular favorite of Chinese women. But what the women enjoy most is sitting at the counters and gossiping with the clerks and shop owners. Such conversations often go on for as much as an hour, yet the dealer does not fly into a rage if the prospect fails to buy; it is even possible that the talk hardly touches on buying. Most women buy eventually; meanwhile, a pleasant exchange of gossip is enjoyed by both parties.

Wing Sing Street, running north off Queen's Road, is a cavernous alley resembling a silent-movie setting for a dark tale of Oriental intrigue. Actually, its most frightening characteristic is its nickname: "Rotten Egg Street." Piles of crates line its wholesale and retail egg stands, yet there is nothing to indicate that the eggs have lingered beyond their normal retirement age. The nickname is simply a local joke applied to all egg-selling streets.

A dozen or so glass-enclosed shops, each no larger than a pair of telephone booths, are located on Man Wa Lane, between Des Voeux Road and Wing Lok Street. All are engaged in cutting dies for business cards, seals and stamps, and the passer-by is welcome to watch their craftsmen at work.

Ladder Street, a flight of steps leading off Queen's Road Central, takes the inquisitive shopper to Upper Lascar Row, popularly called Cat Street. Cat Street's dingy shops sell everything from jade carvings to used bottles, from rare china to chipped and broken junk, valuable antiques to outright fakes. The customer has nothing but his own wits to protect him. Americans would be unduly optimistic to expect a Comprehensive Certificate of Origin from merchants who don't know and seldom care whether their goods are "hot" or legitimate. But Europeans who know Chinese antiques thoroughly have come to Cat Street, bargained shrewdly, and resold their purchases at home with sufficient profit to pay for their Hong Kong vacations.

Man Mo Temple, at 128-130 Hollywood Road, stands a short way back from the street. Buddha enjoys the most prominent altar in its gloomy interior, but the temple mixes Buddhist and Taoist elements, with Kwan Tai and Man Cheong as two of its honored deities. Legions of minor divinities line the walls, including several seated in tall, glass-enclosed boxes. In former days, such boxes were equipped with long handles so that the faithful could carry them through the streets in times of disaster to soothe the angry spirits.

Visitors are free to enter the temple if they behave as they would in any other house of worship. Straight and spiral incense sticks burn before the numerous shrines, and the many statues looming in dark corners suggest a spiritual serenity.

A more urgent reminder of other worlds may be had at the Tak Sau coffin shop, 252 Hollywood Road. Massive pine coffins, ordered in advance of the prospective occupant's death and tailored to his physical dimensions, are stacked about in plain sight. An ordinary model, costing from $50 to $150, can be turned out by a pair of carpenters in about 20 hours. The larger boxes once required 16 men to carry them, but modern trucks have now assumed the burden. A millionaire's coffin, lined with silk and elaborately carved, may cost $3,000 or more. To demonstrate their continuing concern for the departed, surviving relatives visit a nearby shop which sells notes written on the "Bank of Hell." No one likes to deliver these notes personally, and so they are burned to assure the deceased that his credit rating will be maintained in the spirit world.

Most of the Western District may be covered on foot, but taxis are necessary for trips to more distant points, such as Stanley or Shek-O, particularly at night. Drivers often have only a sketchy knowledge of English, but the passenger can usually make his destination clear by pointing to it on a road map, or by printing the address on a sheet of notepaper; if the driver cannot read it, he will find a colleague to translate it for him. Taxis are about 25 cents for the first mile and 18 cents for each succeeding mile on Hong Kong Island. Kowloon taxis are slightly lower. Holders of valid drivers' licenses from their home country, or international drivers' licenses, may hire cars for $11.50 a day or $70 a week, plus gasoline costs. In the English fashion, all cars have right-hand drive.

Sightseers operating on a tight budget may cover almost every part of the island on its 18 bus routes. Most of these start from the Vehicular Ferry Pier and their routes are fully outlined on the reverse side of Jan Jan's Map. Trams give smoother rides and more fequent service along the island's densely populated waterfront, but the only low-cost means of visiting outlying places, such as Shek-O, Stanley and Sandy Bay—all worth seeing—is by bus. This transportation is not for the timorous or those with queasy stomachs; Hong Kong bus-jockeys are competent, but they slam and jolt their passengers about as they whirl through a never-ending succession of upgrades, downgrades and hairpin turns.

Foreign passengers unfamiliar with Hong Kong public transportation may be startled at times to hear their fellow-riders yelling at one another. What sounds to a greenhorn like a violent exchange of insults is nothing more than cheerful gossip. The Cantonese are naturally gabby and exuberant, and only the Gwai-lo (foreign devil) seems subdued and inscrutable.

Transportation to Kowloon, directly across the harbor from Hong Kong Island, is by Star Ferry for most tourists, although there are many other trans-harbor ferries. The Star Ferry terminal in Kowloon is the focal point of practically every kind of transportation on the peninsula. Most Kowloon bus lines turn around directly in front of the ferry terminal. The Kowloon-Canton Railway, which runs through Kowloon and the New Territories to the Red Chinese border, is situated next to the bus terminal. Taxis and rickshaws start from the same area—a big, multiple loop that keeps vehicles moving with a minimum of congestion or delay. The Kowloon side of the colony has no streetcars, but its double-deck buses are almost as bulky as trams.

The greatest concentration of tourist shops and hotels is in the Tsim Sha Tsui section at the tip of the Kowloon Peninsula and within a five-minute walk of the Star Ferry terminal. Nine-tenths of the Kowloon hotels and luxury shops are strung along Nathan Road, the central thoroughfare, and its intersecting streets. At its best, Tsim Sha Tsui is a tourists' Happy Hunting Ground; at its worst, it is an outrageously over-priced deadfall.

The refugee resettlement estates spread across the upper end of the Kowloon Peninsula, several miles north of Tsim Sha Tsui. Visitors who want to see what has been done to help the colony's refugees—and to appreciate how much must still be undertaken—should visit the resettlement estates and the remaining squatter shacks with either a guide or an experienced Hong Kong welfare worker. The terrain is too irregular and the estates too extensive to be covered on foot.

Visitors with an archaeological turn of mind may want to

have a look at the Li Cheng Uk tomb in Sham Shui Po, about a mile north of the Kowloon-New Territories boundary. Workmen excavating for the Li Cheng Uk Resettlement Estate discovered the tomb in August, 1955. Its T-shaped chambers and barrel-vault roof containing pottery and bronze objects from the Later Han Dynasty (A.D. 25-220) and Six Dynasties (A.D. 220-589) indicate that the Chinese may have settled in Hong Kong and neighboring Kwangtung Province many centuries earlier than had been supposed. The colony government preserved the tomb by encasing it in an outer shell of concrete, built a small garden and museum around it, and opened it to the public in 1957.

A guided motor tour, probably the best way of seeing the New Territories, carries the visitor through the manufacturing center at Tsuen Wan, then west past the beaches and eroded hillsides to Castle Peak. The tour proceeds through some of the colony's best farmland to the marketing and shopping center at Yuen Long.

Brown cattle and water buffalo are the only aids to human labor on these farms, and every square foot of land is fertilized, weeded, irrigated and tilled with unsparing diligence. Walled cities, such as Kam Tin, appear along the way. Once they were fortresses to protect the farming families against marauding bands; today they are packed with poor people living in cubicles.

If border conditions are stable, the driver may continue to Lak Ma Chau, a hillside overlooking Red China's farming communes on the far side of the Sham Chun River. The return route is through the fishing settlement at Tai Po, with a view of Tolo Harbor, one of the finest in Hong Kong. In the Shatin Valley, with its intricate pattern of terraced rice fields, the sightseer may catch a glimpse of Amah Rock, a natural formation resembling a woman with an infant on her back.

Chinese legend depicts the rock as the survival of a woman whose husband left to fight in China many centuries ago. For days and months she climbed the hill and looked out to sea, awaiting her husband's return. Their child was born before she at last caught sight of her husband's ship, and she was so overcome by excitement and joy that she died on the spot. After her death, her neighbors were astonished to see a heap of rocks take on the appearance of a woman carrying a child on her back.

As the car passes through the reservoir area above Kowloon, a wild rhesus monkey of the surrounding forests may be seen begging for a roadside handout. Game of any kind is not abundant in the colony, but there are a few ferret-badgers, civet cats, otter, barking deer, rodents and an exceedingly rare leopard. There are 38 kinds of snakes, including the banded krait, king cobra and pit viper, although deaths from snake bites very seldom occur. Over 300 species of birds have been identified. Hundreds of kinds of tropical butterflies, including the Atlas Moth, with a maximum wingspread of nine inches, present the brightest specks on the countryside, sometimes covering a forest grove like an extra set of leaves.

Since Hong Kong embraces 237 islands besides the Kowloon Peninsula and the mainland portions of the New Territories, a tourist must take to the boats if he is to see more than a fraction of its varied topography. Boat service to the larger inhabited islands is fequent and cheap.

Every Saturday afternoon at 3 o'clock an excursion boat leaves the Vehicular Ferry Pier for a three-hour circuit of

Hong Kong Island. It cruises east along the waterfront, through Lei Yue Mun pass at the eastern harbor entrance, then turns south off the island's east coast. The rugged coast and fine homes of Shek-O are at the right, with the outlying islands of Tung Lung and Waglan at the left. The course swings past the south shore resort coast, around the west end of the island and back to the starting point. This trip, at 50 cents for adults and a quarter for children, is the sea-going bargain of Hong Kong.

A more leisurely round-island voyage, taking 4½ hours, leaves the Kowloon and Queens piers every morning, and includes a close-up of the Yau Ma Tei Typhoon Shelter on the west side of Kowloon Peninsula. Going west around the island, it sails as far as Repulse Bay, turns back toward Deep Water Bay and stops at Aberdeen for lunch before returning around the west end of the island to its starting point. A variation of the trip permits the excursionist to leave the boat at Aberdeen and complete the tour with a motor trip via Stanley, Tai Tam Reservoir, Shau Kei Wan, Tiger Balm Gardens, Wanchai, and Victoria Peak. Lunch and soft drinks are included, but this is not a low-price attraction.

A two-hour afternoon water tour offers tourists a view of the harbor, including the island waterfront, Kai Tak airstrip and the harbor islands. If one prefers travel in a craft rather loosely resembling a junk, he may cover most of the same harbor points visited by the regular launch.

The brigantine *Wan Fu*, in addition to its evening cruise to Aberdeen, puts on a plush inter-island tour lasting five hours, with cocktails, canapés and a catered buffet luncheon served aboard. The *Wan Fu* sails through Yau Ma Tei Typhoon Shelter, westward past Stonecutters Island, Lantau, and the little island of Peng Chau before tying up at Cheung Chau for an informal walking tour around this fishermen's settlement, scene of the annual Bun Festival.

Cheung Chau is one of the pleasantest islands in the colony, with neat vegetable gardens planted in its interior hollows, a long stretch of sandy beach and a cluster of English summer homes on its low hills. The village shopping area is a busy place, with narrow, crowded streets, an old temple and a sidewalk shrine to a tree-god. Cost of the *Wan Fu* cruise is in line with its luxurious accommodations.

Ferry services to Cheung Chau, Peng Chau, Tsing Yi Island and Lantau are operated by the Hongkong and Yaumati Ferry Co. Excursion boats may also be hired at fixed rates for reaching any of these islands. Once the visitor gets to the islands, he will have to depend mostly on his feet to get around. As a matter of course, he should determine in advance when the next boat is scheduled to return to Hong Kong Island; otherwise, he may spend the night in some rural retreat with no tourist hotels.

Peng Chau, with a population of about 4,000 persons, has several small industries typical of an earlier day in Hong Kong, such as tanning and lime burning. It was an important match manufacturing center before Macao competition overshadowed it. It also harbors small farming and fishing settlements.

Hei Ling Chau, a nearby island, houses the colony's leprosarium, run by the local auxiliary of the Mission to Lepers. It has 540 patients, including refugees from Red China who were turned out of a leprosarium near Canton when the Communists closed it down. A visit to the island may be arranged through the Mission in Hong Kong and is worthwhile on two counts; it will clear up many common misconceptions about the disease and show the visitor how far medicine has progressed in treating a disease that was once considered fatal. When a Chinese became a known sufferer from the disease, he was, until a few years ago, driven from the community and his family were subjected to abuse by their former friends.

Hei Ling Chau conveys no sense of hopelessness today. Its well-kept stone cottages, workshops, hospital and chapel are arranged around a thriving vegetable garden cultivated by the patients. The unsatisfactory chaulmoogra oil treatment has been replaced by streptomycin, sulfones and other new drugs. Surgery has helped to restore the function of hands crippled by the disease. It is not true that the fingers of lepers drop off; the bones shrink if the disease is not checked.

Most cases on the island are infectious, but chances that a visitor will catch the disease are almost nil. Its chief victims are the undernourished poor. Although leprosy is not hereditary, children may contract it from parents. About 30 young victims of leprosy presently attend a primary school on Hei Ling Chau while being treated. Their chances of recovery are excellent. Early, mild infections can often be cleared up within a year; advanced cases may take many years to cure.

Under staff instruction, many patients have become competent tailors, embroiderers, carpenters, cabinet makers or basket weavers. Very few are bedridden, unless they have an additional disease such as tuberculosis. About a third of the patients are women. Everything concerned with the operation of Hei Ling Chau reflects intelligence and devotion in helping lepers to find their way back to useful living.

Tsing Yi Island, off Tsuen Wan, has a few minor industries such as lime burning and brick making, and its steep hillsides grow an especially sweet variety of pineapple. There is also a community of fishermen and a small village with stores where one may purchase food and soft drinks. Chickens and chow dogs, unmenaced by autos, roam its streets. When cold weather comes, some of the chows will vanish. Many Chinese regard chow meat as a delicacy that will keep the consumer warm in winter, increase his strength and fortify his virility. Killing chows for food is illegal, but every winter the police arrest dozens of dog killers, and the courts hand them high fines and jail sentences.

Lantau Island has only one stretch of paved road in its 55-square-mile extent, but it is a favorite spot for hikers and religious pilgrims. There is a good bathing beach at Silvermine Bay, where the ferry stops, and the paved road, traveled by a new bus line, connects it with the dam-building site at Shek Pik.

Some years ago the island was so isolated that its people built stone towers as redoubts against the forays of pirates. By government permission, residents were allowed to keep arms to defend themselves against raiders. Several of the old towers still stand.

The Buddhist monastery of Po Lin Chi, on a mountain plateau two miles north of Shek Pik, is inhabited by a small community of monks and nuns living from the produce of its fruit trees and gardens and the contributions of pilgrims who struggle up a mountain path to visit the retreat. Visitors are welcome and may stay overnight at a guest house on the grounds. Meals are prepared on wood fires in an ancient, smoke-stained kitchen. Surrounded by its orchards and with two or three massive tombs on the surrounding hills, Po Lin Chi is a quiet echo of James Hilton's *Shangri-La*.

There are other monasteries on Lantau, with the Trappist Monastery at Tai Shui Hang, in the northeast part of the island, perhaps the best-known. In the last decade its community of 22 priests, lay brothers and novices has planted and redeveloped its large farm acreage.

Tai O town, on the west coast of Lantau, is its largest settlement, with nearly 8,000 inhabitants. Tai O has a community of Tanka fishing people living in wooden huts raised on stakes over a muddy inlet. A regular ferry service brings hiking parties from Hong Kong Island to toil up the hillsides to Po Lin Chi. They stay overnight at its guest house and descend on the opposite side of the mountains to catch the ferry at Silver Mine Bay for the trip home.

For a completely different kind of scenery, the inquisitive traveler may visit Tap Mun Chau, an island at the eastern edge of the New Territories. The Kowloon-Canton Railway takes him to Tai Po Station on Tolo Harbor, where he may catch the Tap Mun Chau ferry. The boat nudges up to the foot of Ma On Shan, a craggy, 2,300-foot peak, unloads a cargo of pigs and a few Hakka farmers, and pushes east through Tolo Channel, bordered by round hills. Three Fathoms Cove is the boat's second stop. It is just south of Plover Cove, the deep inlet from Tolo Channel which colony engineers propose to seal off, pump out its salt-water contents, and replace with a fresh-water reservoir.

Most of the stops along this six-hour run are made offshore, disembarking passengers reaching land in small sampans. The boat turns south at the seaward end of Tolo Channel and travels the length of Long Harbor between high, barren hills. Looking at these hills, the passenger may understand how easily Chinese pirates of the last century could slip out of this hidden harbor, pounce on passing ships and make their escape behind the sheltering mountains.

Villages are strung along the water's edge at intervals, but their shallow harbors and small docks cannot handle the ferry boat. The usual sampan, sometimes adroitly propelled by a pair of half-grown boys, rows out to meet the larger boat. There is a dock-side stop at Tap Mun town, where the harbor is crowded with fishing junks, but the layover is too short to permit a walk ashore.

Darkness comes on slowly while the boat heads back, non-stop, to Tai Po, but there are bright patches of light along the water—fishermen using gasoline lanterns to lure their catch into a net spread between two boats. The stars look down from a cloudless sky, and through a gap in the bulky hills, the lights of Hong Kong Island glow in the distance. By early evening, the traveler has gotten his train and is back in Kowloon.

There is so much to see in this colony that no one can compress it into a single visit. Many tourists have returned a dozen times, knowing that each trip would bring some new revelation of unsuspected beauty, some fresh insight into the character of Hong Kong's people.

No book, map nor brochure can tell a colony visitor exactly what to expect. He walks down a street and comes upon the unexpected every day. It may be a Chinese funeral procession with a marching band playing "Bye Bye Blackbird." Or a professional letter-writer, taking dictation with a stylus at his sidewalk table. Or the clatter of Mah Jongg players as they slam the pieces on the table.

It may be a visit to Temple Street in Kowloon, with its odd restaurants and all-night bustle of activity. Or the Kee Heung

Tea House at 597 Shanghai Street, Kowloon, where customers bring their caged birds and discuss them while they sip.

Even the hardiest tourist will be exhausted long before he has exhausted the sights and sounds of Hong Kong.

CHAPTER TEN

Shopping before Dinner

"The culinary art is certainly above all others in Hong Kong."

—Harold Ingrams, *Hong Kong*, 1952

Something happens to the spending habits of all tourists when they reach Hong Kong. Wallets fly open, purse-strings snap and money gushes forth in a golden shower.

It is a matter of record that in Hong Kong more tourists spend more money in a shorter time than in any other port of the Far East or the Pacific west of the American mainland. They shell out $120 a day during an average visit of five days, and almost 70 percent of the $600 five-day total is spent on things the tourist intends to take home. (The figures come, not from Hong Kong, but from an exhaustive study of Pacific and Far Eastern tourism made for the United States Department of Commerce.)

This $120-a-day spending average is applicable to all the colony's civilian visitors except Overseas Chinese. In 1961, the total of such visitors was 210,000, and it was made up of 72,000 Americans, 67,000 British and 71,000 visitors of other nationalities. The number of tourists has more than doubled in the last four years. The Department of Commerce study estimates that the total may climb to 490,000 in 1968, and that tourists could be expected to spend $270 million in the crown colony during the same year. If all this comes to pass, it will carry the merchants of Hong Kong into the full sunlight of a golden age.

But how about the tourist? What does he get for his money that causes him to run hog-wild in Hong Kong shops? The answers are as varied as the shrewdness or the gullibility of the individual tourist.

Let's consider the gullible ones; they are so numerous and vulnerable. The plump lady stuffing herself into a form-fitting Cheongsam. The overnight Beau Brummel, swallowed alive by the 24-hour "custom-tailored" suit he bought with-out taking the time for proper fittings. The customer who ac-cepts the first price quoted by a Chinese merchant. The pho-tography bug who buys a standard West German camera at the most exclusive department store in the heart of the high-rent district, when he could get the same thing for 20 percent less at a number of small, reliable photo-supply shops. The op-timist who thinks he can persuade a British clerk to knock down a fixed price. The lamb who lets a sidewalk "shopping guide" lead him to a fleecing. The poor soul who buys a Swiss watch, a Japanese camera, or any other name product with-out comparing prices of several Hong Kong shops or know-ing the minimum sale price of the same article in his own country. The woman who buys a particular line of famous pearls from anyone except the authorized dealer.

Above all, the American who buys a piece of rare jade

without a Comprehensive Certificate of Origin, and conse-
quently has it confiscated by Customs when he reenters the
United States. For that matter, any American who buys a
"presumptive item"—an article which the U. S. government
suspects was made in Red China or North Korea—without a
Comprehensive Certificate of Origin.

This business of the Comprehensive Certificate of Origin
is a recurrent pain in the neck to American shoppers and
Hong Kong merchants alike. Nevertheless, as an item of
United States foreign policy, it must be deferred to by American tourists in Hong Kong. Many reputable shop-owners will
not apply to the colony's Commerce and Industry Department for the right to issue Comprehensive Certificates of Origin, because it involves so much paperwork, red tape, and
delay that the shops would just as soon skip the American
market and concentrate on the British and others who can
buy without these pesky certificates.

The list of items considered to be presumptive is by no
means clear-cut, and the items on it may change from time
to time, further clouding the issue. Some of the articles considered presumptive are: brassware, brocade, ceramics, cotton goods, embroidery, figurines, wood furniture, greeting
cards, handicrafts, ivory ware, jade, semiprecious jewelry,
lacquerware, porcelain ware, woolen rugs, silks and wall-
paper.

The nonpresumptive articles, or those that can be freely
imported into the U. S., include: binoculars, cameras, cashmere items, enamelware, furs (but not all furs), precious
stones, leather goods, mosaics, mother-of-pearl, plastic articles, rattan ware, sporting goods, umbrellas, watches, wool
clothing and yachts.

These lists are merely indicative; up-to-date and official

information can be obtained in Hong Kong by calling the Foreign Assets Control division of the U. S. Consulate General. If in any doubt about the status of a purchase, pay no attention to the merchant who declares that a Comprehensive Certificate of Origin is unnecessary; if his advice is erroneous, he will not post the buyer's bail.

A Comprehensive Certificate of Origin costs five Hong Kong dollars, or 87.5 cents, and will cover many articles bought at the same store, provided that their value does not exceed HK $1,500, or US $262. It is applied for when the purchase is made. The store sends it to the colony government for official clearance, and when this comes through, usually in about a week, the articles are shipped to the U. S. address designated.

The amount of duty-free goods an American tourist could buy abroad was cut from $500 to $100 in 1961, but merchants of the crown colony say it has not seriously affected their business. At Hong Kong prices, Americans apparently feel they can pay duties and still have a bargain. They are still permitted to buy duty-free any number of items intended as gifts valued at less than $10 each, provided they do not mail more than one gift a day to the same person.

Colony shops with the right to issue Comprehensive Certificates of Origin always post a sign in their windows to advertise the fact; it helps to attract American customers. But there are a few tricksters who will attempt to palm off a fraudulent or nonapplicable certificate. The only certificate of value to an American purchaser, it should be stressed, is the Comprehensive Certificate of Origin.

There are two main shopping areas in the colony: the Central District of Hong Kong Island, and the Tsim Sha Tsui section at the tip of the Kowloon Peninsula. Both areas can easily be covered on foot, and the shopper's budget is guaranteed to wear out much sooner than his shoe leather. King's Road, the main avenue through North Point in the northeastern part of Hong Kong island, is also a good shopping area for tourists. The Chinese and knowledgeable Caucasian residents, however, shop over a much wider area on both sides of the harbor.

Central District shopping for tourists runs west along Queen's Road Central, Des Voeux Road Central, Chater Road and Connaught Road Central from Statue Square, opposite the Star Ferry terminal, to the Vehicular Ferry Pier at Jubilee Street. The best British department stores are toward the eastern end of this small zone, such as Whiteaway Laidlaw & Co. on Connaught Road near the General Post Office, and Lane, Crawford's on Des Voeux Road. Both have Kowloon branches as well, and their prices range from fairly high to forbidding. They are comparable to top-quality department stores in New York or San Francisco, and their marked price is unalterable. No dickering. Even so, they undersell many stores overseas because Hong Kong is with very few exceptions a duty-free port.

The American shopper will need to keep the Comprehensive Certificate of Origin problem in mind constantly as he branches out to other stores, but there's no harm in looking. The larger Chinese stores in the area include Chinese Arts & Crafts and China Emporium, both on Queen's Road, and the Shui Hing Co., The Sincere Co. and Wing On, Ltd., all on Des Voeux Road. The Man Yee Building on Des Voeux Road has two floors of shops with radios, typewriters, curios, watches and tape recorders, plus many other articles; they are well worth checking, either to buy or for comparing prices. The Japanese have opened a large department store, Daimaru, at Causeway Bay, just west of the North Point section.

The Gloucester Building at Des Voeux Road and Pedder Street has an extensive shopping arcade with many quality shops. Alexandra House, just across Des Voeux, also has its quota of fine shops, and there are other first-rate stores throughout this area. The streets intersecting with Queen's Road and Des Voeux Road should not be overlooked either. Only a dozen blocks or so are involved, but the shops are so numerous and their goods so varied that it will take even an industrious shopper a full day to see them and compare prices. Wise tourists looking for values usually spend a day surveying the shops and their merchandise before they are ready to spend a cent. It is a sound procedure, for hundreds of hasty shoppers have prematurely congratulated themselves on a wonderful buy, only to see the same article in another shop the next day for 15 to 25 percent less than they have paid.

What are the good buys in Hong Kong? They particularly include custom-made clothes for men and women, because the workmanship is cheap and the quality high—this applies to coats, suits, dresses and shoes. For women, silk and woolen garments are good buys, especially when they require extensive hand work on beading and embroidery. If planning to wash the garment, make sure that the outer material and the inner lining are pre-shrunk and color-fast.

The Cheongsam, with its side-slit skirt and carefully fitted collar, is worth individual attention here. The Cheongsam is a closely fitted, shape-clinging dress that shows to best advantage on a slim, small-boned Chinese girl. Put the average Western woman in one and she looks beefy, which certainly isn't the effect she is striving for. If she's overweight, the sight of her in a Cheongsam is enough to make Chinese children hide behind their mother's slit-skirt where their howls and giggles won't be too evident.

Men can get excellent bargains in custom-tailored suits of English woolens, Japanese woolens, Dacron, mixed silk and wool, or cashmere and wool. Pure cashmere looks and feels luxurious in the shop, but it is extremely expensive and doesn't wear as well as a cashmere-and-wool combination. If the tailor puts in cheap lining, the collar and lapels will look like an elephant's hide after a few cleanings. If he skimps on the thread, and some do, the suit may pull apart under strenuous circumstances. The worldwide story about the $20 Hong Kong suit that can be perfectly fitted in 24-hours may have been circulated by some show-business comedian trying to impress his friends; it is not, and never was, true.

Assuming that a good Hong Kong tailor is located—and there are scores of them—a man will be able to get the finest kind of custom-made suit for a little less than he would pay for a ready-made suit of the same materials in the United States. That would be around $75 for a pure cashmere sport jacket, $40 for a cashmere-and-wool jacket, $70 for a tuxedo of English worsteds, and $40 to $60 for a suit, with the higher-priced one of English woolen and the cheaper of a lightweight wool. A custom-tailored shirt of Sea Island cotton will cost about $6—considerably less than an American ready-made shirt of the same material.

The chances are that an established Hong Kong tailor will start by asking a higher price for all of these articles. By patient haggling and comparison-shopping, he may be wheedled down by 5 to 20 percent. And don't be afraid that hard bargaining will drive him out of business; he always allows a comfortable profit margin for himself. Ignore his claims based on the famous people he has made suits for; they may have been given the ultimate in special care at a price far below the going rate for serving to advertise the shop.

One thing a tailor cannot do is to turn out a well-fitted suit without three or four fittings. This will require no less than five days, and two weeks would yield even better results. In busy periods, before the Christmas and Chinese New Year holidays, a tailor might need three weeks. One can buy a better-looking ready-made suit in the United States than almost any Hong Kong tailor can turn out in 24 hours; he's good, but he's not a miracle worker.

Women shopping for top-grade American and British ready-made clothing should have a look at Mackintosh's in Alexandra House, Paquerette (in the Gloucester Arcade), Lane, Crawford's, and Whiteaway Laidlaw & Co. A wide range of high-style tailored clothing for women is offered by Charlotte Horstmann of Duddell Street and Town and Country of Queen's Road, both on the Hong Kong side, and at three Kowloon shops in the arcade of the Hotel Peninsula: Dynasty Salon, Betty Clemo, and Star of Siam.

Men's tailoring shops are most numerous on the Kowloon side, and many of them also make women's clothing. A sample survey might include Y. William Yu and Frank L. Chan of Kimberley Road, Ying Tai & Co., and Harilela's of Nathan Road, James S. Lee & Co. of Nathan Road (and Gloucester Road, Hong Kong), and Tailor Young & Co. of Humphreys Avenue. In the blocks from Mody Road to Kimberley Road, all branching east from Nathan Road, tailors seem to occupy about every third storefront. Take nothing for granted at any of them, and be watchful to see that the cloth ordered is supplied.

Hong Kong has outstanding bargains in handmade shoes, handbags, jewelry, watches, cameras, radios and furniture. It is desirable to know prices and to shop around extensively, comparing values. The Man Yee Building, previously mentioned, the Gloucester Arcade, and the arcades of the Ambassador and Miramar Hotels in Kowloon should give an idea of what's available, though they may be undersold by some side-street shop.

Kowloon has dozens of small shops, often combined with back-room "factories," where one can buy Chinese handicrafts or watch them being turned out by superlative craftsmen. These products are duplicates of those that China has produced for centuries, and may require a Comprehensive Certificate of Origin to get them through U. S. Customs.

Hankow Road, just west of the Hotel Peninsula, has the greatest number of wood-carving shops. They all stock sets of wooden horses in several sizes; also Buddhas, Gods and Goddesses in profusion, wild animals, fish and birds. The asking price is outrageous, but can be whittled down as much as 50 percent by patient haggling. A well-made carved horse about four inches high can be bought for 75 cents. It would cost six times as much in New York.

No other article more convincingly demonstrates the skill of the Chinese craftsman than carved ivory. There are ivory factories along Nathan Road and its side streets that produce beautifully carved chess sets, intricately fashioned concentric balls of ivory, and miniature temples, flower boats and pagodas.

Fine cabinetmakers turn out highly polished teak and rosewood chests trimmed with brass and lined with silk. Each one is a masterpiece of workmanship, but there's one catch—if the wood has not been carefully kiln-dried, the chest may split when it is shipped home. This is a point on which a customer will want to quiz the dealer, then decide whether his answers are satisfactory. Carved and lacquered screens can be an artistic delight, but don't forget to include the shipping costs when figuring their price. Carved and full-rigged Chinese junks are sold in a wide range of sizes.

The shopper can forget about the give-no-quarter type of bargaining when he enters one of the stores operated by Hong Kong welfare organizations for the benefit of physically handicapped refugees. These are strictly nonprofit operations, with all but basic overhead costs being turned over to the needy people who make the handicrafts. The quality of their products is high and their prices are reasonable. Two of these shops are the Welfare Handicrafts on Salisbury Road, opposite the Kowloon Post Office, and The Rice Bowl, on Minden Row. To find The Rice Bowl, turn east off Nathan Road at Mody Road; Minden Row is the first street south off Mody. Both stores have Comprehensive Certificates of Origin.

The Tsim Sha Shui section of Kowloon is developing so rapidly that it will probably have a dozen shopping arcades by the end of 1963. The Central District of Hong Kong Island is also planning new arcades.

Tourists may wind up a day's shopping by attending one of the 72 movie theaters in the colony. Of these, 16 show English-language films and 13 are first-run houses. Foreign films reach Hong Kong as soon as they appear in the world market. In Kowloon, Nathan Road is the main movie avenue; in Hong Kong, they are spotted along the principal streets from Kennedy Town to Shau Kei Wan. All seats are reserved, and selected from a seating-chart at the box office; daily show-times are carried in the local press. Chinese films have a big following, but many colony Chinese prefer American movies with plenty of action and spectacle. English films strike them as stodgy and slow, European art films bore them, and sexy importations from Italy and France offend their sensibilities.

English-language films usually carry Chinese subtitles which look like embroidery to Western viewers.

If it's night clubs the tourist is looking for, there's nothing to get wildly excited about. Floor shows run to jugglers, acrobats and pony chorus lines, with an occasional comedian as a star attraction. Vaudeville isn't dead; it simply shuffled off to Hong Kong. Prices are steeper than the entertainment warrants. Most of the musicians are Filipinos; individually able, but their band arrangements follow the blast-off traditions of American stage bands in the 1930s.

For a predinner cocktail with a magnificent view, two of the best locations are the lounge on top of the Imperial Hotel, Nathan Road, and the 11th floor Marigold Lounge of the Park Hotel at Cameron and Chatham Roads, both in Kowloon. Just as the finest daytime view is from the upper slopes of Victoria Peak on Hong Kong Island, the most satisfying after-dark panorama is from Kowloon. From either of these lounges you can see the banks of lighted apartment houses along the Hong Kong hillside, tied together by festoons of streetlamps as the roads zig-zag up the slopes, shining blue at the lower levels, then turning to vapor-piercing amber as they climb above the fog line. The Imperial has the closest view of the multi-colored neon signs glowing along the Hong Kong side of the harbor in English and Chinese characters. The Park Hotel overlooks the whole sweep of Kowloon Bay and the wavy, mountainous horizon of the island, with the brilliantly lighted boats of a dozen ferry lines criss-crossing the harbor in every direction. A line of lights passes directly under the window—a Kowloon-Canton train returning from a trip to the Red China border. If one could compress all of his memories of Hong Kong into a single glance, this would be it.

Kowloon holds two-thirds of the colony's fifty hotels, and many of these are quite new. Hong Kong Island will add two major hotels in 1963, the 1,000-room American and the 600-room Queen's, but Kowloon will retain its leadership in room capacity for many years. Altogether, about a dozen hotels will be added by the end of 1964 if business holds up.

The tremendous surge in hotel growth means that after years of lagging behind, Hong Kong has finally roused itself to meet the needs of tourists, in room capacity, at least. The expansion has been so frantic that a number of the newer hotels have shaved every possible corner in construction, skimping on the number of elevators and unduly shrinking the size of rooms to squeeze every cent out of their cubic-foot capacity. Hotel help is scarce, and as each new hotel opens, it raids the staffs of existing hotels; this raises wages slightly, but saves the raider the time and expense of training his own people. It also lowers the quality of service and leaves the older hotels to scramble for replacements.

With these limitations in mind, it is remarkable that hotel service is as good as it is, and much of the credit must go to the staff people themselves. They are hard-working, cheerful and obliging to a degree seldom seen in large cities. Because of inadequate training and the inevitable language difficulties, they are sometimes caught off-base, but when they know what a guest wants, they will do everything possible to get it. Americans and British whose democratic principles do not always prevent them from getting pretty high-handed about the way they are served will just have to be a little less fussy.

The Peninsula Hotel and its jointly managed addition, the Peninsula Court, occupy the same place in the colony that the Plaza does in New York—smart, eminently respectable and expensive. The Park, the Imperial and the Ambassador are among the best of the large, new hotels in Kowloon. The Gloucester has the greatest status of the Central District hotels, and the Repulse Bay, on the south shore of Hong Kong Island, rates as the island's most luxurious resort hotel. There are about a dozen other first-rate hotels and approximately 30 additional ones that range from satisfactory to catch-as-catch-can. All those recommended by the Hong Kong Tourist Association are acceptable, but their quality varies with their rates, though not always in proportion.

Two outlying hotels worth noting are the Carlton and the Shatin Heights, both in the New Territories but not far from Kowloon. The Luk Kwok in Wanchai, once the locale for Richard Mason's *The World of Suzie Wong*, prospered so handsomely from the publicity that it is now a quiet, middle-class hotel.

Confirmed hotel reservations, arranged well in advance of your arrival, are advisable for all tourists who are not thoroughly familiar with Hong Kong. Certainly it would be unwise to arrive without them and be forced to rely on sheer luck or the noisy touts who besiege incoming passengers at Kai Tak. The touts are kept behind a fence nowadays, but if the unsuspecting visitor lets them steer him to a hotel, their kick-back will be added to the bill. Experienced visitors sometimes check into a modestly priced hotel for the night and spend the next day bargaining for the lowest rates at one of the better places which, when business is slow, regularly knock 30 percent off the stated charges. For newcomers, this is seldom done.

Some European and American visitors cannot be persuaded to try Chinese food. Either they think it will make them ill, which it certainly will not, or they believe they'll look silly fumbling with chopsticks. It must be conceded that inexperienced users of chopsticks usually look rather foolish, but practically every Chinese restaurant will provide a knife and fork if asked for them.

No difficulty should arise from a determination to stick to one's usual diet. Every first-class hotel serves an international cuisine. Prices are tailored to the room rents; high at the Peninsula, cheap at the Y.M.C.A. next door to it. In general, the meals are as good as those at American hotels and they cost considerably less. Steaks are tougher than Choice U. S. beef, and occasionally one resembles a small portion of a welcome mat. Apart from the hotels, there are about a dozen good European restaurants.

In Mandarin Chinese, there is a saying that "food is the heaven of the ordinary people," and the Chinese in Hong Kong, like their countrymen all over the world, do their remarkable best to impart a foretaste of heaven to their cooking. Their food reaches the table in edible form, and does not have to be slashed and hacked before the guest is ready to eat it. Chopsticks are all that is needed to lift the food to the mouth. (Foreigners take weeks to get over the shock of seeing a three-year-old Chinese child manipulating chopsticks; it seems so infernally clever.)

Chinese restaurants of the colony serve four different kinds of cuisine: Cantonese (from southern China); Shanghainese (from east-central China); Pekinese (from northern China) and Szechuan (central China).

Cantonese is the type most familiar to Americans, since most of the Chinese restaurants in the U.S. are owned by Southern Chinese. Chop suey and chow mein are not Chinese at all, except that they were invented by Chinese cooks in the United States to please their American customers. None the less, Cantonese restaurants serve them in Hong Kong, as well as egg rolls, egg foo yung, and sweet-and-sour pork, if only to keep the visiting foreigners happy.

Authentic Cantonese dishes are strong on seafoods. Steamed fish seasoned with ginger, mushrooms, spring onion, salted black soya beans, garlic, salad oil, sherry, soy sauce, and sugar is a particular favorite. Shark's fin soup which includes not only the fins but crab meat, sliced chicken, chicken broth, cornstarch, and peanut oil is a floating potpourri.

Other Cantonese delicacies are gut lee hai kim, shelled fat crabs dipped in butter, fried in deep oil and served with a tart wine-and-vinegar sauce; goo low yuk, the Cantonese name for sweet-and-sour pork; and ho yau ngau yuk, slices of beef tenderloin quick-fried with an oyster sauce and garnished with greens. Cantonese cooks are sparing in their use of salt and grease.

A lunchtime specialty of Cantonese restaurants is dim sun (tiny bits of food), which includes twenty different kinds of sweet and salty dishes; among them, steamed biscuits with various meat fillings, rice cakes, sweet buns and chicken rolls.

A few of the better Cantonese restaurants are: Tai Tung, 234 Des Voeux Road; Golden City, 122-126 Queen's Road Central; Miramar and Ambassador (both in hotels), Nathan Road; and the Sky, 8 Queen's Road Central. They're accustomed to tourists, and will help with the ordering, if need be. Tai Tung is typical of the large Cantonese restaurants, catering to family parties and group dinners. Kam Ling, at 484 Queen's Road West in the West Point section of the island, is another Cantonese giant.

Dinner at one of the multi-story Chinese restaurants may cause a shock to the nerves from a series of violent and unexpected explosions. The blasts, which sound like closely bunched machine-gun fire, seem to be coming from right out-side the window. No cause for alarm—it's just a string of firecrackers celebrating a wedding or some other joyous fam-ily event. A solid string of firecrackers is suspended from a crane at the top of the building, then lighted at the bottom; as the bursting crackers eat their way up the string, a man with a guide rope slowly lowers the string to keep the explosions at street level, thus preventing the paper from blowing all over the surrounding streets. A portable, circular wire screen is also placed around the explosion zone to confine the mess, and a policeman stands by to see that the fireworks are being handled according to law. All large restaurants have a swing-out firecracker crane, and when they book a family party for a special celebration, a police permit is obtained for the noise-making. The rattle of explosions often lasts ten minutes or more, costing the host from $100 to $300, depending on the length and elaborateness of the string.

Shanghainese cooking, which became more popular in Hong Kong after the arrival of Shanghai refugees in the late 1940s, is sweeter and more salty than Cantonese food, and uses a lot more oil. Its characteristic dishes include: la dze jee ding, fresh chicken diced and fried with peppers and flavored with soy sauce; chao ha yen, small shelled shrimp garnished with green herbs or bean sprouts; and sze tze tao, pork sautéed with Chinese white cabbage and often served in a casserole.

Beggar's chicken is highly regarded by colony residents, both Chinese and English, and can be ordered at Tien Hong Lau on Woosung Street, Kowloon; or other Shanghai places such as Winter Garden, Nathan Road; or Four Five Six, 340 King's Road, North Point. Bamboo shoots, boiled crab and fried eel, in season, are also Shanghai treats.

Szechuan food is hot and spicy, with such representative

dishes as: suan la tang, sour peppery soup; dried beef with peppers; and Szechuan duck, deep-fried to cook both the skin and
the flesh brown, spiced with pungent black pepper and served
with the meat so tender that it may be picked off the bones
with chopsticks. The Ivy, at 11 D'Aguilar Street, in the Central District, is a familiar Szechuan establishment. There are
others in the Diamond Hill section of New Kowloon, north
of Kai Tak Airport, but one would probably need the guid-
ance of a long-time colony resident to find them.

The Pekinese cuisine is best known for Peking duck,
served as a suitable entrée for a meal that begins with assorted
cold meats and proceeds through chicken and walnuts to the
celebrated bird. The duck is basted with salad oil and roasted
until brown, then the skin is dipped in soya paste with scallions
and wrapped in thin pancakes to be eaten as a kind of sandwich; the meat is dipped and eaten in a similar manner and the
bones of the duck are made into a soup with cabbage and
mushrooms. Toffee apples and caramelized bananas (sugared
and deep-fried, then immersed in cold water) top off the feast.

Two of the popular Pekinese restaurants are the Peking, 1
Great George Street, Causeway Bay; and the Princess Garden, Kimberley Road, Kowloon.

Hard to classify but too good to miss is the Mongolian
steamboat, a cooking utensil used for Northern and Cantonese
dishes. Hot coals are placed in the bottom of the vessel from
which the heat rises through a chimney at the center. Water or
soup stock boils in a little open-top tank that encircles the
chimney. In the Cantonese style, tiny baskets of sea food, meat
and vegetables are hung into the boiling water until they are
done, then the contents are fished out with chopsticks. In the
Northern Chinese variation, a soup stock is put in the
reservoir with very thin slices of meat and sea food being

dipped in until they are cooked, which takes only a few seconds. Both styles use various sauces and condiments to flavor the food after it is cooked and drawn out with chopsticks. The steamboat sits in the center of the table, puffing energetically, and every diner has a fine time dipping and fishing for his food.

The Peking Restaurant at Causeway Bay and the Wong Heung Min, at 191-193 Gloucester Road along the Wanchai waterfront, are two steamboat anchorages of note.

The various styles of Chinese cooking do not differ so radically that the same restaurant cannot prepare food in two or more regional ways. Many restaurants do so and quite capably. Americans sometimes choke at the thought of bird's nest soup, which is made from the saliva that swallows use to build their nests. The saliva is separated from the straw and feathers by boiling and evaporation, and the dried saliva extract is added to a stock of chicken broth, combined with sliced ham and minced chicken. The end-product, served in most Chinese restaurants, is a prince among fine soups.

If one wants to prowl around a bit, he can locate a restaurant or two that serves snake meat or civet cat. The Chinese have a theory that they can make anything taste good with the right amount of cooking and a judicious use of sauces, spices and condiments. What is more, they usually prove to be correct. But a taste for snake meat is like the appreciation of Cantonese opera; it takes years of conditioning.

For those who enjoy sukiyaki and other Japanese dishes, they are available at the Tokyo Restaurant, on the 17th floor of the Imperial Hotel, and in the dining room of the Daimaru department store at Causeway Bay. The Bombay Restaurant at 19 Prat Avenue, Kowloon, has a good selection of Indian dishes. For Russian specialties, especially fine cakes and pastries, Rikki's restaurant at Cameron and Carnarvon Roads, Kowloon, is a plain but acceptable spot.

Assuming that one has had at least a one-week stay in Hong Kong, and has applied himself to eating, shopping and sightseeing to the limit of his energies, there is every reason to believe that he will go home happy, stimulated, exhausted, and broke.

It is the common lot of Hong Kong's 210,000 annual visitors.

Index